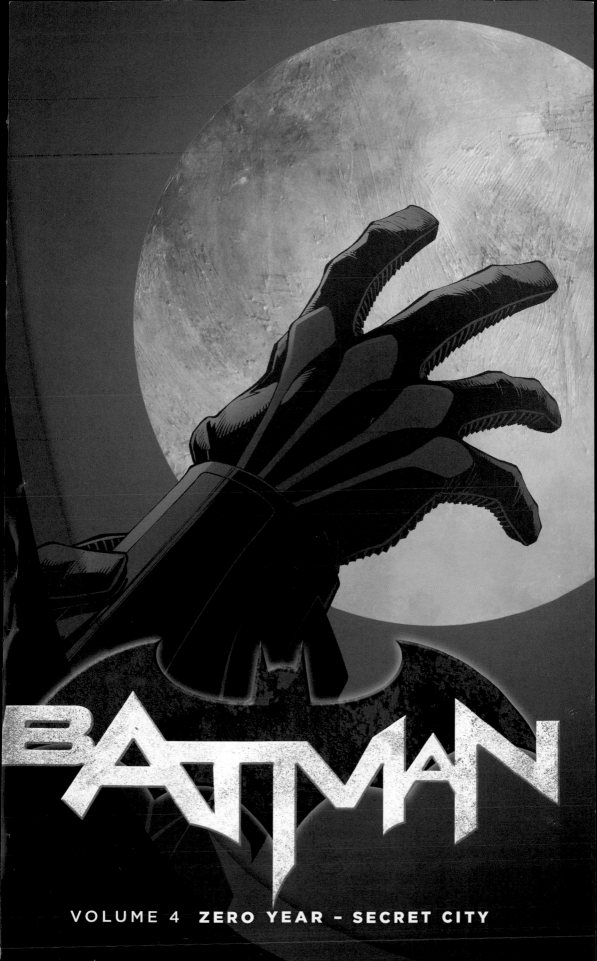

BATMAN

VOLUME 4 ZERO YEAR - SECRET CITY

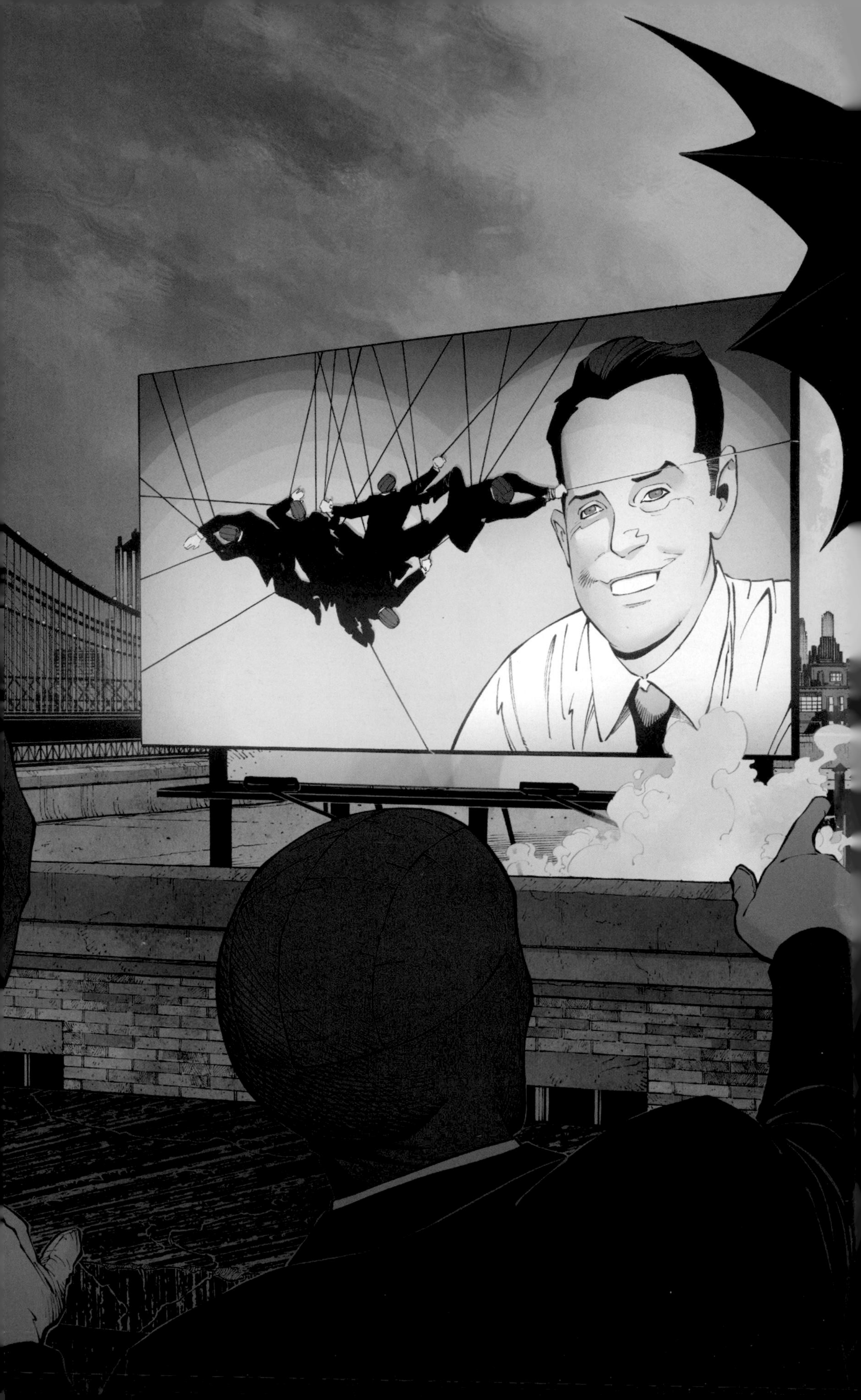

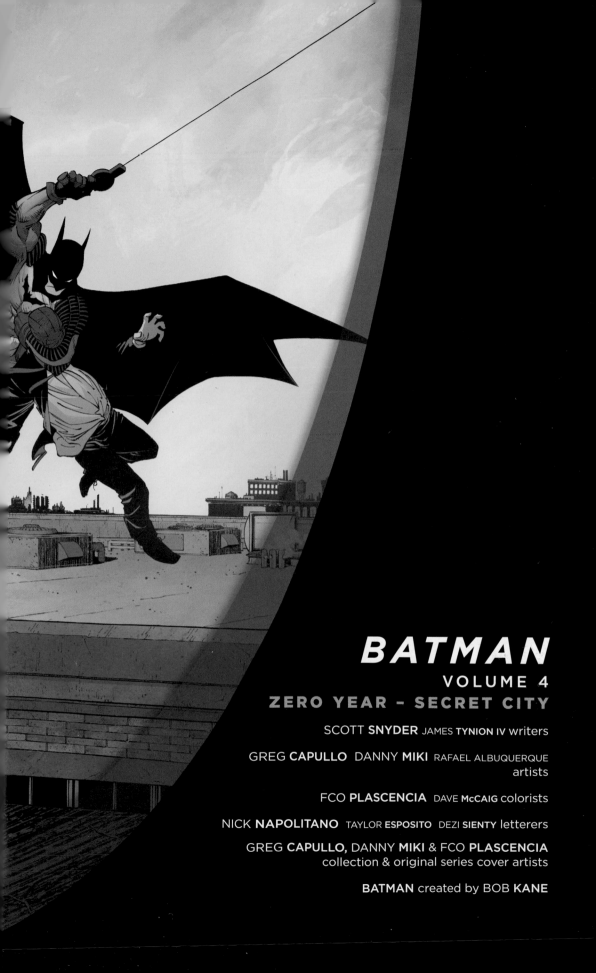

BATMAN

VOLUME 4
ZERO YEAR - SECRET CITY

SCOTT **SNYDER** JAMES **TYNION IV** writers

GREG **CAPULLO** DANNY **MIKI** RAFAEL ALBUQUERQUE
artists

FCO **PLASCENCIA** DAVE **McCAIG** colorists

NICK **NAPOLITANO** TAYLOR **ESPOSITO** DEZI **SIENTY** letterers

GREG **CAPULLO**, DANNY **MIKI** & FCO **PLASCENCIA**
collection & original series cover artists

BATMAN created by BOB **KANE**

MIKE MARTS Editor – Original Series   KATIE KUBERT Associate Editor – Original Series   PETER HAMBOUSSI Editor
ROBBIN BROSTERMAN Design Director – Books   ROBBIE BIEDERMAN Publication Design

BOB HARRAS Senior VP – Editor-in-Chief, DC Comics

DIANE NELSON President   DAN DIDIO and JIM LEE Co-Publishers
GEOFF JOHNS Chief Creative Officer
JOHN ROOD Executive VP – Sales, Marketing and Business Development
AMY GENKINS Senior VP – Business and Legal Affairs   NAIRI GARDINER Senior VP – Finance
JEFF BOISON VP – Publishing Planning   MARK CHIARELLO VP – Art Direction and Design
JOHN CUNNINGHAM VP – Marketing   TERRI CUNNINGHAM VP – Editorial Administration
ALISON GILL Senior VP – Manufacturing and Operations   HANK KANALZ Senior VP – Vertigo and Integrated Publishing
JAY KOGAN VP – Business and Legal Affairs, Publishing   JACK MAHAN VP – Business Affairs, Talent
NICK NAPOLITANO VP – Manufacturing Administration   SUE POHJA VP – Book Sales
COURTNEY SIMMONS Senior VP – Publicity   BOB WAYNE Senior VP – Sales

BATMAN VOLUME 4: ZERO YEAR – SECRET CITY

DC Comics, 1700 Broadway, New York, NY 10019
A Warner Bros. Entertainment Company.
Printed by RR Donnelley, Salem, VA, USA. 4/4/14. First Printing.

HC ISBN: 978-1-4012-4508-5
SC ISBN: 978-1-4012-4933-5

Library of Congress Cataloging-in-Publication Data

Snyder, Scott, author
Batman. Volume 4, Zero Year-Secret City / Scott Snyder ; illustrated by Greg Capullo.
pages cm. — (The New 52!)
ISBN 978-1-4012-4508-5 (hardback)
1. Graphic novels. I. Capullo, Greg, illustrator. II. Title. III. Title: Zero Year-Secret City.
PN6728.B36S685 2014
741.5'973—dc23
2014000326

SUSTAINABLE
FORESTRY
INITIATIVE

Certified Chain of Custody
At Least 20% Certified Forest Content
www.sfiprogram.org
SFI-01042
APPLIES TO TEXT STOCK ONLY

ZERO
YEAR

ZERO
YEAR

Gotham City,
IX YEARS AGO...

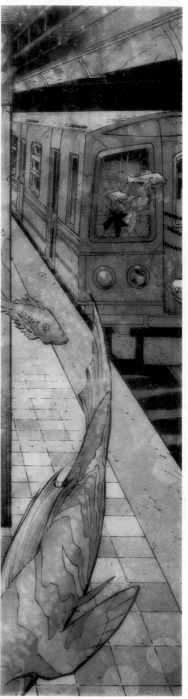

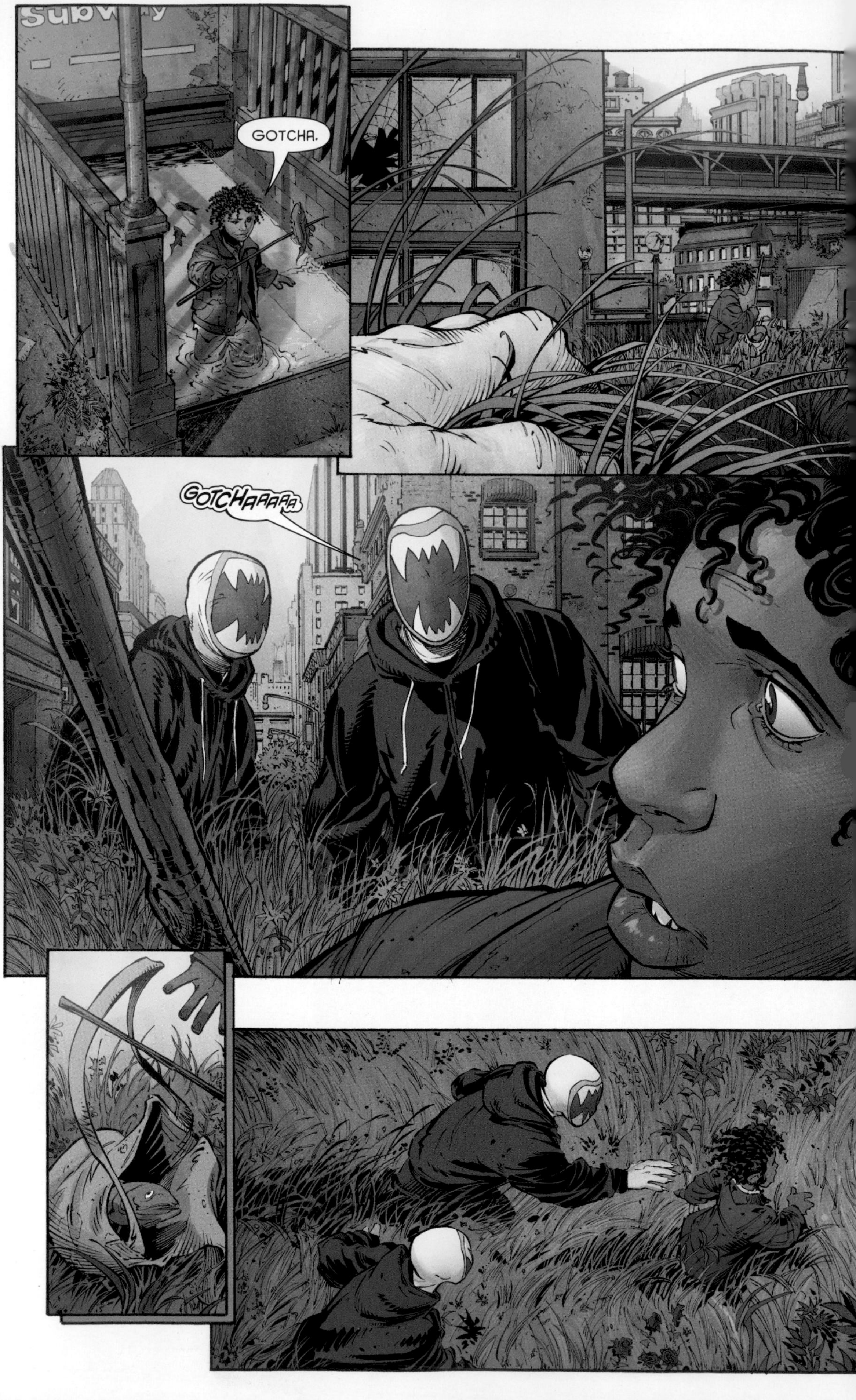
Subway
GOTCHA.
GOTCHAAAAAA

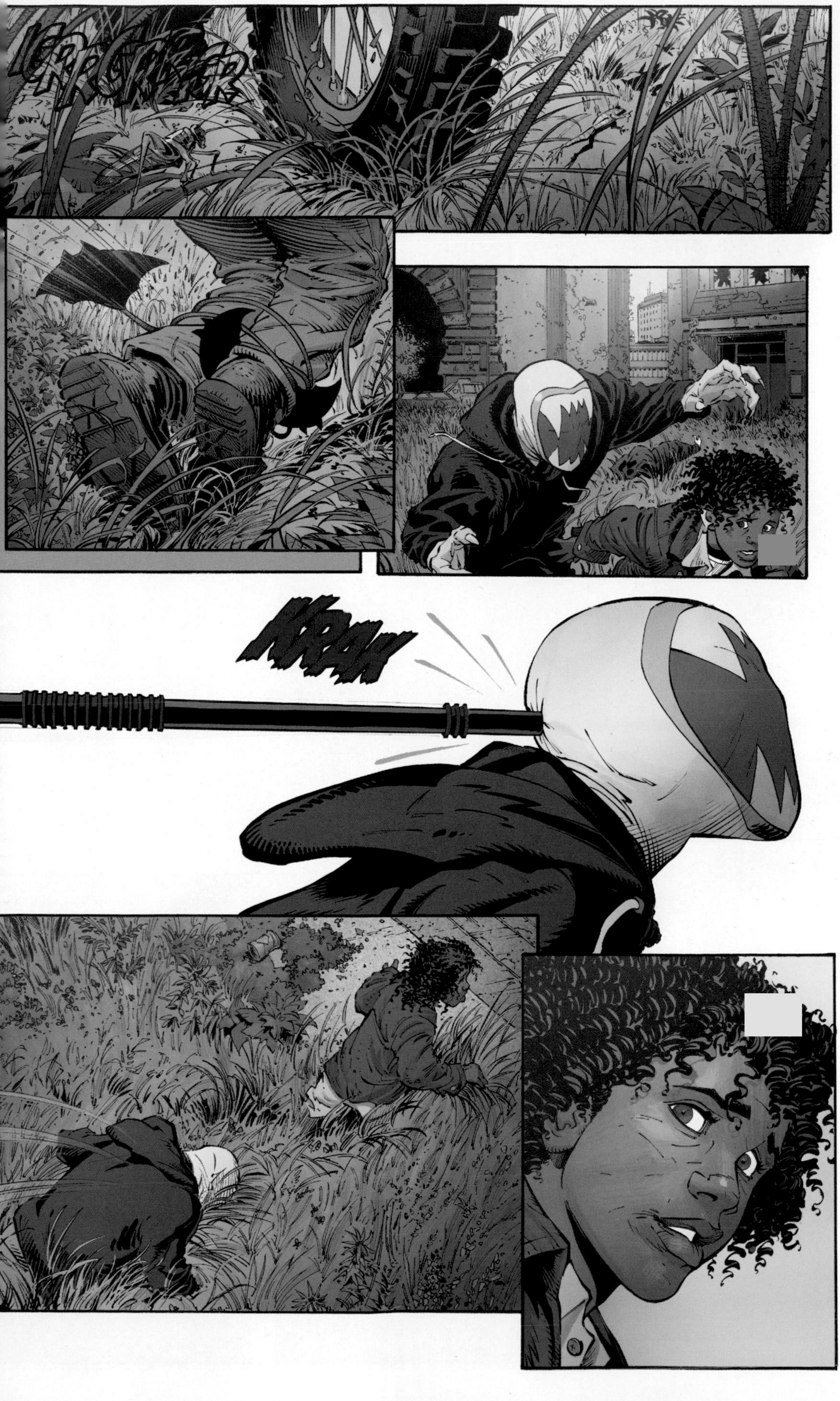
KRAK

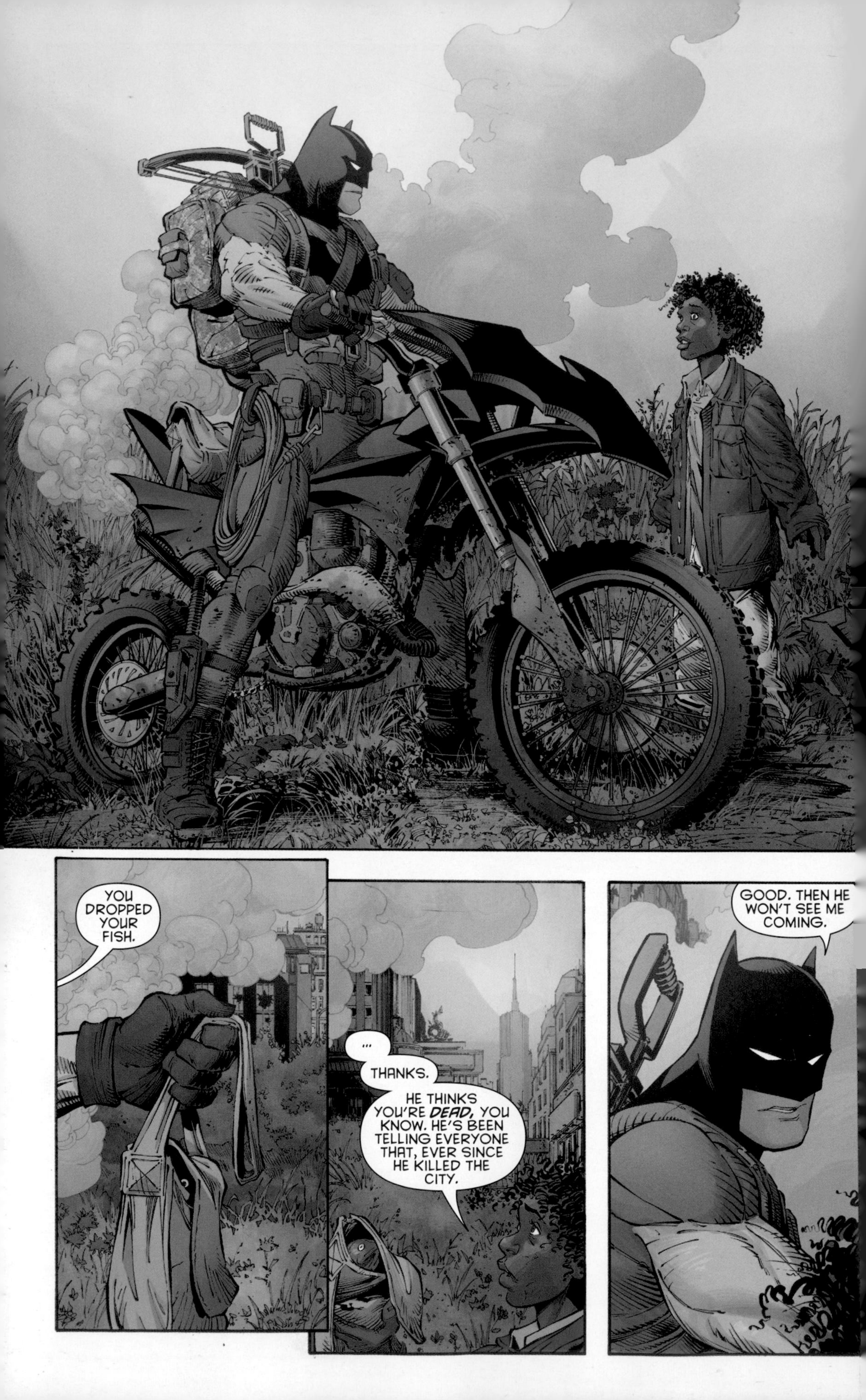
YOU DROPPED YOUR FISH.
...
THANKS.
HE THINKS YOU'RE *DEAD,* YOU KNOW. HE'S BEEN TELLING EVERYONE THAT, EVER SINCE HE KILLED THE CITY.
GOOD. THEN HE WON'T SEE ME COMING.

ZERO YEAR

SECRET CITY: PART ONE

SCOTT SNYDER
WRITER

GREG CAPULLO
PENCILLER

DANNY MIKI - INKER

FCO PLASCENCIA - COLORIST

NICK NAPOLITANO - LETTERER

CAPULLO & PLASCENCIA - COVER

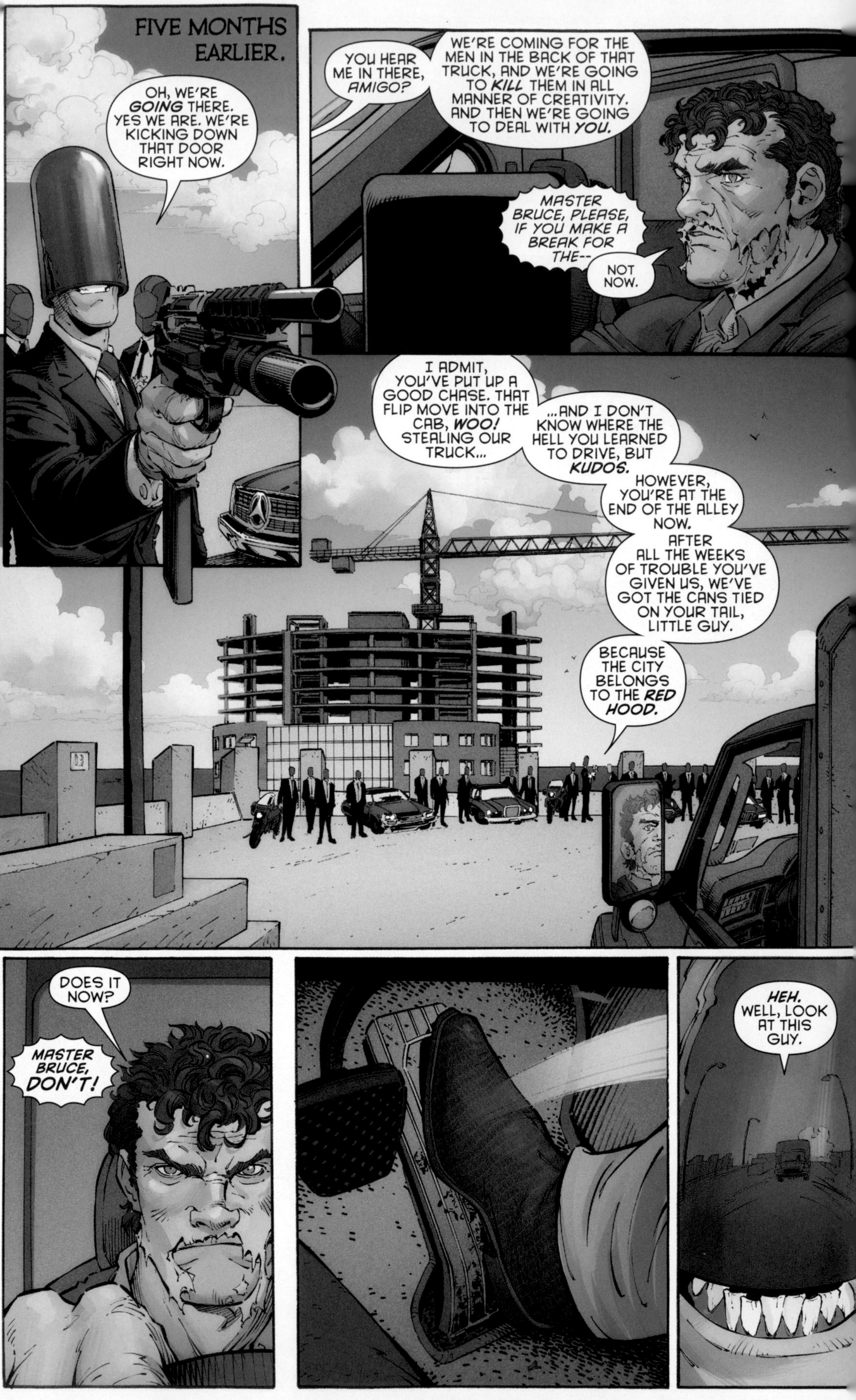

FIVE MONTHS EARLIER.
OH, WE'RE GOING THERE. YES WE ARE. WE'RE KICKING DOWN THAT DOOR RIGHT NOW.
YOU HEAR ME IN THERE, AMIGO?
WE'RE COMING FOR THE MEN IN THE BACK OF THAT TRUCK, AND WE'RE GOING TO KILL THEM IN ALL MANNER OF CREATIVITY. AND THEN WE'RE GOING TO DEAL WITH YOU.
MASTER BRUCE, PLEASE, IF YOU MAKE A BREAK FOR THE--
NOT NOW.
I ADMIT, YOU'VE PUT UP A GOOD CHASE. THAT FLIP MOVE INTO THE CAB, WOO! STEALING OUR TRUCK...
...AND I DON'T KNOW WHERE THE HELL YOU LEARNED TO DRIVE, BUT KUDOS.
HOWEVER, YOU'RE AT THE END OF THE ALLEY NOW.
AFTER ALL THE WEEKS OF TROUBLE YOU'VE GIVEN US, WE'VE GOT THE CANS TIED ON YOUR TAIL, LITTLE GUY.
BECAUSE THE CITY BELONGS TO THE RED HOOD.
DOES IT NOW?
MASTER BRUCE, DON'T!
HEH. WELL, LOOK AT THIS GUY.

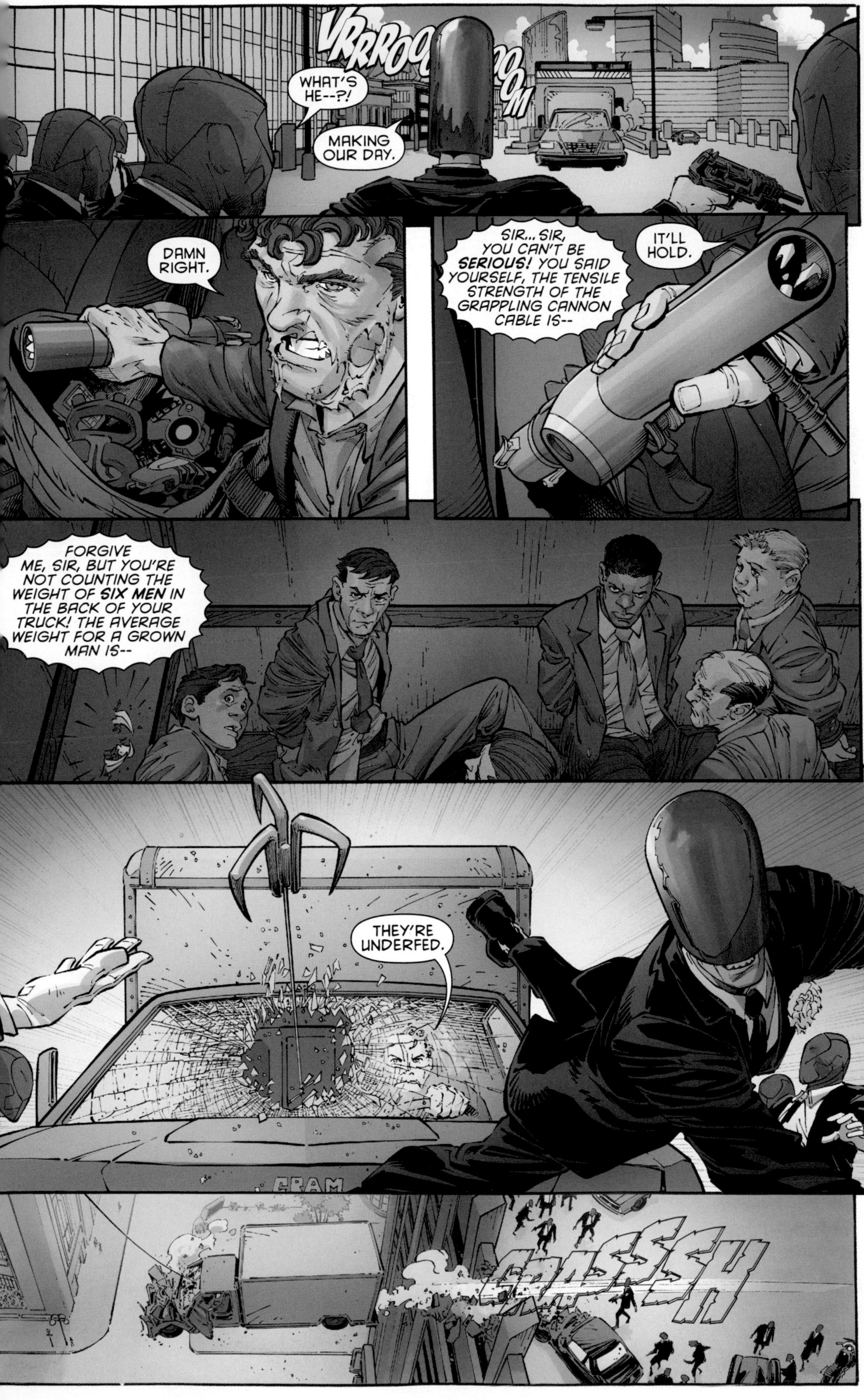
VRRROOOOOOOOOM
WHAT'S HE--?!
MAKING OUR DAY.
DAMN RIGHT.
SIR... SIR, YOU CAN'T BE SERIOUS! YOU SAID YOURSELF, THE TENSILE STRENGTH OF THE GRAPPLING CANNON CABLE IS--
IT'LL HOLD.
FORGIVE ME, SIR, BUT YOU'RE NOT COUNTING THE WEIGHT OF SIX MEN IN THE BACK OF YOUR TRUCK! THE AVERAGE WEIGHT FOR A GROWN MAN IS--
THEY'RE UNDERFED.
CRASSSH

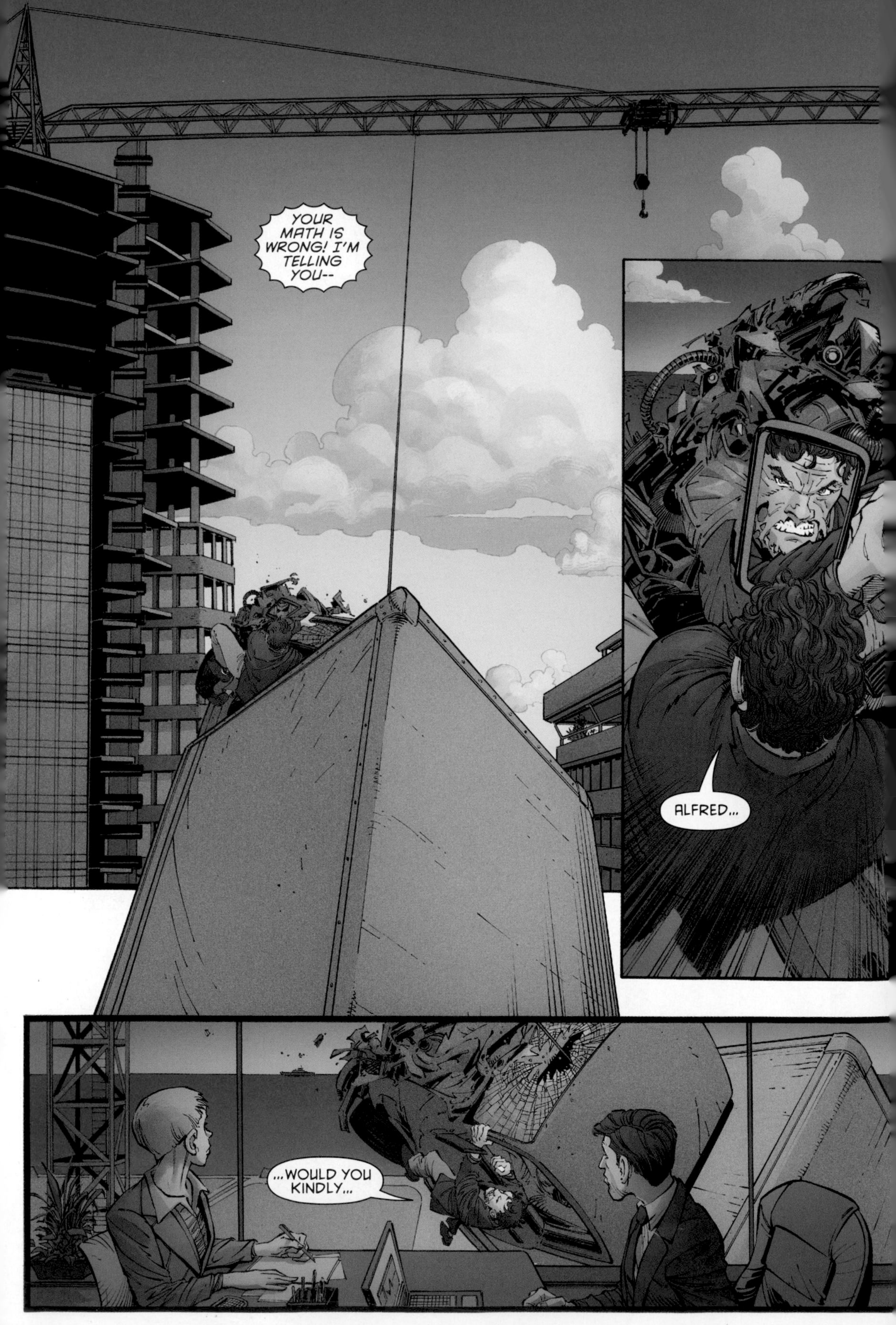
YOUR MATH IS WRONG! I'M TELLING YOU--
ALFRED...
...WOULD YOU KINDLY...

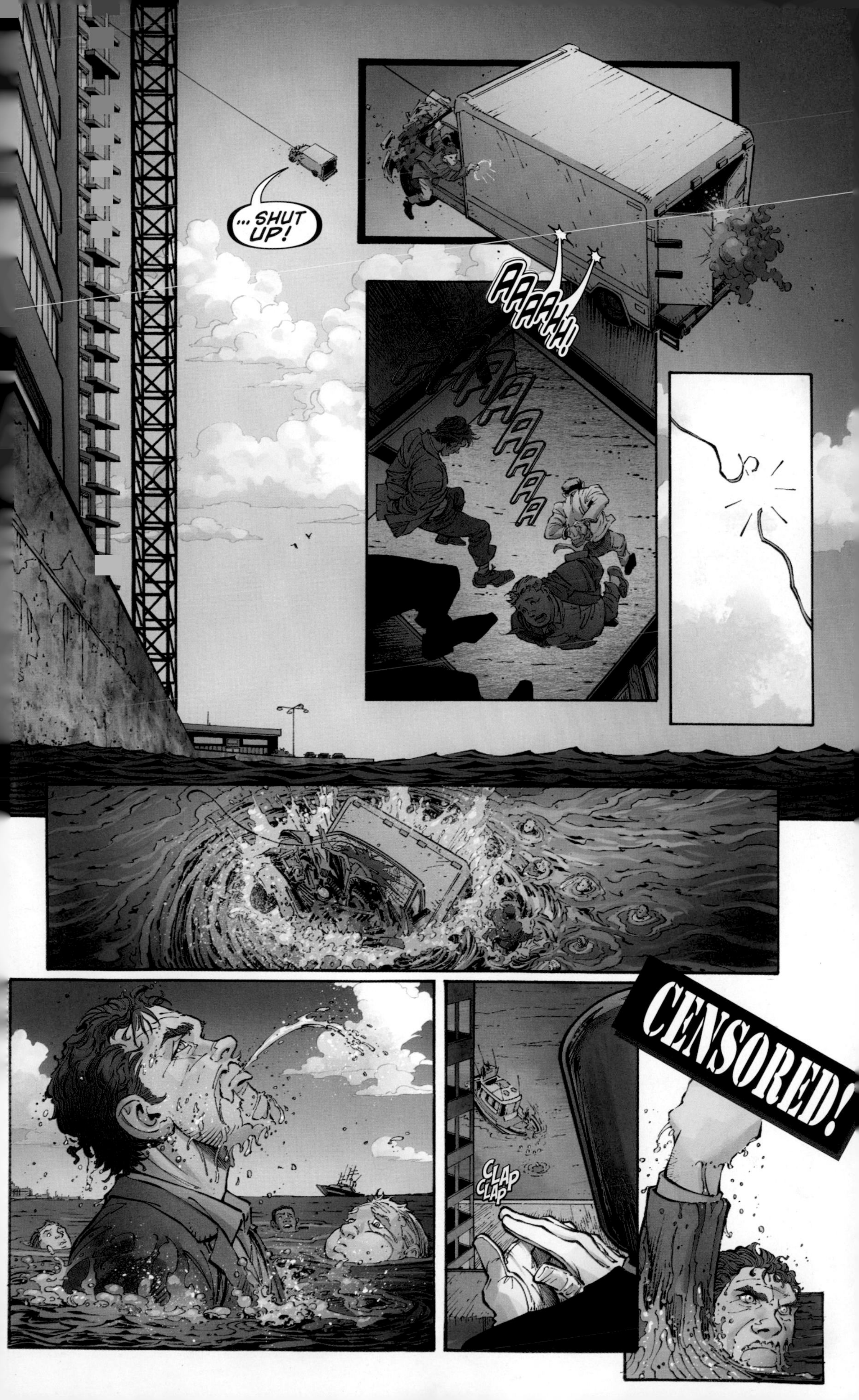
...SHUT UP!
AAAAAH!
CLAP CLAP
CENSORED!

"WHAT DO YOU LOVE ABOUT THE CITY, BRUCE?"

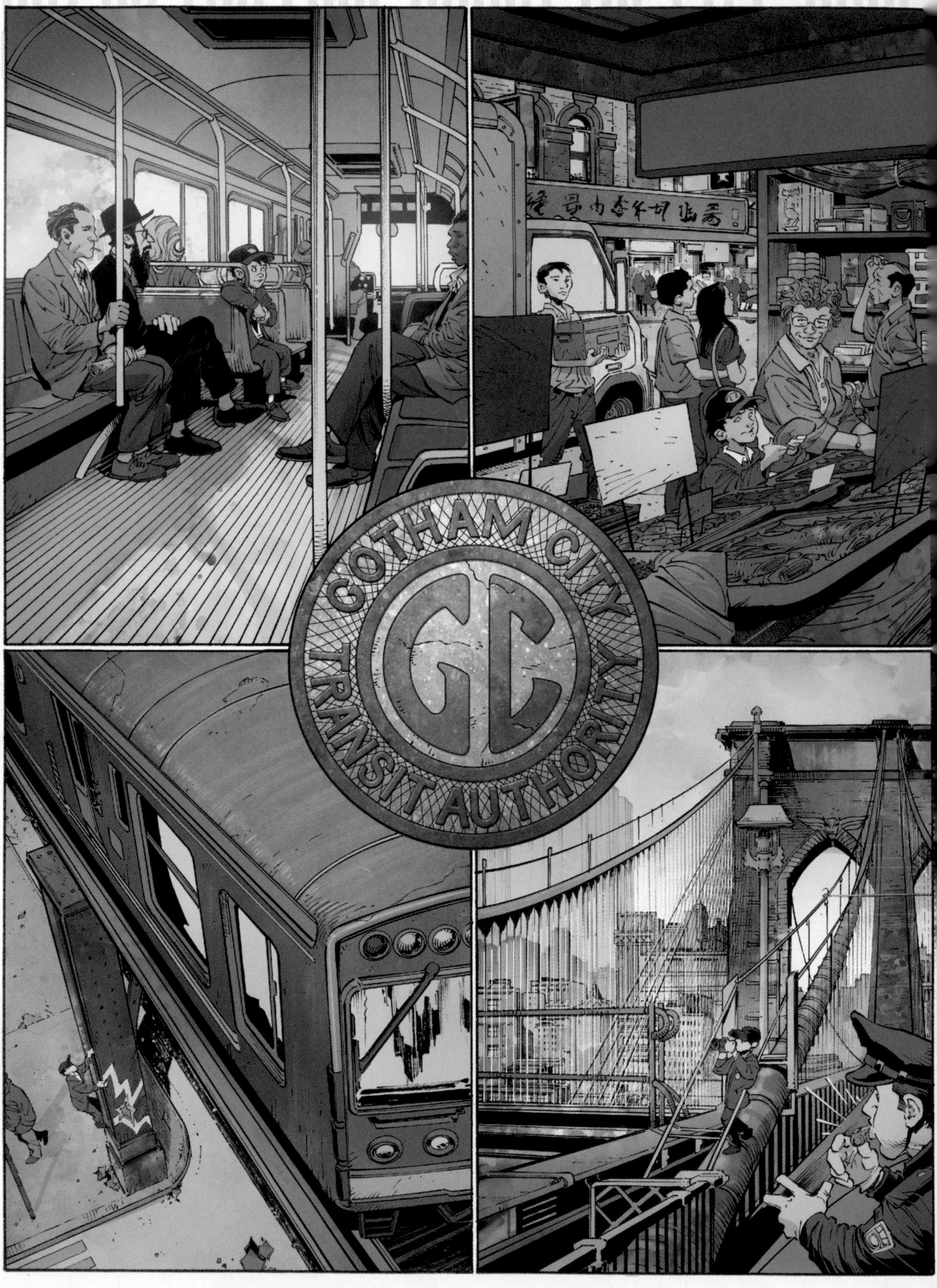
GOTHAM CITY
GC
TRANSIT AUTHORITY

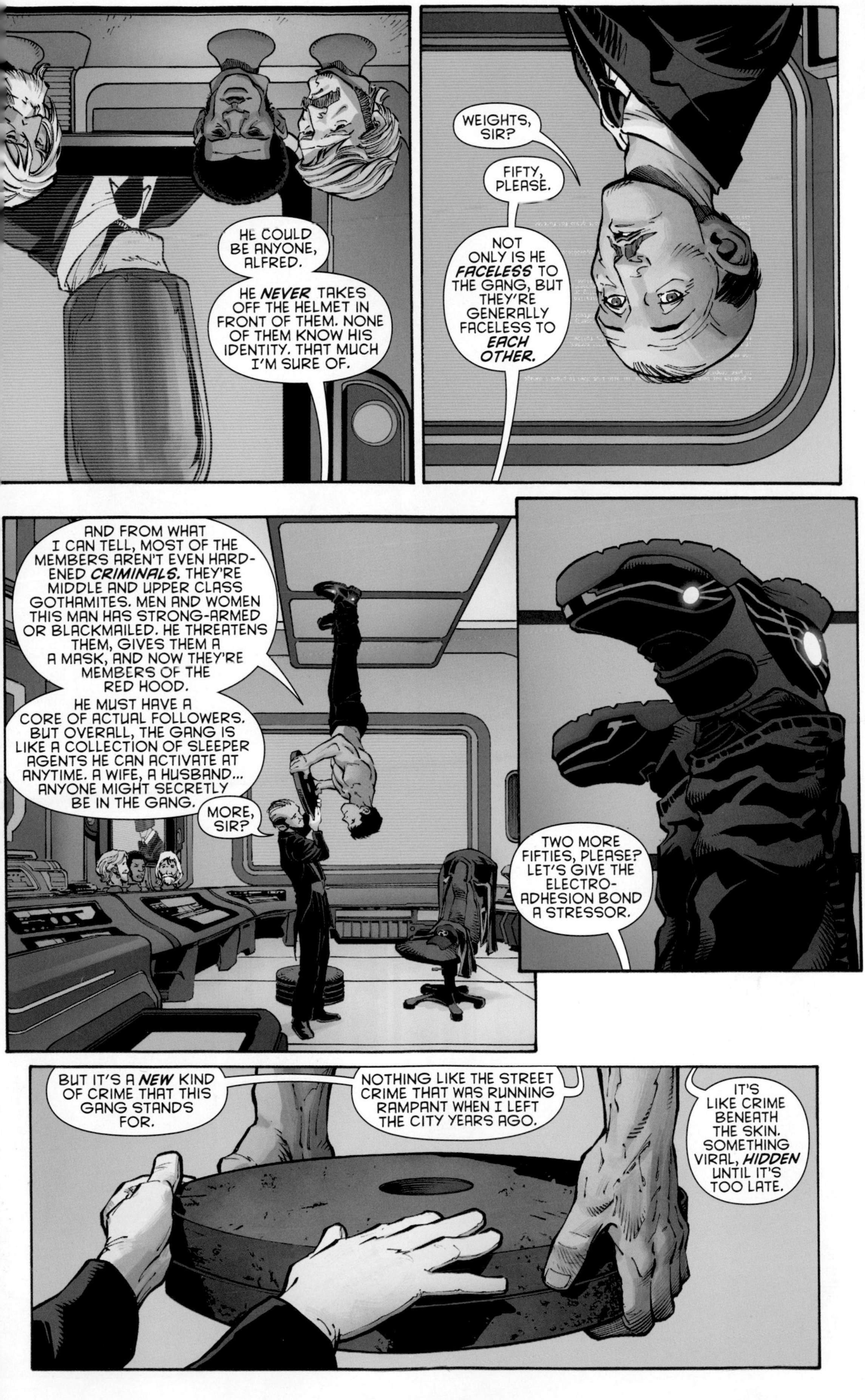

HE COULD BE ANYONE, ALFRED.
HE NEVER TAKES OFF THE HELMET IN FRONT OF THEM. NONE OF THEM KNOW HIS IDENTITY. THAT MUCH I'M SURE OF.
WEIGHTS, SIR?
FIFTY, PLEASE.
NOT ONLY IS HE FACELESS TO THE GANG, BUT THEY'RE GENERALLY FACELESS TO EACH OTHER.
AND FROM WHAT I CAN TELL, MOST OF THE MEMBERS AREN'T EVEN HARDENED CRIMINALS. THEY'RE MIDDLE AND UPPER CLASS GOTHAMITES. MEN AND WOMEN THIS MAN HAS STRONG-ARMED OR BLACKMAILED. HE THREATENS THEM, GIVES THEM A A MASK, AND NOW THEY'RE MEMBERS OF THE RED HOOD.
HE MUST HAVE A CORE OF ACTUAL FOLLOWERS. BUT OVERALL, THE GANG IS LIKE A COLLECTION OF SLEEPER AGENTS HE CAN ACTIVATE AT ANYTIME. A WIFE, A HUSBAND... ANYONE MIGHT SECRETLY BE IN THE GANG.
MORE, SIR?
TWO MORE FIFTIES, PLEASE? LET'S GIVE THE ELECTRO-ADHESION BOND A STRESSOR.
BUT IT'S A NEW KIND OF CRIME THAT THIS GANG STANDS FOR.
NOTHING LIKE THE STREET CRIME THAT WAS RUNNING RAMPANT WHEN I LEFT THE CITY YEARS AGO.
IT'S LIKE CRIME BENEATH THE SKIN. SOMETHING VIRAL, HIDDEN UNTIL IT'S TOO LATE.

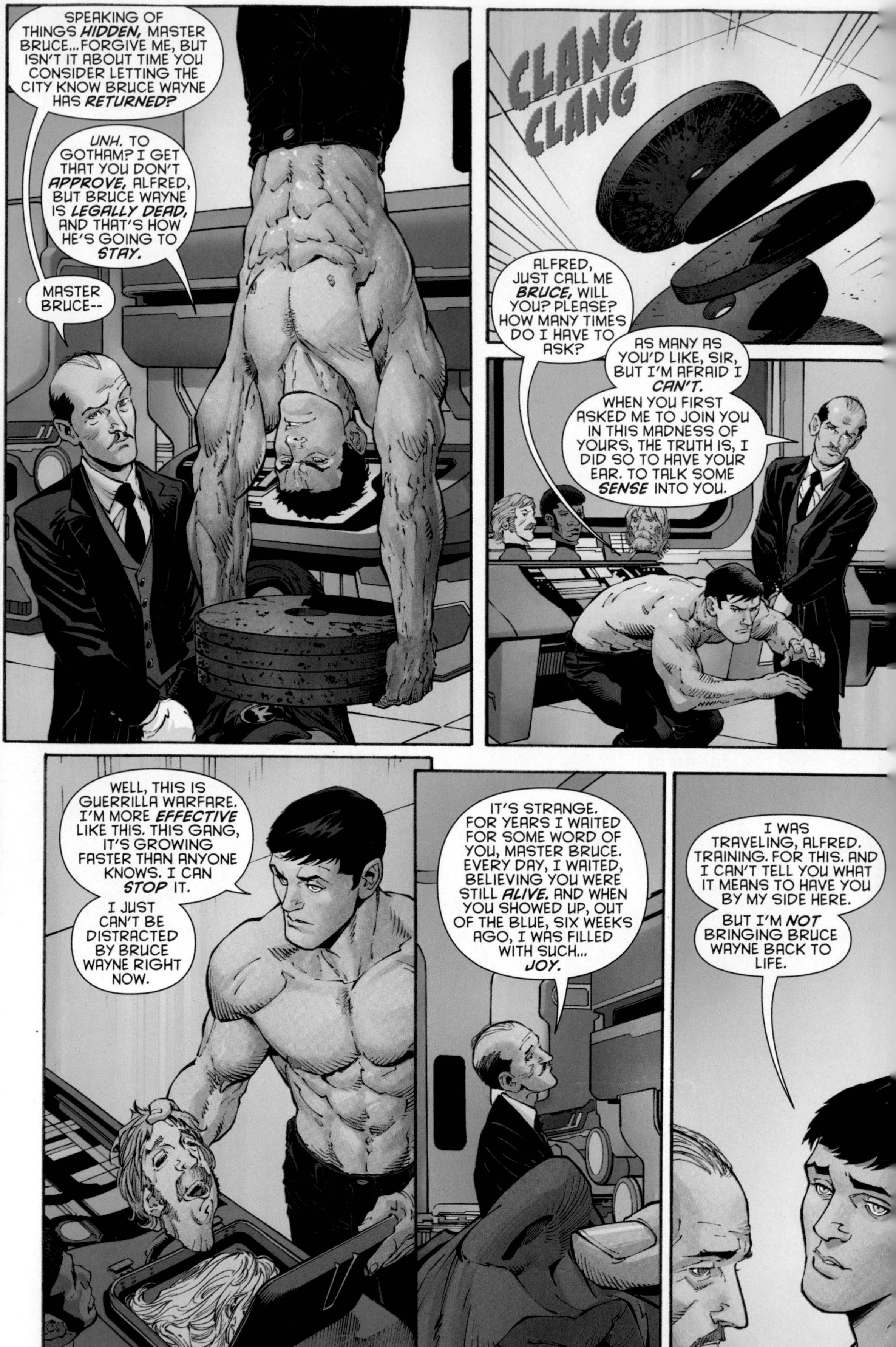

SPEAKING OF THINGS HIDDEN, MASTER BRUCE...FORGIVE ME, BUT ISN'T IT ABOUT TIME YOU CONSIDER LETTING THE CITY KNOW BRUCE WAYNE HAS RETURNED?
UNH. TO GOTHAM? I GET THAT YOU DON'T APPROVE, ALFRED, BUT BRUCE WAYNE IS LEGALLY DEAD, AND THAT'S HOW HE'S GOING TO STAY.
MASTER BRUCE--
CLANG CLANG
ALFRED, JUST CALL ME BRUCE, WILL YOU? PLEASE? HOW MANY TIMES DO I HAVE TO ASK?
AS MANY AS YOU'D LIKE, SIR, BUT I'M AFRAID I CAN'T.
WHEN YOU FIRST ASKED ME TO JOIN YOU IN THIS MADNESS OF YOURS, THE TRUTH IS, I DID SO TO HAVE YOUR EAR. TO TALK SOME SENSE INTO YOU.
WELL, THIS IS GUERRILLA WARFARE. I'M MORE EFFECTIVE LIKE THIS. THIS GANG, IT'S GROWING FASTER THAN ANYONE KNOWS. I CAN STOP IT.
I JUST CAN'T BE DISTRACTED BY BRUCE WAYNE RIGHT NOW.
IT'S STRANGE. FOR YEARS I WAITED FOR SOME WORD OF YOU, MASTER BRUCE. EVERY DAY, I WAITED, BELIEVING YOU WERE STILL ALIVE. AND WHEN YOU SHOWED UP, OUT OF THE BLUE, SIX WEEKS AGO, I WAS FILLED WITH SUCH... JOY.
I WAS TRAVELING, ALFRED. TRAINING. FOR THIS. AND I CAN'T TELL YOU WHAT IT MEANS TO HAVE YOU BY MY SIDE HERE.
BUT I'M NOT BRINGING BRUCE WAYNE BACK TO LIFE.

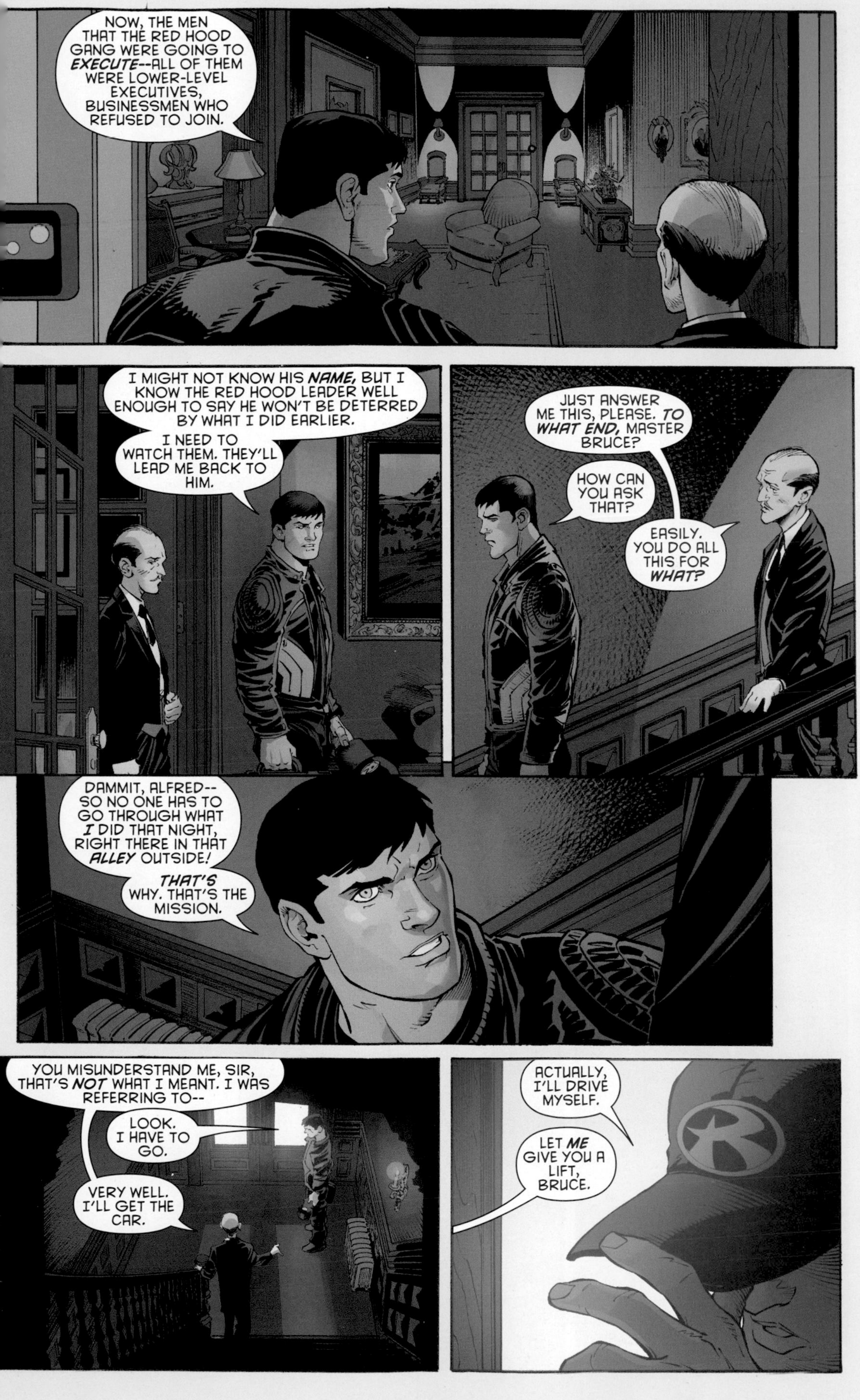
NOW, THE MEN THAT THE RED HOOD GANG WERE GOING TO EXECUTE--ALL OF THEM WERE LOWER-LEVEL EXECUTIVES, BUSINESSMEN WHO REFUSED TO JOIN.
I MIGHT NOT KNOW HIS NAME, BUT I KNOW THE RED HOOD LEADER WELL ENOUGH TO SAY HE WON'T BE DETERRED BY WHAT I DID EARLIER.
I NEED TO WATCH THEM. THEY'LL LEAD ME BACK TO HIM.
JUST ANSWER ME THIS, PLEASE. TO WHAT END, MASTER BRUCE?
HOW CAN YOU ASK THAT?
EASILY. YOU DO ALL THIS FOR WHAT?
DAMMIT, ALFRED-- SO NO ONE HAS TO GO THROUGH WHAT I DID THAT NIGHT, RIGHT THERE IN THAT ALLEY OUTSIDE!
THAT'S WHY. THAT'S THE MISSION.
YOU MISUNDERSTAND ME, SIR, THAT'S NOT WHAT I MEANT. I WAS REFERRING TO--
LOOK. I HAVE TO GO.
VERY WELL. I'LL GET THE CAR.
ACTUALLY, I'LL DRIVE MYSELF.
LET ME GIVE YOU A LIFT, BRUCE.

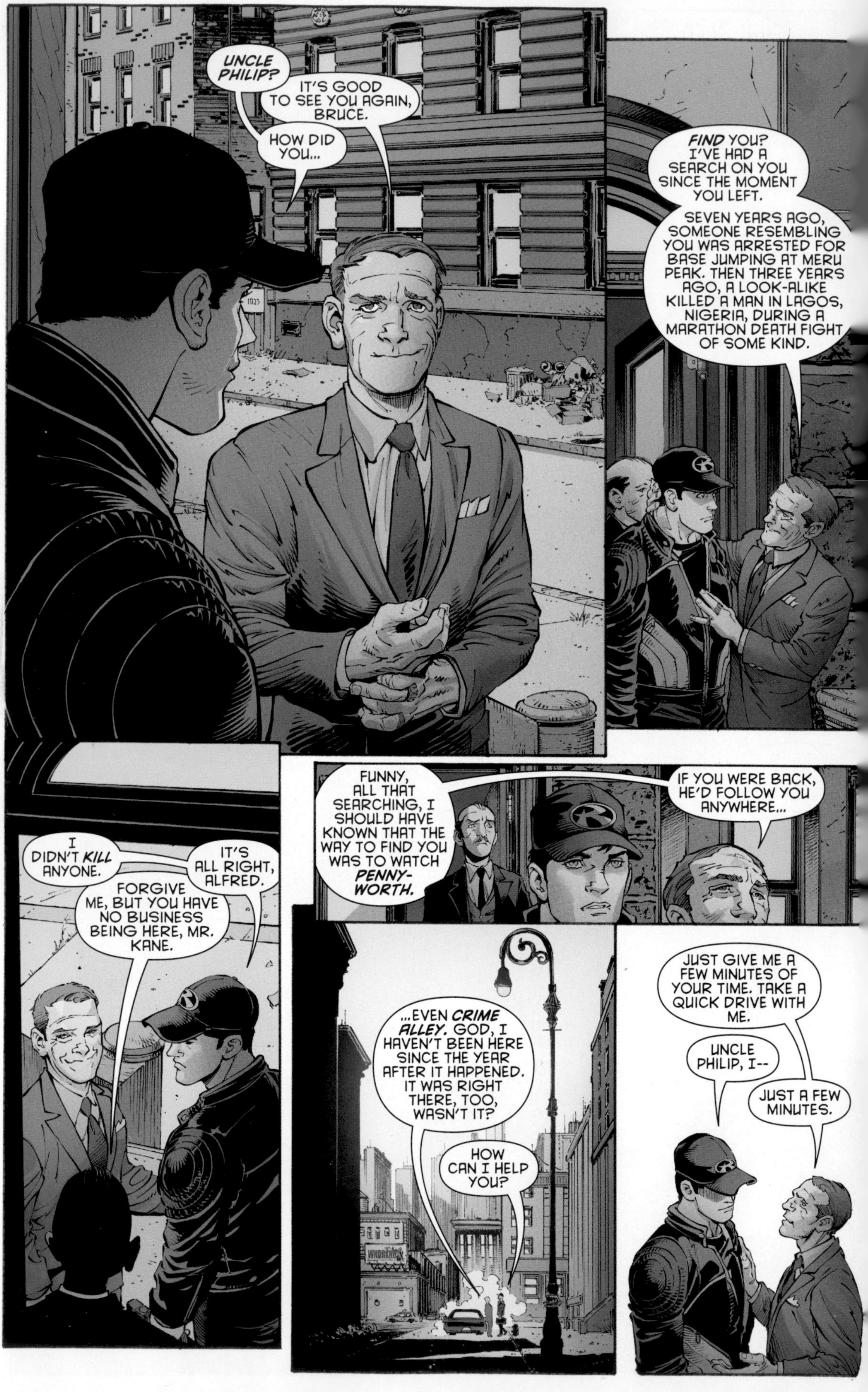
UNCLE PHILIP?
IT'S GOOD TO SEE YOU AGAIN, BRUCE.
HOW DID YOU...
FIND YOU? I'VE HAD A SEARCH ON YOU SINCE THE MOMENT YOU LEFT.
SEVEN YEARS AGO, SOMEONE RESEMBLING YOU WAS ARRESTED FOR BASE JUMPING AT MERU PEAK. THEN THREE YEARS AGO, A LOOK-ALIKE KILLED A MAN IN LAGOS, NIGERIA, DURING A MARATHON DEATH FIGHT OF SOME KIND.
I DIDN'T KILL ANYONE.
IT'S ALL RIGHT, ALFRED.
FORGIVE ME, BUT YOU HAVE NO BUSINESS BEING HERE, MR. KANE.
FUNNY, ALL THAT SEARCHING, I SHOULD HAVE KNOWN THAT THE WAY TO FIND YOU WAS TO WATCH PENNYWORTH.
IF YOU WERE BACK, HE'D FOLLOW YOU ANYWHERE...
...EVEN CRIME ALLEY. GOD, I HAVEN'T BEEN HERE SINCE THE YEAR AFTER IT HAPPENED. IT WAS RIGHT THERE, TOO, WASN'T IT?
HOW CAN I HELP YOU?
JUST GIVE ME A FEW MINUTES OF YOUR TIME. TAKE A QUICK DRIVE WITH ME.
UNCLE PHILIP, I--
JUST A FEW MINUTES.

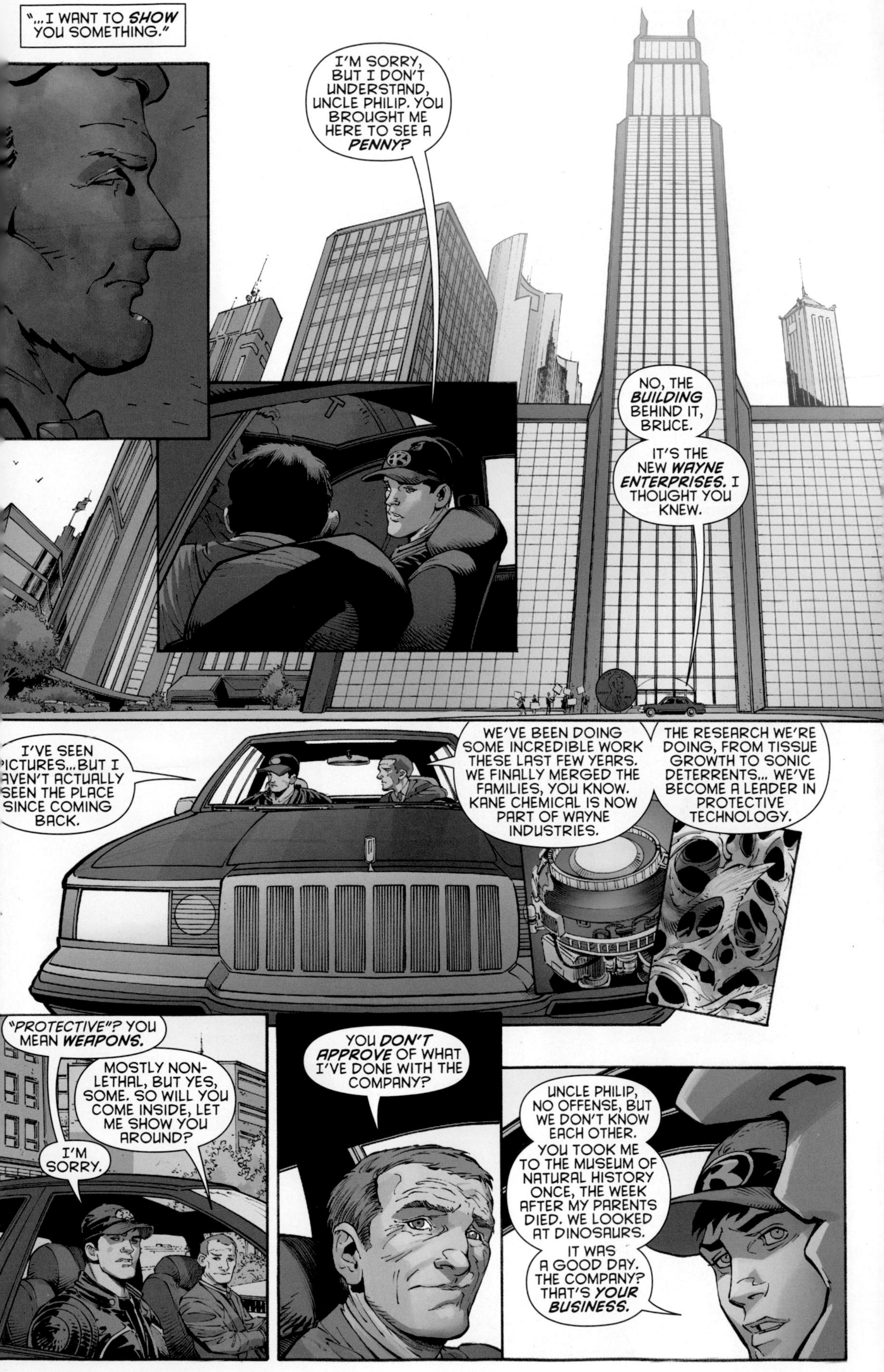
"...I WANT TO SHOW YOU SOMETHING."
I'M SORRY, BUT I DON'T UNDERSTAND, UNCLE PHILIP. YOU BROUGHT ME HERE TO SEE A PENNY?
NO, THE BUILDING BEHIND IT, BRUCE.
IT'S THE NEW WAYNE ENTERPRISES. I THOUGHT YOU KNEW.
I'VE SEEN PICTURES...BUT I HAVEN'T ACTUALLY SEEN THE PLACE SINCE COMING BACK.
WE'VE BEEN DOING SOME INCREDIBLE WORK THESE LAST FEW YEARS. WE FINALLY MERGED THE FAMILIES, YOU KNOW. KANE CHEMICAL IS NOW PART OF WAYNE INDUSTRIES.
THE RESEARCH WE'RE DOING, FROM TISSUE GROWTH TO SONIC DETERRENTS... WE'VE BECOME A LEADER IN PROTECTIVE TECHNOLOGY.
"PROTECTIVE"? YOU MEAN WEAPONS.
MOSTLY NON-LETHAL, BUT YES, SOME. SO WILL YOU COME INSIDE, LET ME SHOW YOU AROUND?
I'M SORRY.
YOU DON'T APPROVE OF WHAT I'VE DONE WITH THE COMPANY?
UNCLE PHILIP, NO OFFENSE, BUT WE DON'T KNOW EACH OTHER.
YOU TOOK ME TO THE MUSEUM OF NATURAL HISTORY ONCE, THE WEEK AFTER MY PARENTS DIED. WE LOOKED AT DINOSAURS.
IT WAS A GOOD DAY. THE COMPANY? THAT'S YOUR BUSINESS.

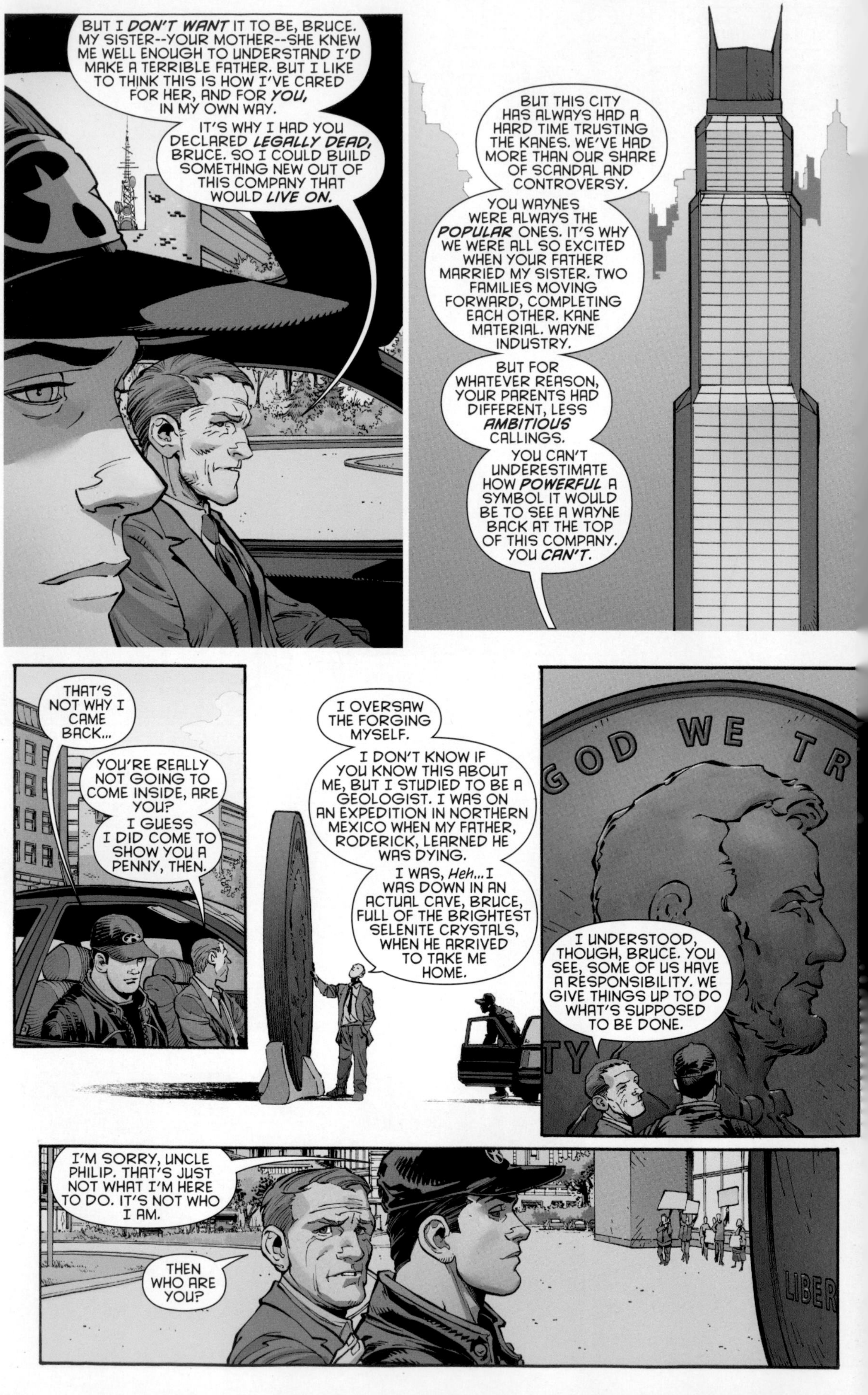
BUT I DON'T WANT IT TO BE, BRUCE. MY SISTER--YOUR MOTHER--SHE KNEW ME WELL ENOUGH TO UNDERSTAND I'D MAKE A TERRIBLE FATHER. BUT I LIKE TO THINK THIS IS HOW I'VE CARED FOR HER, AND FOR YOU, IN MY OWN WAY.
IT'S WHY I HAD YOU DECLARED LEGALLY DEAD, BRUCE. SO I COULD BUILD SOMETHING NEW OUT OF THIS COMPANY THAT WOULD LIVE ON.
BUT THIS CITY HAS ALWAYS HAD A HARD TIME TRUSTING THE KANES. WE'VE HAD MORE THAN OUR SHARE OF SCANDAL AND CONTROVERSY.
YOU WAYNES WERE ALWAYS THE POPULAR ONES. IT'S WHY WE WERE ALL SO EXCITED WHEN YOUR FATHER MARRIED MY SISTER. TWO FAMILIES MOVING FORWARD, COMPLETING EACH OTHER. KANE MATERIAL. WAYNE INDUSTRY.
BUT FOR WHATEVER REASON, YOUR PARENTS HAD DIFFERENT, LESS AMBITIOUS CALLINGS.
YOU CAN'T UNDERESTIMATE HOW POWERFUL A SYMBOL IT WOULD BE TO SEE A WAYNE BACK AT THE TOP OF THIS COMPANY. YOU CAN'T.
THAT'S NOT WHY I CAME BACK...
YOU'RE REALLY NOT GOING TO COME INSIDE, ARE YOU?
I GUESS I DID COME TO SHOW YOU A PENNY, THEN.
I OVERSAW THE FORGING MYSELF.
I DON'T KNOW IF YOU KNOW THIS ABOUT ME, BUT I STUDIED TO BE A GEOLOGIST. I WAS ON AN EXPEDITION IN NORTHERN MEXICO WHEN MY FATHER, RODERICK, LEARNED HE WAS DYING.
I WAS, Heh... I WAS DOWN IN AN ACTUAL CAVE, BRUCE, FULL OF THE BRIGHTEST SELENITE CRYSTALS, WHEN HE ARRIVED TO TAKE ME HOME.
GOD WE TR
I UNDERSTOOD, THOUGH, BRUCE. YOU SEE, SOME OF US HAVE A RESPONSIBILITY. WE GIVE THINGS UP TO DO WHAT'S SUPPOSED TO BE DONE.
TY
I'M SORRY, UNCLE PHILIP. THAT'S JUST NOT WHAT I'M HERE TO DO. IT'S NOT WHO I AM.
THEN WHO ARE YOU?
LIBER

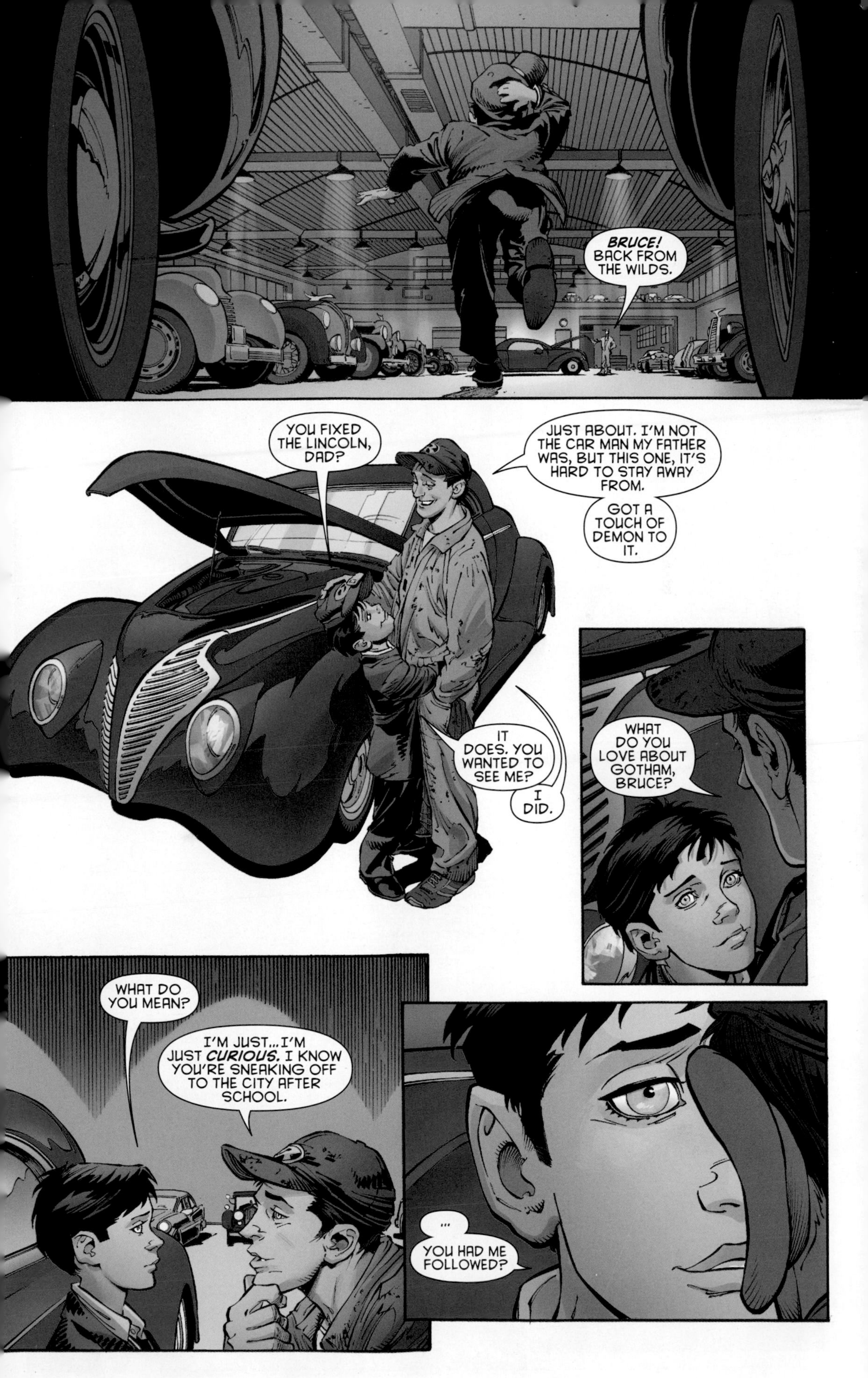
BRUCE! BACK FROM THE WILDS.
YOU FIXED THE LINCOLN, DAD?
JUST ABOUT. I'M NOT THE CAR MAN MY FATHER WAS, BUT THIS ONE, IT'S HARD TO STAY AWAY FROM.
GOT A TOUCH OF DEMON TO IT.
IT DOES. YOU WANTED TO SEE ME?
I DID.
WHAT DO YOU LOVE ABOUT GOTHAM, BRUCE?
WHAT DO YOU MEAN?
I'M JUST...I'M JUST CURIOUS. I KNOW YOU'RE SNEAKING OFF TO THE CITY AFTER SCHOOL.
...
YOU HAD ME FOLLOWED?

BRUCE, WHEN YOU'RE FROM A FAMILY LIKE OURS, IT ISN'T *SAFE* TO--

THAT'S *WHY*, THOUGH.

THAT'S WHY *WHAT*?

THAT'S WHY I LOVE GOTHAM, DAD. BECAUSE IT'S A PLACE WHERE YOU CAN BE *ANYONE*. WHERE I CAN BE...*NOT* BRUCE WAYNE. I MEAN, NOBODY KNOWS WHO I AM THERE. NOT LIKE SCHOOL. THE CITY LETS ME BE *ANYONE* I WANT.

WELL, WHO DID THE CITY TELL YOU TO BE TODAY?

I DON'T KNOW. NO ONE, REALLY.

Heh. WELL, WHOEVER YOU ARE, BRUCE, KNOW THAT WE'RE *PROUD* OF YOU, YOUR MOM AND I. AND DO ME A FAVOR, WILL YOU? GO EASY ON YOURSELF IN THAT DEPARTMENT. YOU'VE GOT A LOT OF TIME TO FIGURE YOURSELF OUT.

MY GREAT-GRANDFATHER, ALAN, HE USED TO SAY THAT FATE FORMS IN THE DARK. AND SPEAKING OF THE *DARK*, TAKE A LOOK AT THIS.

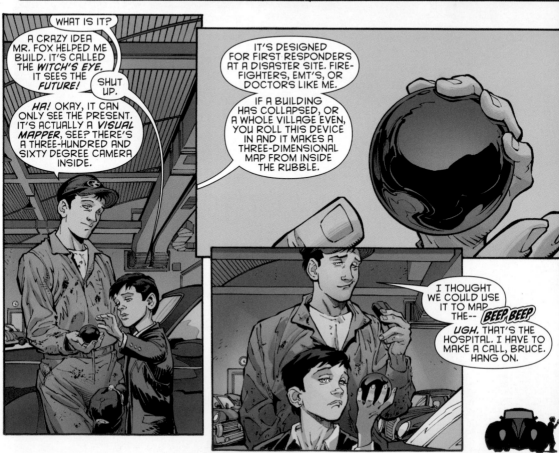

WHAT IS IT?

A CRAZY IDEA MR. FOX HELPED ME BUILD. IT'S CALLED THE *WITCH'S EYE.* IT SEES THE *FUTURE!*

SHUT UP.

HA! OKAY, IT CAN ONLY SEE THE PRESENT. IT'S ACTUALLY A *VISUAL MAPPER,* SEE? THERE'S A THREE-HUNDRED AND SIXTY DEGREE CAMERA INSIDE.

IT'S DESIGNED FOR FIRST RESPONDERS AT A DISASTER SITE. FIRE-FIGHTERS, EMT'S, OR DOCTORS LIKE ME.

IF A BUILDING HAS COLLAPSED, OR A WHOLE VILLAGE EVEN, YOU ROLL THIS DEVICE IN AND IT MAKES A THREE-DIMENSIONAL MAP FROM INSIDE THE RUBBLE.

I THOUGHT WE COULD USE IT TO MAP THE-- *BEEP BEEP*

UGH. THAT'S THE HOSPITAL. I HAVE TO MAKE A CALL, BRUCE. HANG ON.

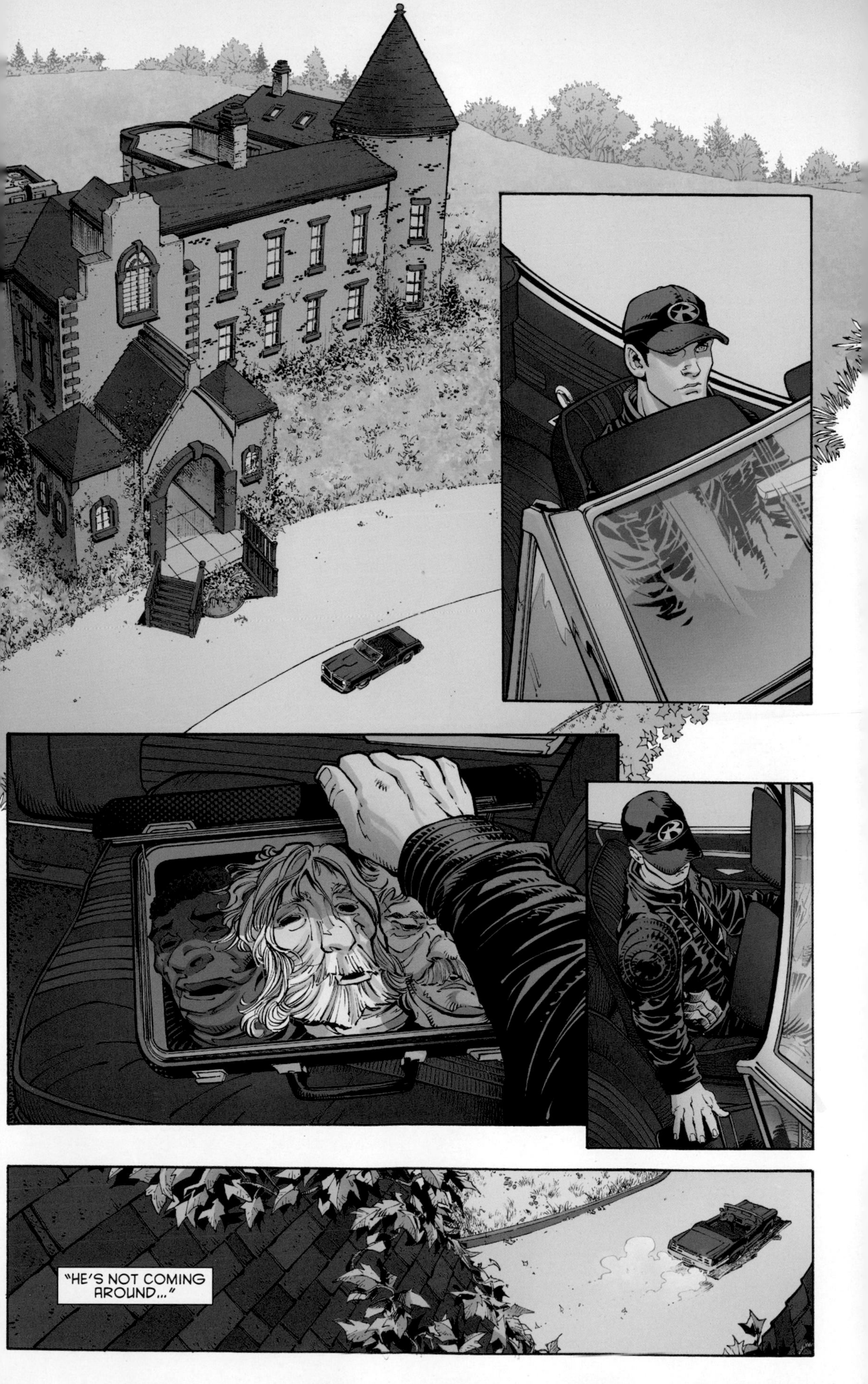
"HE'S NOT COMING AROUND..."

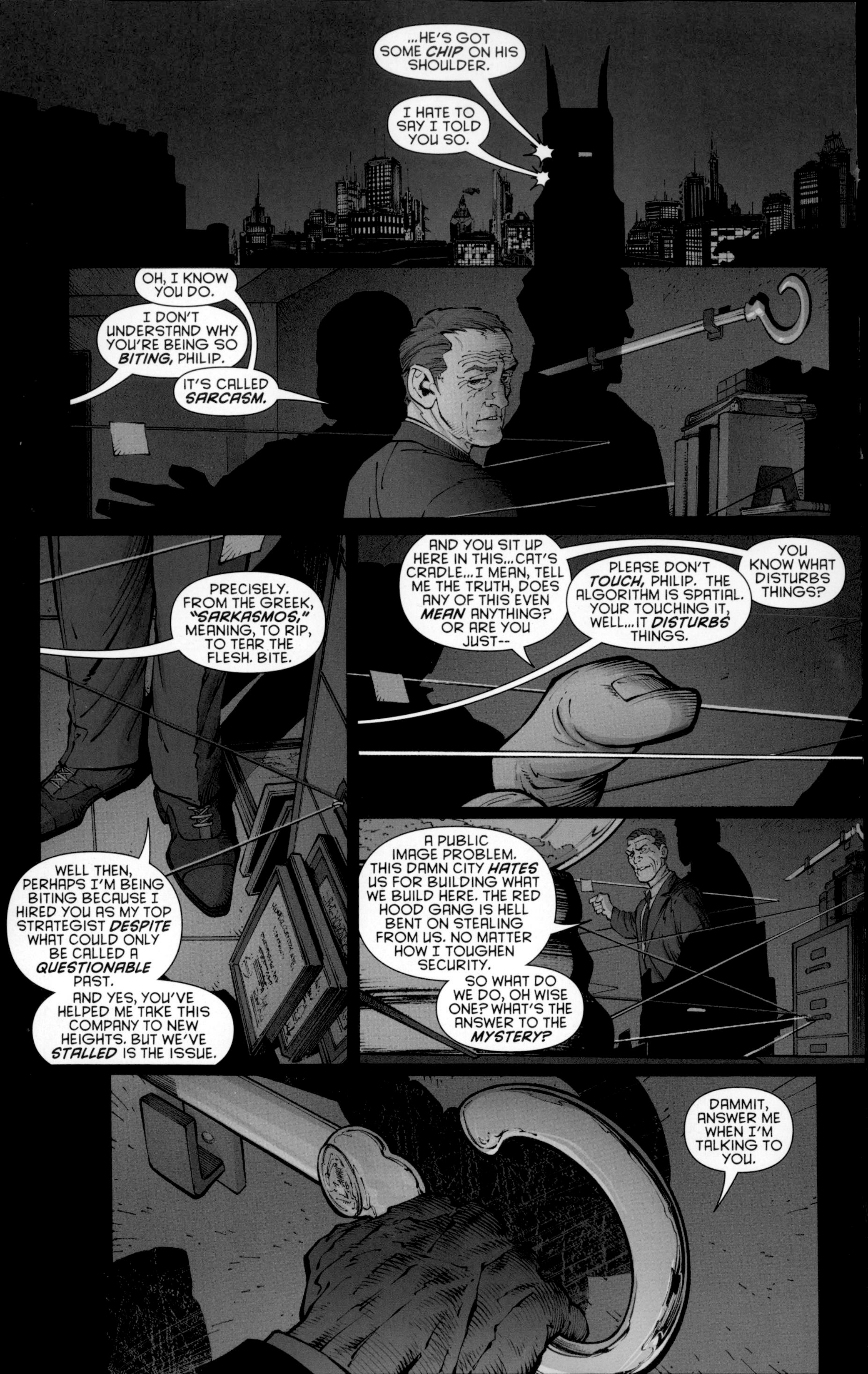
...HE'S GOT SOME CHIP ON HIS SHOULDER.
I HATE TO SAY I TOLD YOU SO.
OH, I KNOW YOU DO.
I DON'T UNDERSTAND WHY YOU'RE BEING SO BITING, PHILIP.
IT'S CALLED SARCASM.
PRECISELY. FROM THE GREEK, "SARKASMOS," MEANING, TO RIP, TO TEAR THE FLESH. BITE.
WELL THEN, PERHAPS I'M BEING BITING BECAUSE I HIRED YOU AS MY TOP STRATEGIST DESPITE WHAT COULD ONLY BE CALLED A QUESTIONABLE PAST.
AND YES, YOU'VE HELPED ME TAKE THIS COMPANY TO NEW HEIGHTS. BUT WE'VE STALLED IS THE ISSUE.
AND YOU SIT UP HERE IN THIS...CAT'S CRADLE...I MEAN, TELL ME THE TRUTH, DOES ANY OF THIS EVEN MEAN ANYTHING? OR ARE YOU JUST--
PLEASE DON'T TOUCH, PHILIP. THE ALGORITHM IS SPATIAL. YOUR TOUCHING IT, WELL...IT DISTURBS THINGS.
YOU KNOW WHAT DISTURBS THINGS?
A PUBLIC IMAGE PROBLEM. THIS DAMN CITY HATES US FOR BUILDING WHAT WE BUILD HERE. THE RED HOOD GANG IS HELL BENT ON STEALING FROM US. NO MATTER HOW I TOUGHEN SECURITY.
SO WHAT DO WE DO, OH WISE ONE? WHAT'S THE ANSWER TO THE MYSTERY?
DAMMIT, ANSWER ME WHEN I'M TALKING TO YOU.

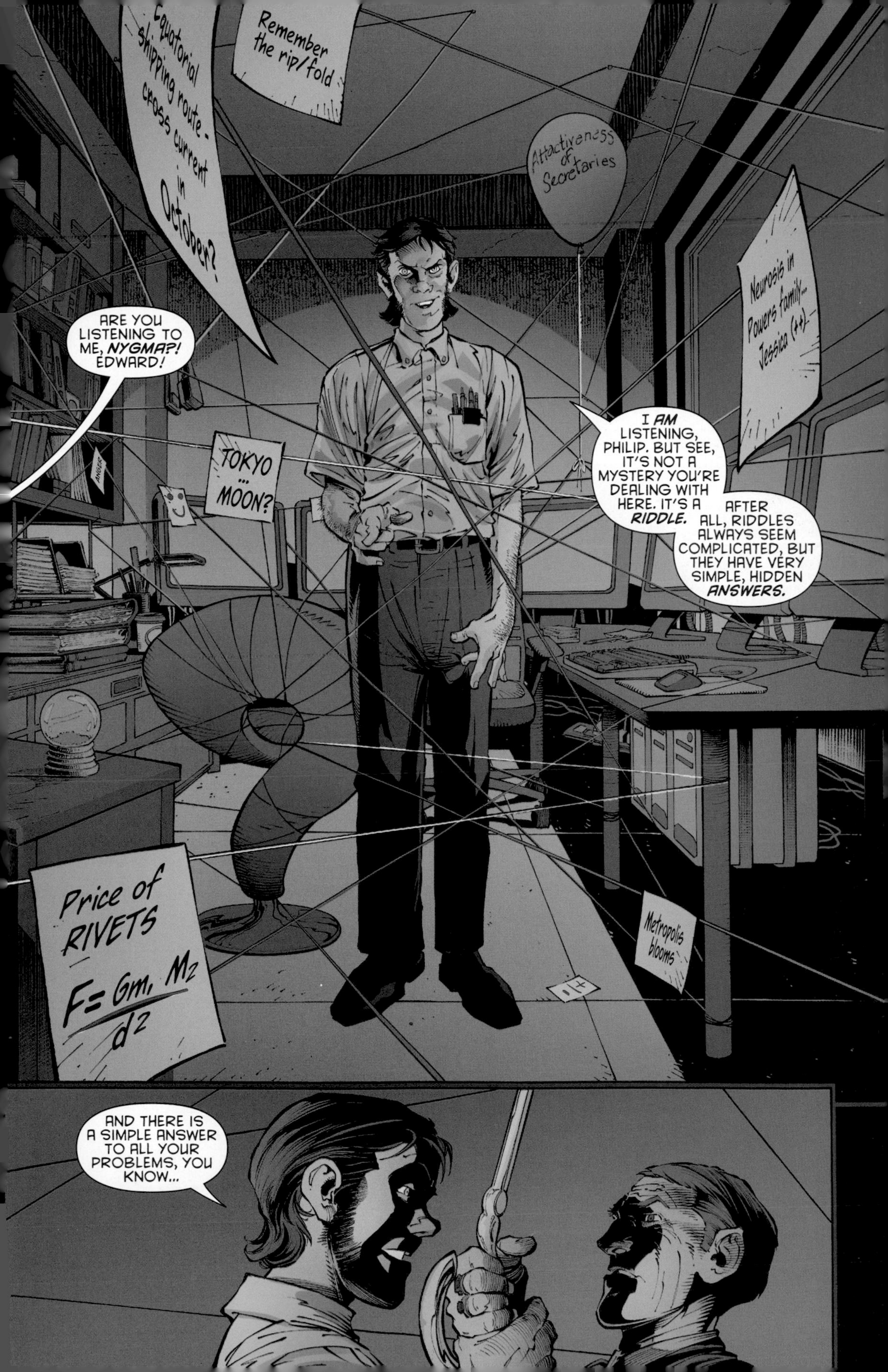
Equatorial shipping route - cross current in October?
Remember the rip/fold
Attractiveness of Secretaries
Neurosis in Powers family... Jessica (++)
ARE YOU LISTENING TO ME, NYGMA?! EDWARD!
TOKYO ... MOON?
ANGER
I AM LISTENING, PHILIP. BUT SEE, IT'S NOT A MYSTERY YOU'RE DEALING WITH HERE. IT'S A RIDDLE.
AFTER ALL, RIDDLES ALWAYS SEEM COMPLICATED, BUT THEY HAVE VERY SIMPLE, HIDDEN ANSWERS.
Price of RIVETS
F= Gm, M2 / d2
Metropolis blooms
AND THERE IS A SIMPLE ANSWER TO ALL YOUR PROBLEMS, YOU KNOW...

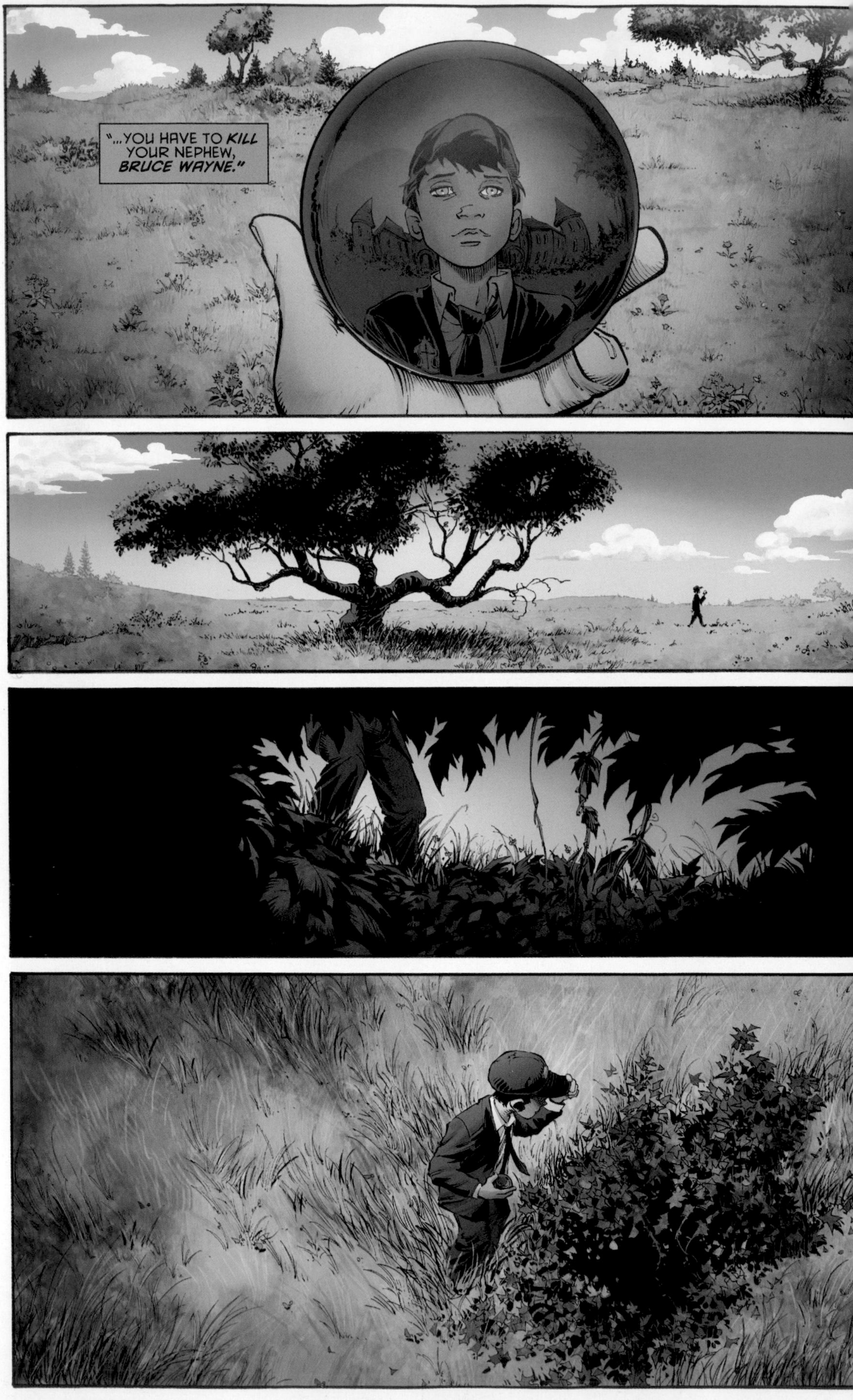
"...YOU HAVE TO KILL YOUR NEPHEW, BRUCE WAYNE."

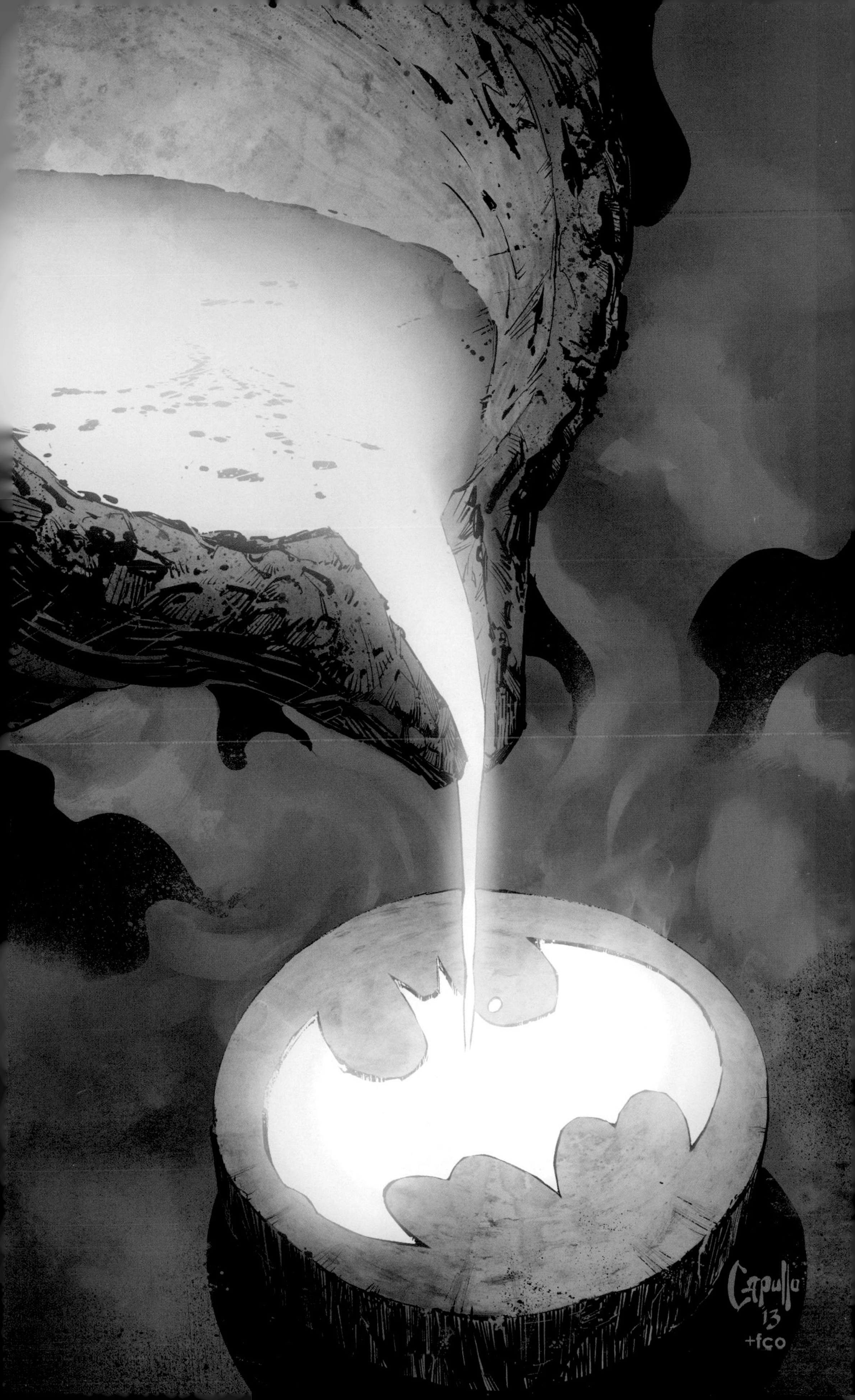
Capullo
13
+fco

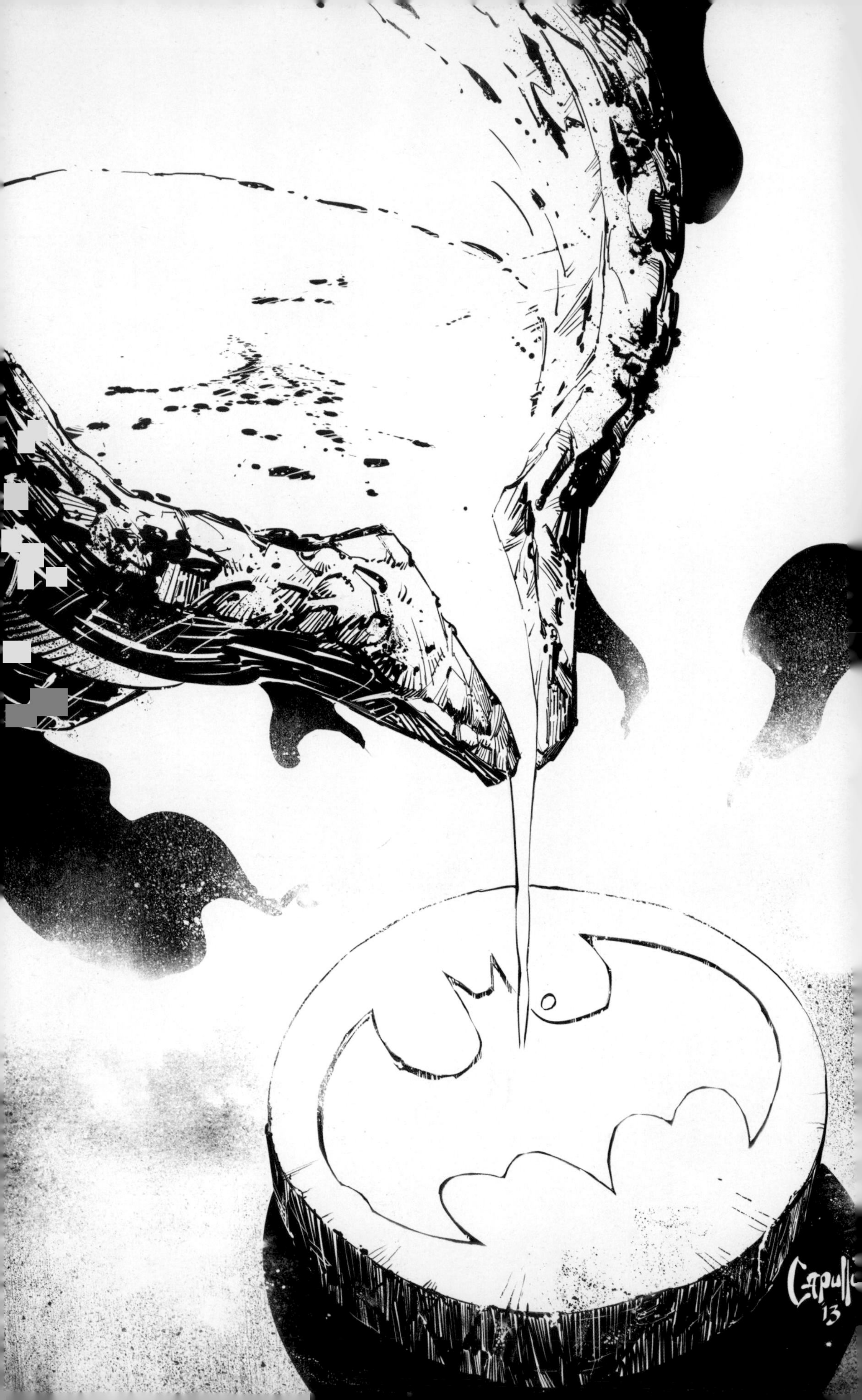

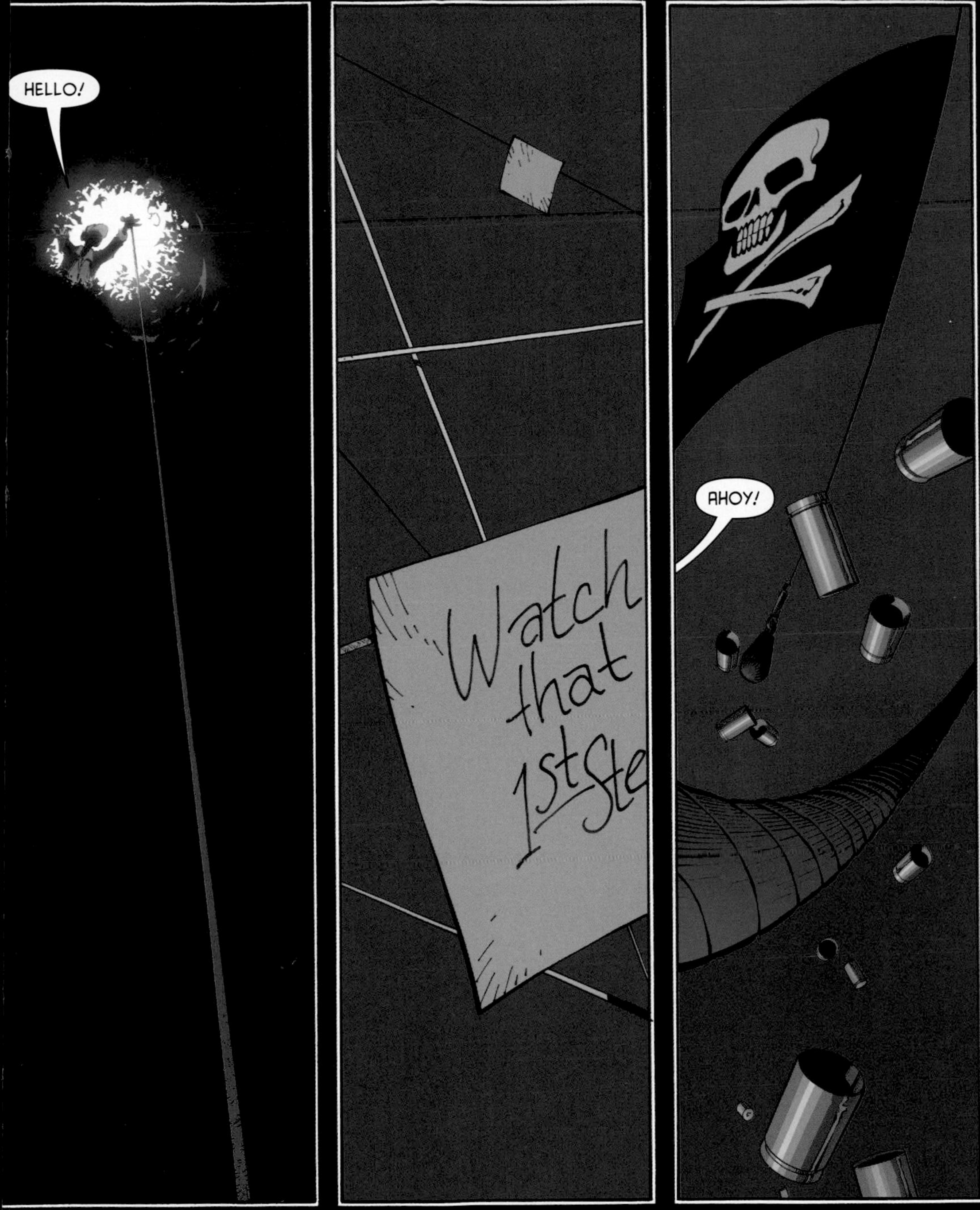
HELLO!
Watch that 1st Ste
AHOY!

ZERO YEAR

SECRET CITY: PART TWO

SCOTT SNYDER WRITER

GREG CAPULLO PENCILLER

DANNY MIKI INKER

FCO PLASCENCIA – COLORIST • **NICK NAPOLITANO** – LETTERER

CAPULLO & PLASCENCIA – COVER

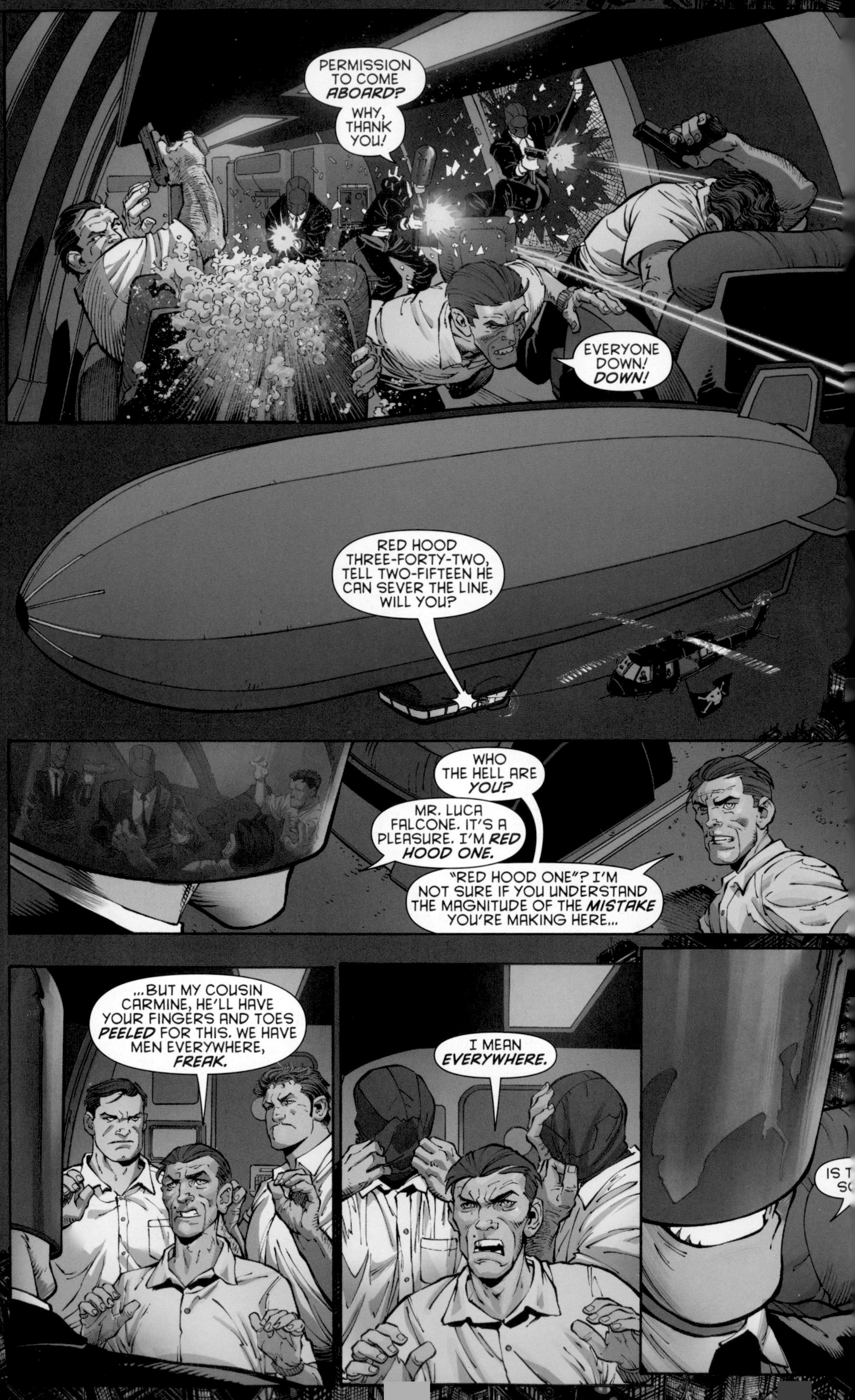

PERMISSION TO COME ABOARD?
WHY, THANK YOU!
EVERYONE DOWN! DOWN!
RED HOOD THREE-FORTY-TWO, TELL TWO-FIFTEEN HE CAN SEVER THE LINE, WILL YOU?
WHO THE HELL ARE YOU?
MR. LUCA FALCONE. IT'S A PLEASURE. I'M RED HOOD ONE.
"RED HOOD ONE"? I'M NOT SURE IF YOU UNDERSTAND THE MAGNITUDE OF THE MISTAKE YOU'RE MAKING HERE...
...BUT MY COUSIN CARMINE, HE'LL HAVE YOUR FINGERS AND TOES PEELED FOR THIS. WE HAVE MEN EVERYWHERE, FREAK.
I MEAN EVERYWHERE.

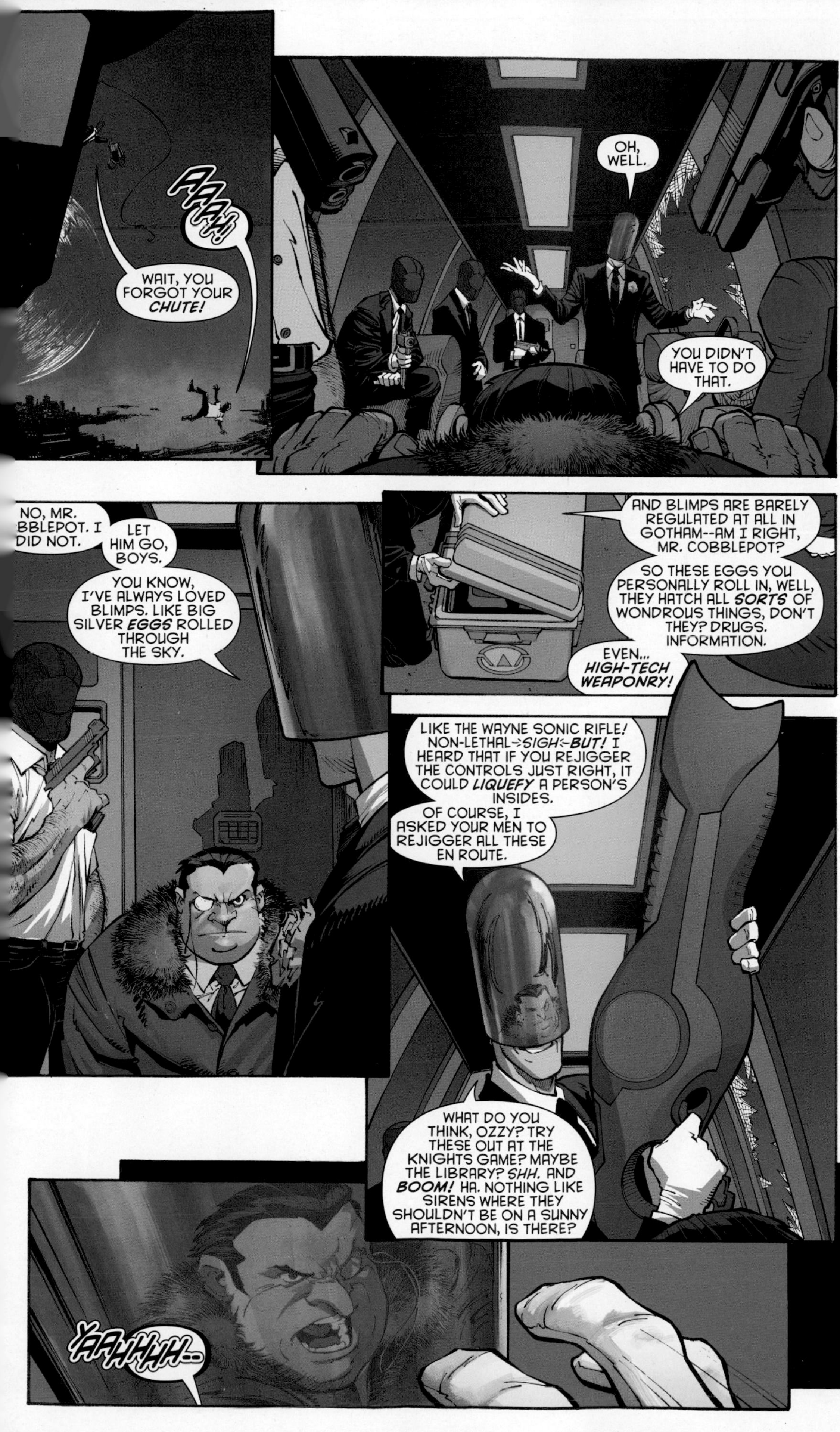
AAAH!
WAIT, YOU FORGOT YOUR CHUTE!
OH, WELL.
YOU DIDN'T HAVE TO DO THAT.
NO, MR. ...BBLEPOT. I DID NOT.
LET HIM GO, BOYS.
YOU KNOW, I'VE ALWAYS LOVED BLIMPS. LIKE BIG SILVER EGGS ROLLED THROUGH THE SKY.
AND BLIMPS ARE BARELY REGULATED AT ALL IN GOTHAM--AM I RIGHT, MR. COBBLEPOT?
SO THESE EGGS YOU PERSONALLY ROLL IN, WELL, THEY HATCH ALL SORTS OF WONDROUS THINGS, DON'T THEY? DRUGS. INFORMATION.
EVEN... HIGH-TECH WEAPONRY!
LIKE THE WAYNE SONIC RIFLE! NON-LETHAL→SIGH←BUT! I HEARD THAT IF YOU REJIGGER THE CONTROLS JUST RIGHT, IT COULD LIQUEFY A PERSON'S INSIDES.
OF COURSE, I ASKED YOUR MEN TO REJIGGER ALL THESE EN ROUTE.
WHAT DO YOU THINK, OZZY? TRY THESE OUT AT THE KNIGHTS GAME? MAYBE THE LIBRARY? SHH. AND BOOM! HA. NOTHING LIKE SIRENS WHERE THEY SHOULDN'T BE ON A SUNNY AFTERNOON, IS THERE?
YAAHHHH--

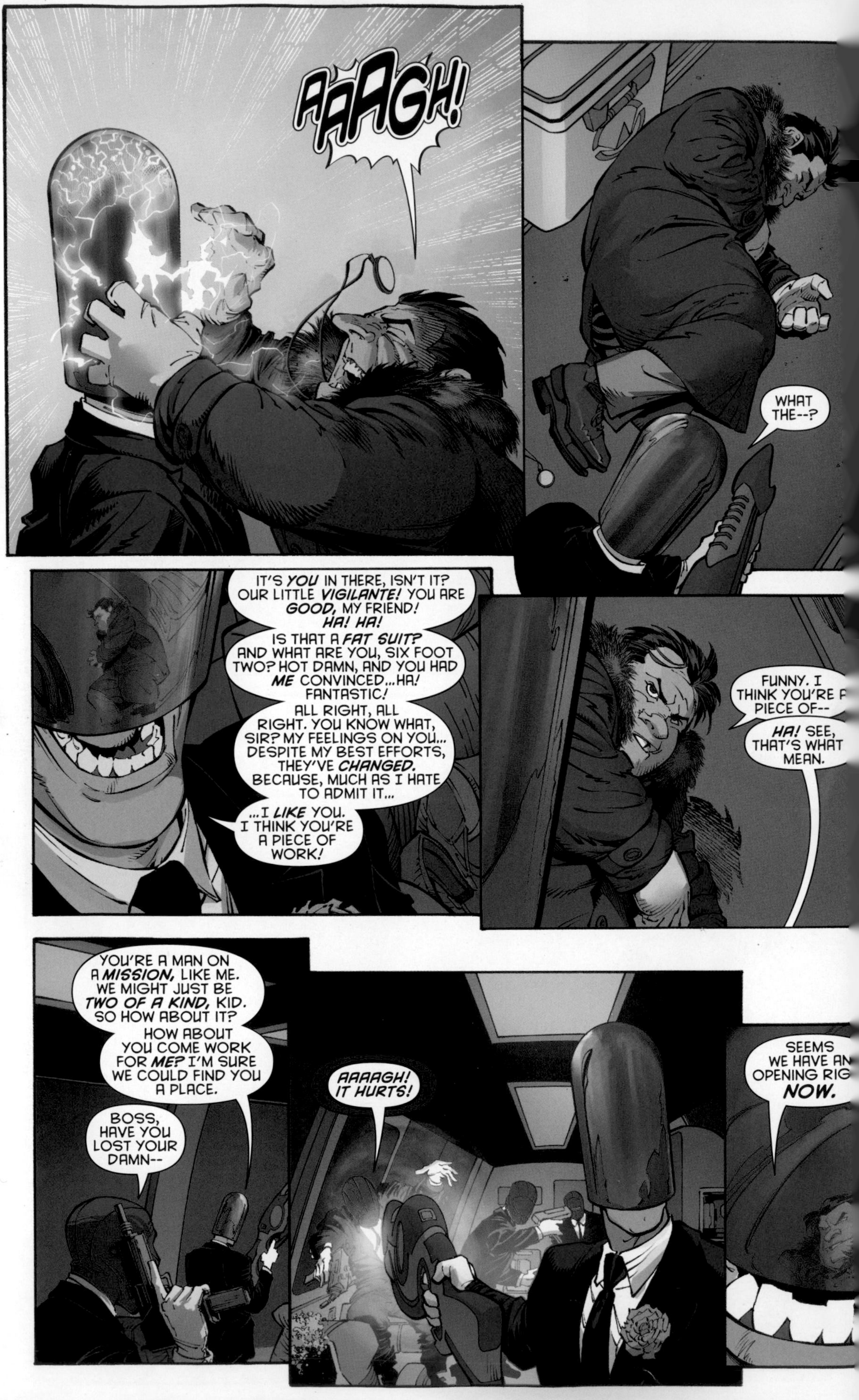
AAAGH!
WHAT THE--?
IT'S YOU IN THERE, ISN'T IT? OUR LITTLE VIGILANTE! YOU ARE GOOD, MY FRIEND! HA! HA!
IS THAT A FAT SUIT? AND WHAT ARE YOU, SIX FOOT TWO? HOT DAMN, AND YOU HAD ME CONVINCED...HA! FANTASTIC!
ALL RIGHT, ALL RIGHT. YOU KNOW WHAT, SIR? MY FEELINGS ON YOU... DESPITE MY BEST EFFORTS, THEY'VE CHANGED. BECAUSE, MUCH AS I HATE TO ADMIT IT...
...I LIKE YOU. I THINK YOU'RE A PIECE OF WORK!
FUNNY. I THINK YOU'RE A PIECE OF--
HA! SEE, THAT'S WHAT MEAN.
YOU'RE A MAN ON A MISSION, LIKE ME. WE MIGHT JUST BE TWO OF A KIND, KID. SO HOW ABOUT IT?
HOW ABOUT YOU COME WORK FOR ME? I'M SURE WE COULD FIND YOU A PLACE.
BOSS, HAVE YOU LOST YOUR DAMN--
AAAAGH! IT HURTS!
SEEMS WE HAVE AN OPENING RIG NOW.

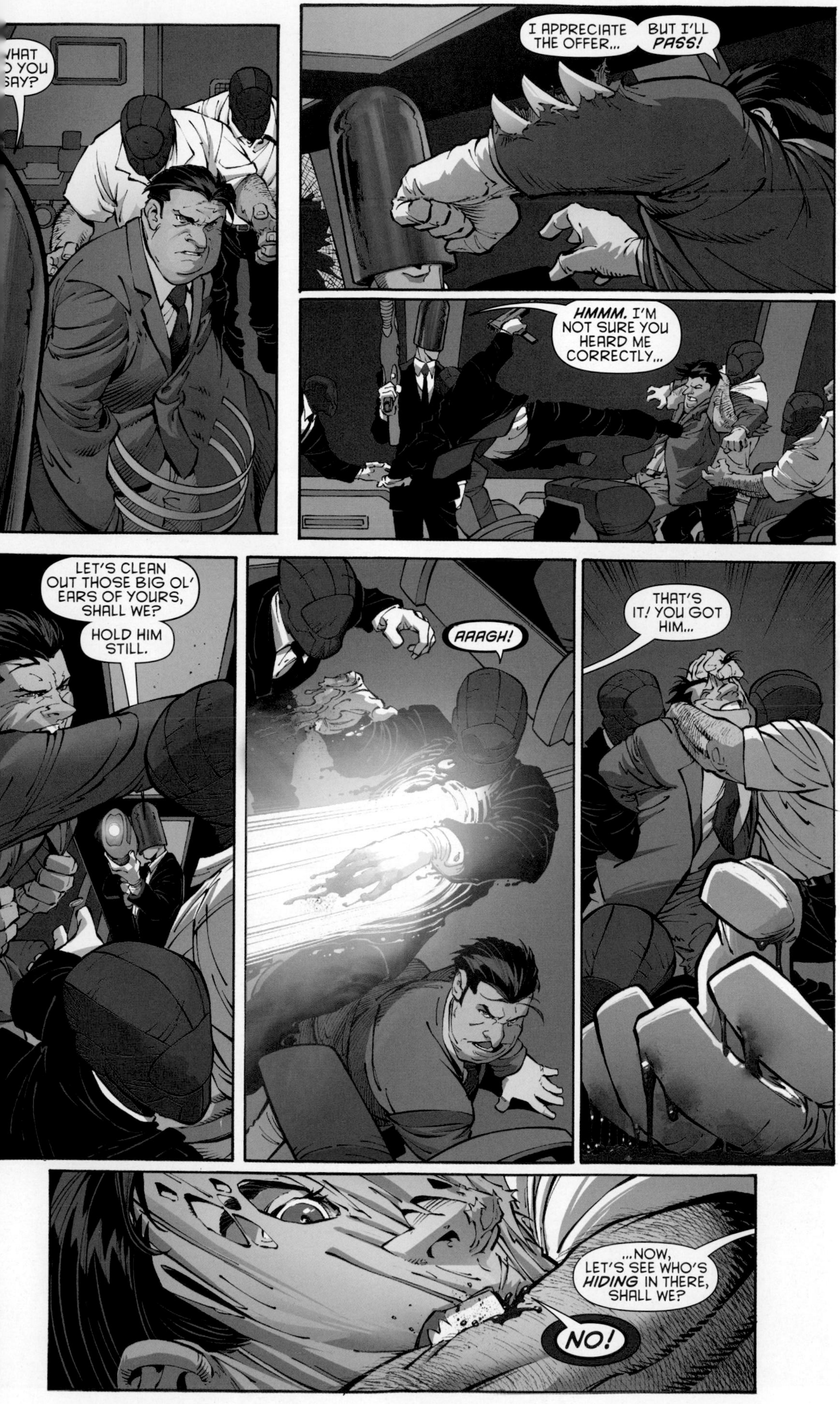
WHAT
DO YOU
SAY?
I APPRECIATE THE OFFER...
BUT I'LL PASS!
HMMM. I'M NOT SURE YOU HEARD ME CORRECTLY...
LET'S CLEAN OUT THOSE BIG OL' EARS OF YOURS, SHALL WE?
HOLD HIM STILL.
AAAGH!
THAT'S IT! YOU GOT HIM...
...NOW, LET'S SEE WHO'S HIDING IN THERE, SHALL WE?
NO!

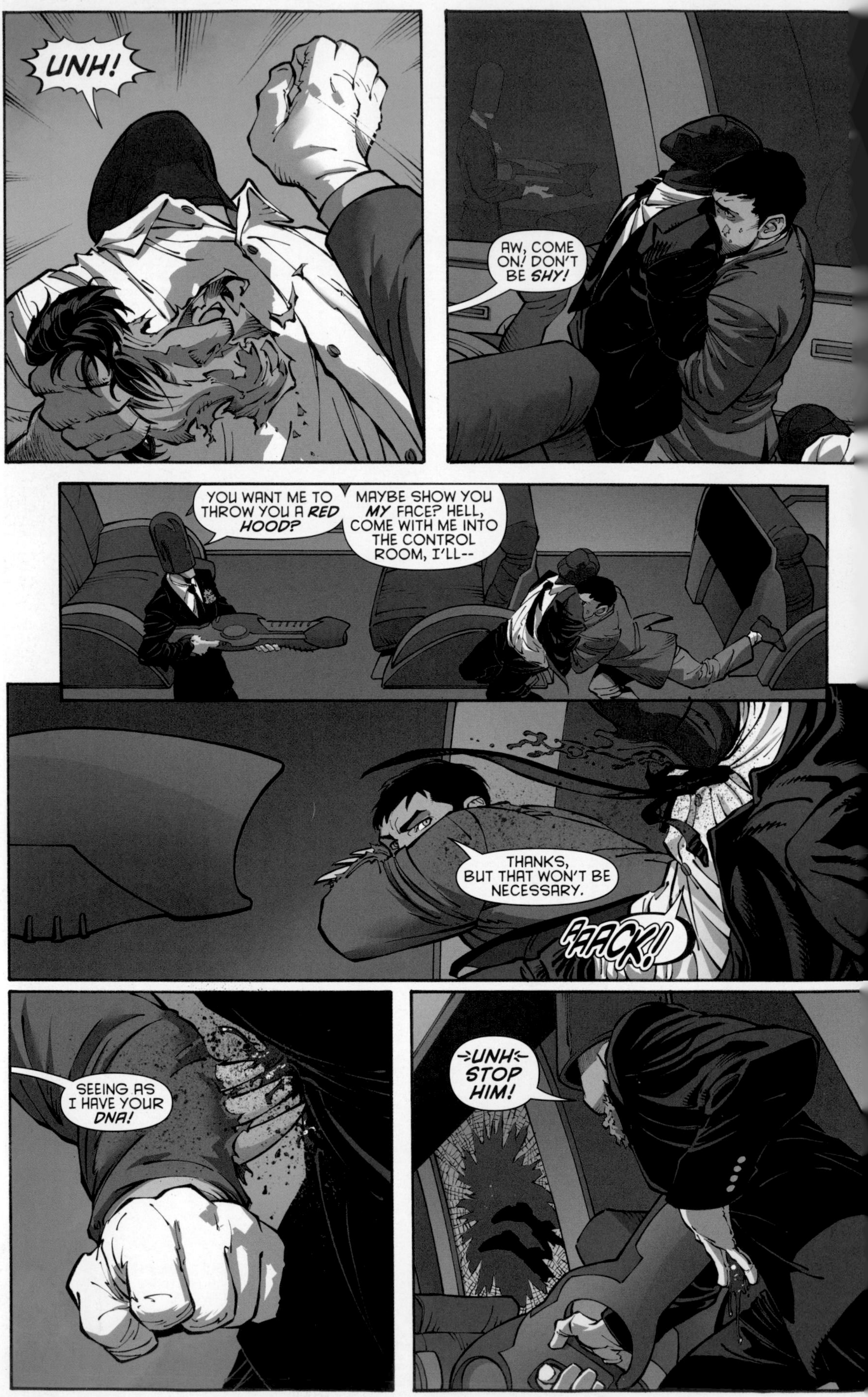
UNH!
AW, COME ON! DON'T BE SHY!
YOU WANT ME TO THROW YOU A RED HOOD?
MAYBE SHOW YOU MY FACE? HELL, COME WITH ME INTO THE CONTROL ROOM, I'LL--
THANKS, BUT THAT WON'T BE NECESSARY.
AAACK!!
SEEING AS I HAVE YOUR DNA!
UNH STOP HIM!

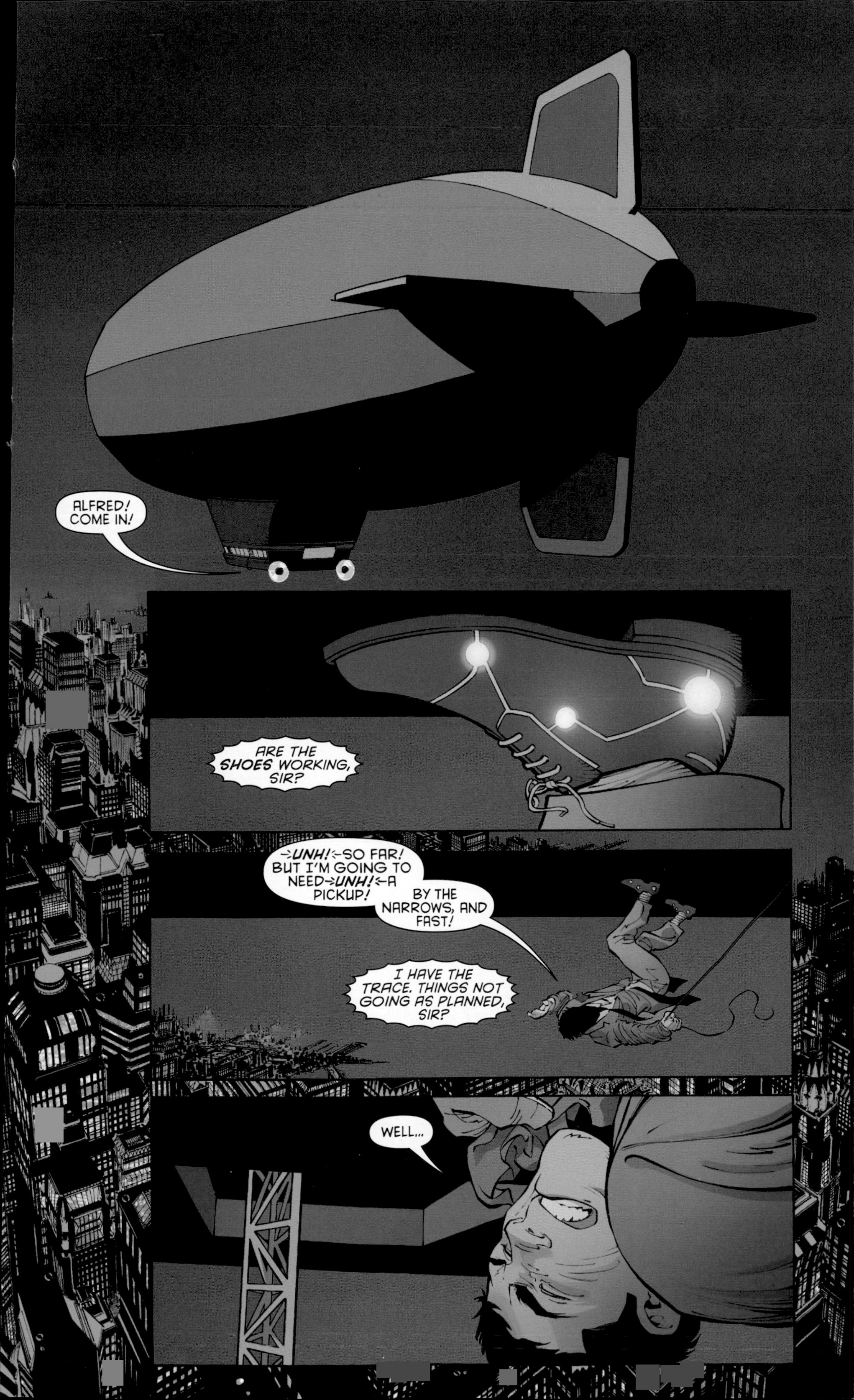

ALFRED! COME IN!
ARE THE SHOES WORKING, SIR?
–UNH!– SO FAR! BUT I'M GOING TO NEED –UNH!– A PICKUP!
BY THE NARROWS, AND FAST!
I HAVE THE TRACE. THINGS NOT GOING AS PLANNED, SIR?
WELL...

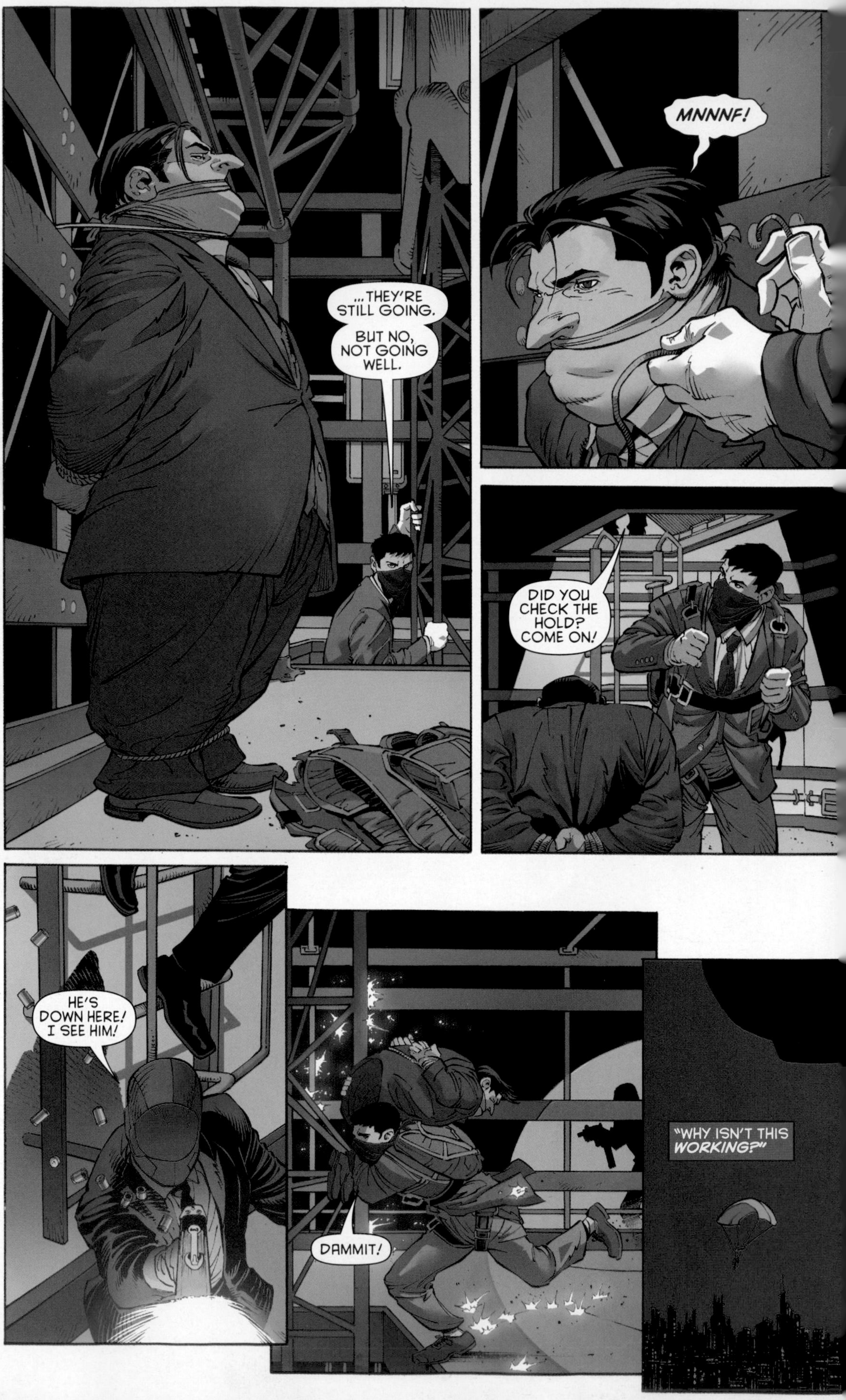
...THEY'RE STILL GOING.
BUT NO, NOT GOING WELL.
MNNNF!
DID YOU CHECK THE HOLD? COME ON!
HE'S DOWN HERE! I SEE HIM!
DAMMIT!
"WHY ISN'T THIS WORKING?"

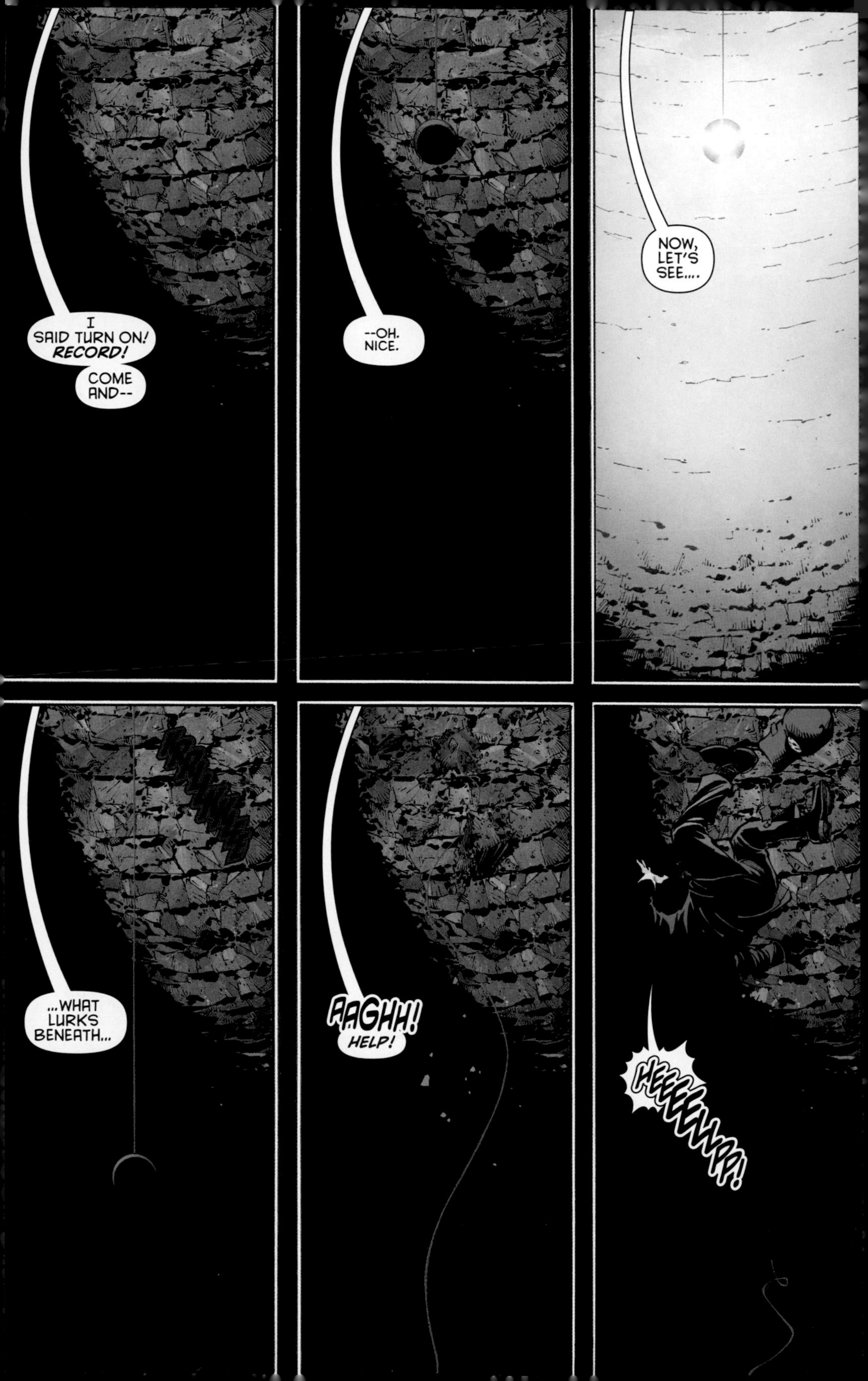
I SAID TURN ON! RECORD!
COME AND--
--OH. NICE.
NOW, LET'S SEE....
...WHAT LURKS BENEATH...
AAGHH! HELP!
HEEEELLPP!

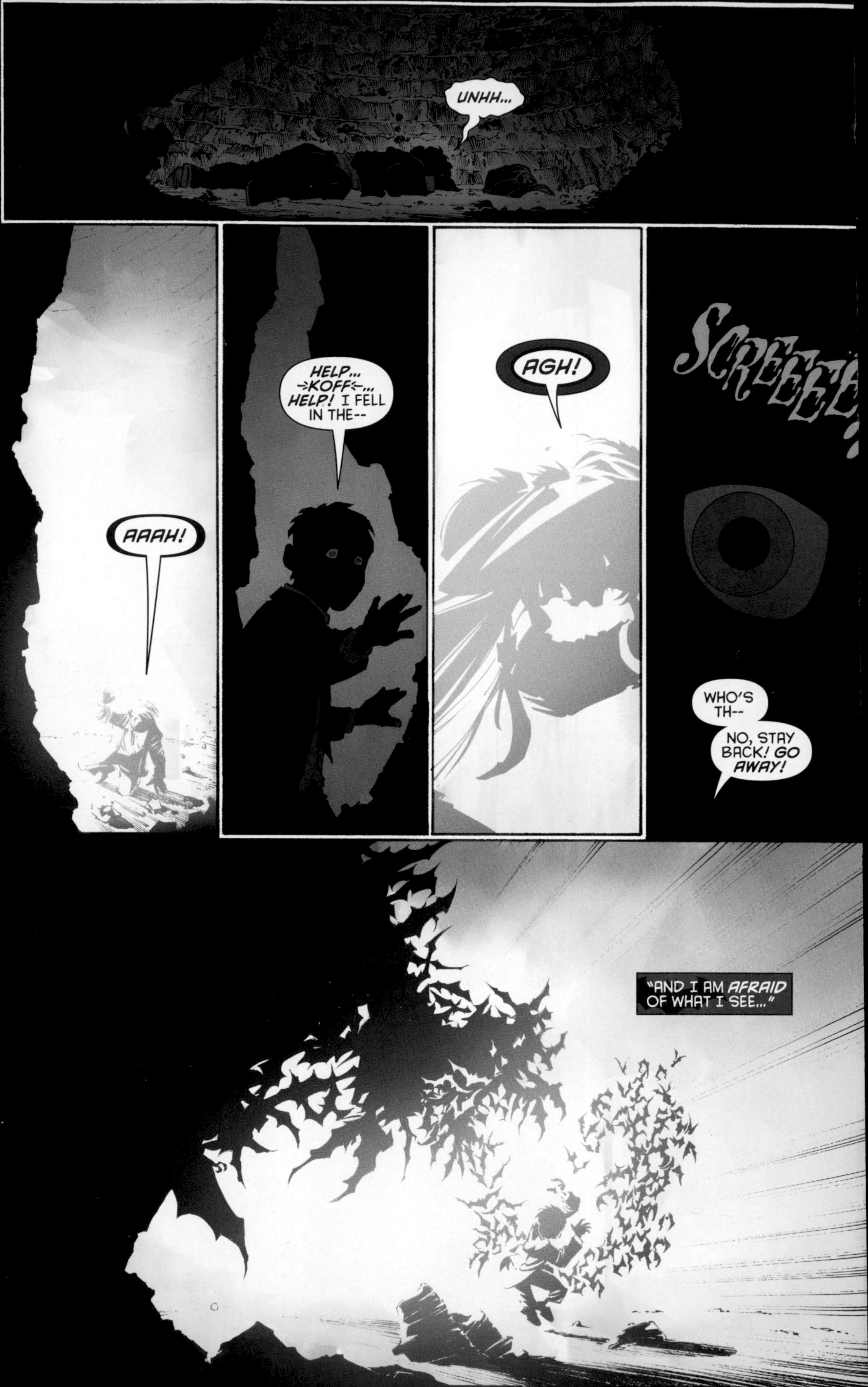
UNHH...
AAAH!
HELP... -KOFF-... HELP! I FELL IN THE--
AGH!
SCREEEE
WHO'S TH--
NO, STAY BACK! GO AWAY!
"AND I AM AFRAID OF WHAT I SEE..."

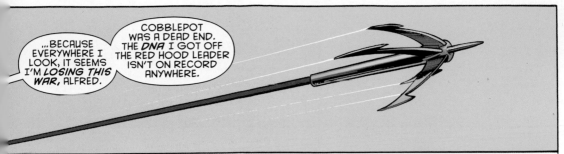

...BECAUSE EVERYWHERE I LOOK, IT SEEMS I'M *LOSING THIS WAR*, ALFRED.

COBBLEPOT WAS A DEAD END. THE *DNA* I GOT OFF THE RED HOOD LEADER ISN'T ON RECORD ANYWHERE.

AND NOW HE'S TAKING OVER RIVAL GANGS. WHILE BEFORE HE ONLY TOOK IN NON-CRIMINALS. IT'S LIKE HE EXPANDS THE GANG TO PROVE HE *CAN*.

A BOMB GOES OFF AT A SCHOOL FOR THE DEAF. SOMEONE IS SHOT FOR NO REASON WALKING IN THE PARK.

THERE'S NO PATTERN EXCEPT TO MAKE THE CITY AFRAID OF ITSELF.

NO ONE KNOWS WHO TO BE AFRAID OF ANYMORE. THE POLICE ARE DESPERATE AND TAXED, SEARCHING EVERYONE THEY CAN. ALL OF IT BREEDS MORE *FEAR*.

NOW THAT HE'S GOT WAYNE INDUSTRIES WEAPONS IN HIS CACHE, HE CAN SHOW THAT *NOTHING'S* OUT OF REACH.

DAMMIT.

HOOK COME BACK.

ALFRED, IF YOU HAVE SOMETHING TO *SAY*, JUST SAY IT. YOU'RE NEVER THIS QUIET. I CAN PRACTICALLY *FEEL* THE WAVES OF DISDAIN ROLLING OFF YOU.

WHAT'S THERE TO *SAY*, SIR? IF YOU CAN'T SEE THE STATE OF THINGS CLEARLY NOW, THERE'S *NO POINT*.

ENLIGHTEN ME.

YOU'RE RIGHT. THIS WAR OF YOURS...IT'S DOOMED. YOU *WILL LOSE*.

I SAID I WAS LOSING. NOT THAT IT WAS *LOST*. I CAN STILL *GET* HIM.

AND IF YOU DO, WHAT THEN? *ANOTHER* LIKE HIM WILL COME.

SO BE IT. THEN I'LL FIGHT THEM, TOO. THE WAR MAY NOT BE WINNABLE, ALFRED, BUT IT'S *MINE*.

AND FRANKLY, I'M GETTING TIRED OF YOUR DAMN SKEPTICISM.

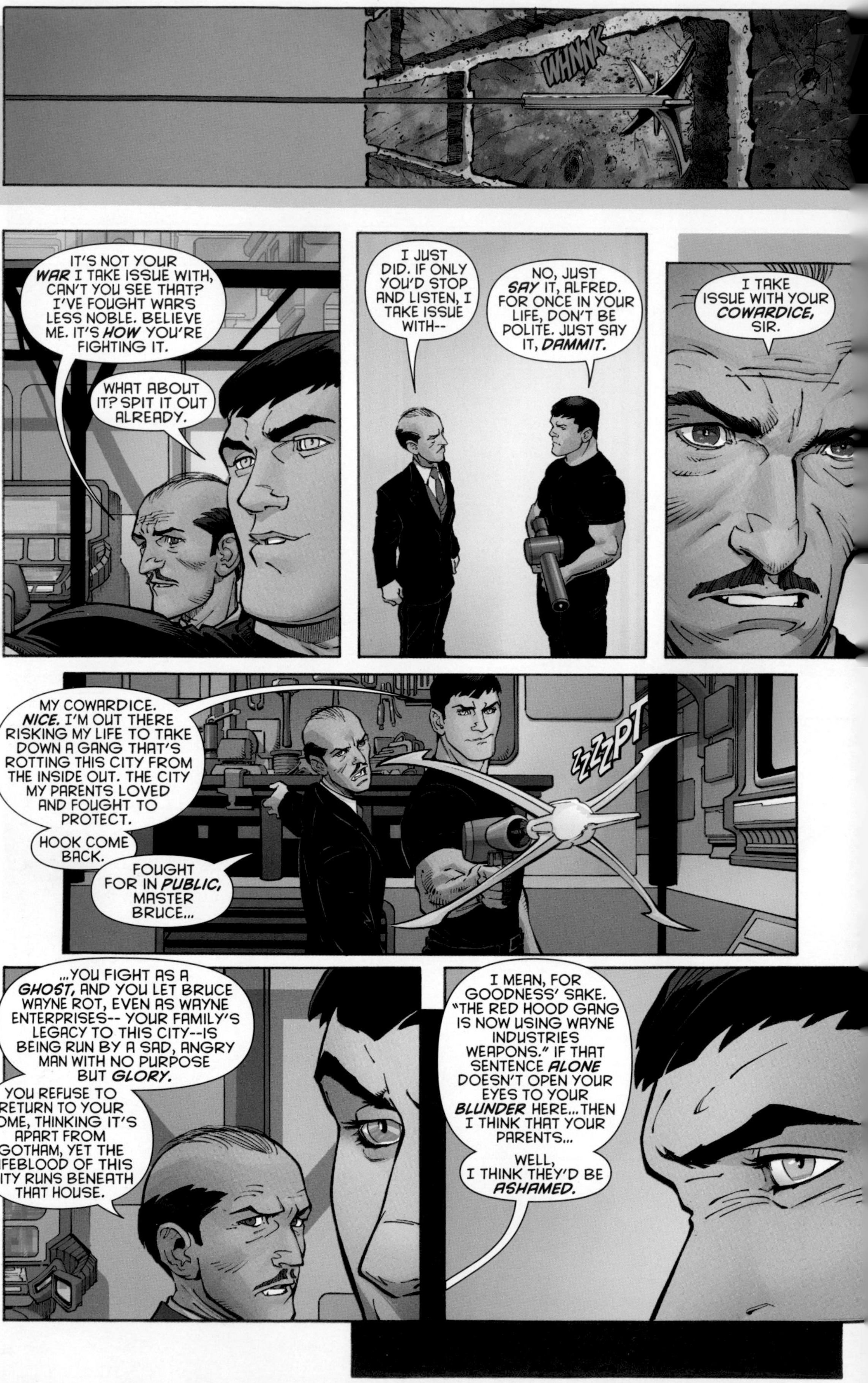
WHHNK
IT'S NOT YOUR WAR I TAKE ISSUE WITH, CAN'T YOU SEE THAT? I'VE FOUGHT WARS LESS NOBLE. BELIEVE ME. IT'S HOW YOU'RE FIGHTING IT.
WHAT ABOUT IT? SPIT IT OUT ALREADY.
I JUST DID. IF ONLY YOU'D STOP AND LISTEN, I TAKE ISSUE WITH--
NO, JUST SAY IT, ALFRED. FOR ONCE IN YOUR LIFE, DON'T BE POLITE. JUST SAY IT, DAMMIT.
I TAKE ISSUE WITH YOUR COWARDICE, SIR.
MY COWARDICE. NICE. I'M OUT THERE RISKING MY LIFE TO TAKE DOWN A GANG THAT'S ROTTING THIS CITY FROM THE INSIDE OUT. THE CITY MY PARENTS LOVED AND FOUGHT TO PROTECT.
HOOK COME BACK.
ZZZZPT
FOUGHT FOR IN PUBLIC, MASTER BRUCE...
...YOU FIGHT AS A GHOST, AND YOU LET BRUCE WAYNE ROT, EVEN AS WAYNE ENTERPRISES-- YOUR FAMILY'S LEGACY TO THIS CITY--IS BEING RUN BY A SAD, ANGRY MAN WITH NO PURPOSE BUT GLORY.
YOU REFUSE TO RETURN TO YOUR HOME, THINKING IT'S APART FROM GOTHAM, YET THE LIFEBLOOD OF THIS CITY RUNS BENEATH THAT HOUSE.
I MEAN, FOR GOODNESS' SAKE. "THE RED HOOD GANG IS NOW USING WAYNE INDUSTRIES WEAPONS." IF THAT SENTENCE ALONE DOESN'T OPEN YOUR EYES TO YOUR BLUNDER HERE... THEN I THINK THAT YOUR PARENTS...
WELL, I THINK THEY'D BE ASHAMED.

IS THAT *RIGHT*?! AND WHAT ABOUT *YOU*, MR. PENNYWORTH?! *HUH*? WHAT EXAMPLE HAVE *YOU* SET?

LIVING IN A MAUSOLEUM, POLISHING SILVER? WHAT GOOD HAVE *YOU* DONE IN THE WORLD? WHO'S THE *REAL* COWARD?

I'M GOING TO GO BACK TO THE MANOR, SIR. THIS WAS A *MISTAKE*. I WISH YOU THE BEST.

COME BACK.

I WAS TALKING TO THE *HOOK*.

RRRGHH!

=SIGH=
CALL PHILIP KANE.

HELLO?

IT'S *ME*, UNCLE PHILIP. BRUCE. I NEED TO TALK TO YOU. IT'S *URGENT*.

KANE, PHILIP

BRUCE, I WAS ABOUT TO SAY THE SAME THING. CAN YOU MEET ME TONIGHT, AT THE MUSEUM? AROUND MIDNIGHT...

"...FOR OLD TIMES' SAKE."

PHILIP?

OVER HERE, BRUCE.

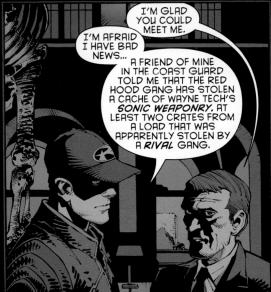

I'M GLAD YOU COULD MEET ME.

I'M AFRAID I HAVE BAD NEWS... A FRIEND OF MINE IN THE COAST GUARD TOLD ME THAT THE RED HOOD GANG HAS STOLEN A CACHE OF WAYNE TECH'S *SONIC WEAPONRY.* AT LEAST TWO CRATES FROM A LOAD THAT WAS APPARENTLY STOLEN BY A *RIVAL* GANG.

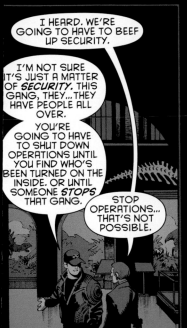

I HEARD. WE'RE GOING TO HAVE TO BEEF UP SECURITY.

I'M NOT SURE IT'S JUST A MATTER OF *SECURITY.* THIS GANG, THEY... THEY HAVE PEOPLE ALL OVER.

YOU'RE GOING TO HAVE TO SHUT DOWN OPERATIONS UNTIL YOU FIND WHO'S BEEN TURNED ON THE INSIDE. OR UNTIL SOMEONE *STOPS* THAT GANG.

STOP OPERATIONS... THAT'S NOT POSSIBLE.

THERE ARE KILLERS AND THIEVES RUNNING AROUND WITH WEAPONS WITH THE *WAYNE NAME* ON THEM.

AND WE'LL PUT A STOP TO THAT. BUT...

LOOK, BRUCE. COME BACK TO THE COMPANY. BE A *PART* OF IT. WE CAN TALK ABOUT THIS.

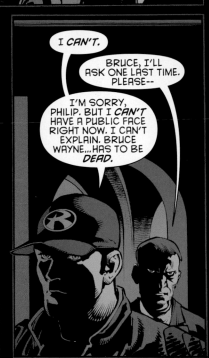

I *CAN'T.*

BRUCE, I'LL ASK ONE LAST TIME. PLEASE--

I'M SORRY, PHILIP. BUT I *CAN'T* HAVE A PUBLIC FACE RIGHT NOW. I CAN'T EXPLAIN. BRUCE WAYNE...HAS TO BE *DEAD.*

IF YOU *INSIST,* BRUCE.

KLIK

PHILIP, WHAT THE HELL ARE YOU *DOING?*

WHEN MY FATHER CAME TO THAT *CAVE* IN MEXICO TO GET ME, BRUCE, I DIDN'T WANT TO GO. WE *FOUGHT*. IN FACT, I SPLIT MY *HEAD* OPEN FIGHTING WITH HIM.

I STILL HAVE THE *METAL PLATE*.

THE POINT IS, HE WAS RIGHT. AND YOU HAVE SOMETHING YOU HAVE TO DO. THIS IS ME, COMING TO YOUR CAVE AND DRAGGING YOU OUT.

BRUCE! THERE YOU ARE!

BRUCE, *VICKI VALE*, GOTHAM GAZETTE! SO FIRST THINGS FIRST! WHY ARE YOU *BACK?*

BRUCE! YOU CAN'T KEEP RUNNING, BRUCE!

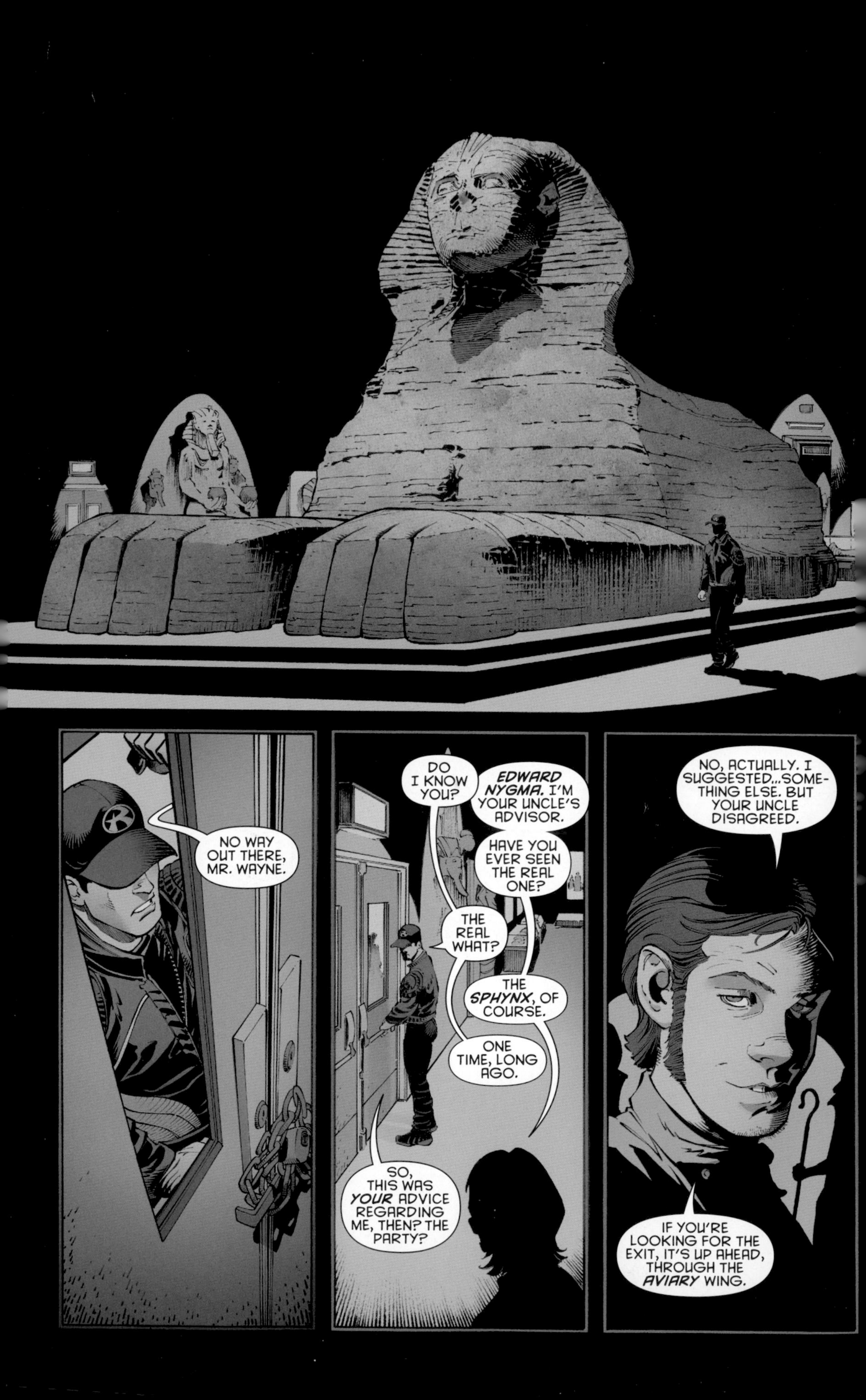
NO WAY OUT THERE, MR. WAYNE.
DO I KNOW YOU?
EDWARD NYGMA. I'M YOUR UNCLE'S ADVISOR.
HAVE YOU EVER SEEN THE REAL ONE?
THE REAL WHAT?
THE SPHYNX, OF COURSE.
ONE TIME, LONG AGO.
SO, THIS WAS YOUR ADVICE REGARDING ME, THEN? THE PARTY?
NO, ACTUALLY. I SUGGESTED...SOMETHING ELSE. BUT YOUR UNCLE DISAGREED.
IF YOU'RE LOOKING FOR THE EXIT, IT'S UP AHEAD, THROUGH THE AVIARY WING.

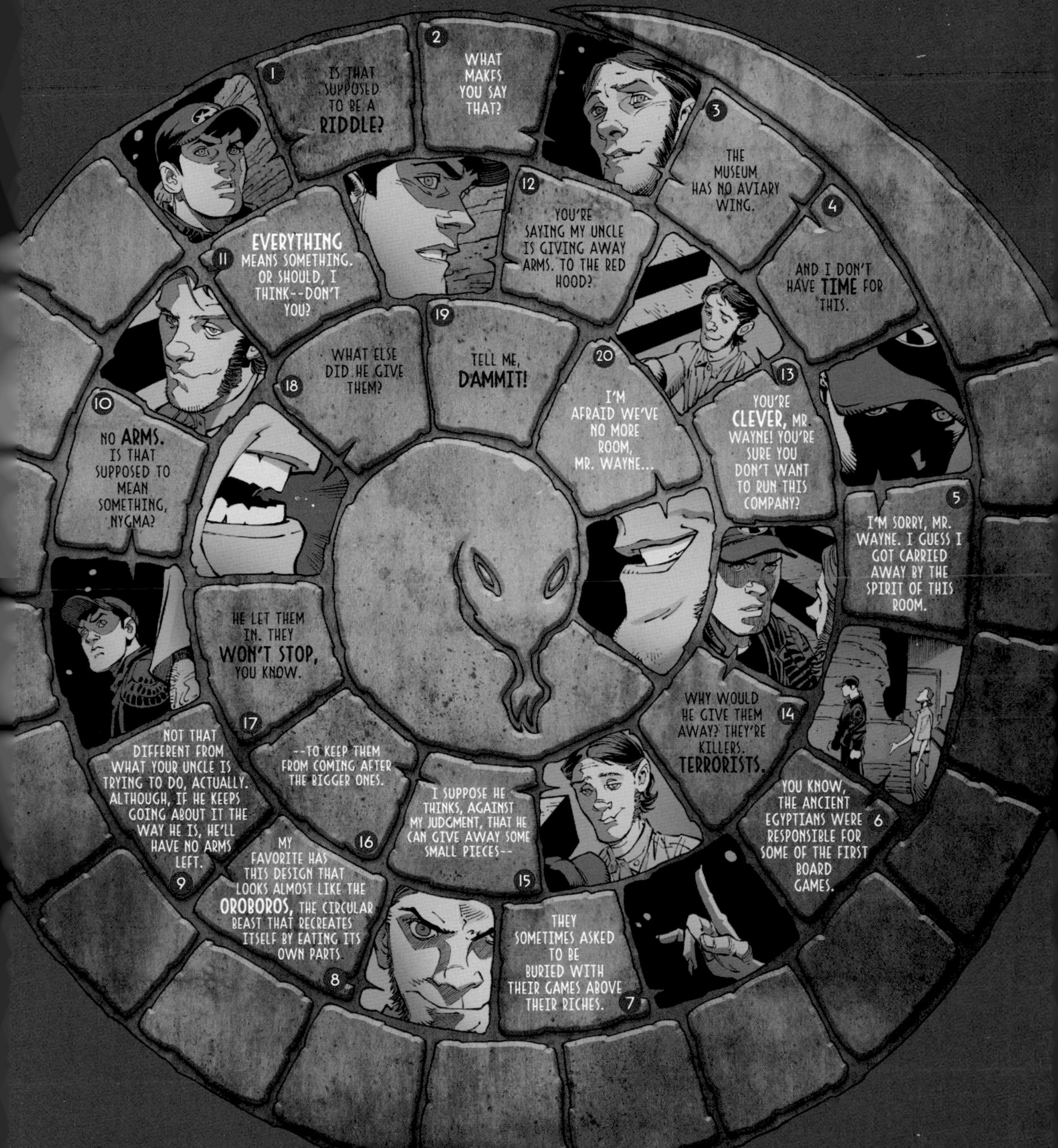
IS THAT SUPPOSED TO BE A RIDDLE?
WHAT MAKES YOU SAY THAT?
THE MUSEUM HAS NO AVIARY WING.
AND I DON'T HAVE TIME FOR THIS.
I'M SORRY, MR. WAYNE. I GUESS I GOT CARRIED AWAY BY THE SPIRIT OF THIS ROOM.
YOU KNOW, THE ANCIENT EGYPTIANS WERE RESPONSIBLE FOR SOME OF THE FIRST BOARD GAMES.
THEY SOMETIMES ASKED TO BE BURIED WITH THEIR GAMES ABOVE THEIR RICHES.
MY FAVORITE HAS THIS DESIGN THAT LOOKS ALMOST LIKE THE OROBOROS, THE CIRCULAR BEAST THAT RECREATES ITSELF BY EATING ITS OWN PARTS.
NOT THAT DIFFERENT FROM WHAT YOUR UNCLE IS TRYING TO DO, ACTUALLY. ALTHOUGH, IF HE KEEPS GOING ABOUT IT THE WAY HE IS, HE'LL HAVE NO ARMS LEFT.
NO ARMS. IS THAT SUPPOSED TO MEAN SOMETHING, NYGMA?
EVERYTHING MEANS SOMETHING. OR SHOULD, I THINK--DON'T YOU?
YOU'RE SAYING MY UNCLE IS GIVING AWAY ARMS. TO THE RED HOOD?
YOU'RE CLEVER, MR. WAYNE! YOU'RE SURE YOU DON'T WANT TO RUN THIS COMPANY?
WHY WOULD HE GIVE THEM AWAY? THEY'RE KILLERS. TERRORISTS.
I SUPPOSE HE THINKS, AGAINST MY JUDGMENT, THAT HE CAN GIVE AWAY SOME SMALL PIECES--
--TO KEEP THEM FROM COMING AFTER THE BIGGER ONES.
HE LET THEM IN. THEY WON'T STOP, YOU KNOW.
WHAT ELSE DID HE GIVE THEM?
TELL ME, DAMMIT!
I'M AFRAID WE'VE NO MORE ROOM, MR. WAYNE...

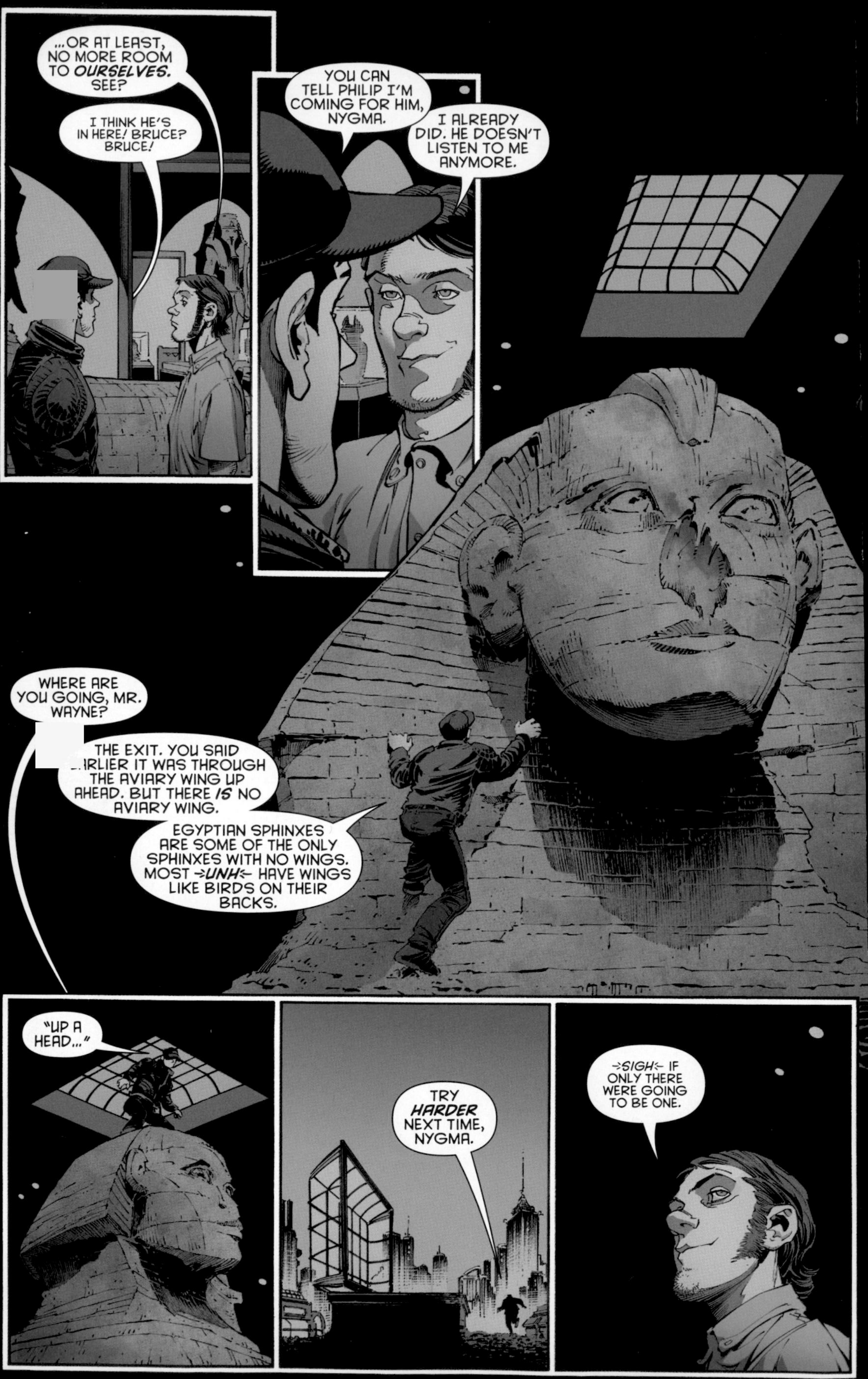
...OR AT LEAST, NO MORE ROOM TO **OURSELVES.** SEE?
I THINK HE'S IN HERE! BRUCE? BRUCE!
YOU CAN TELL PHILIP I'M COMING FOR HIM, NYGMA.
I ALREADY DID. HE DOESN'T LISTEN TO ME ANYMORE.
WHERE ARE YOU GOING, MR. WAYNE?
THE EXIT. YOU SAID ARLIER IT WAS THROUGH THE AVIARY WING UP AHEAD. BUT THERE ***IS*** NO AVIARY WING.
EGYPTIAN SPHINXES ARE SOME OF THE ONLY SPHINXES WITH NO WINGS. MOST ⇒*UNH*⇐ HAVE WINGS LIKE BIRDS ON THEIR BACKS.
"UP A HEAD..."
TRY ***HARDER*** NEXT TIME, NYGMA.
⇒*SIGH*⇐ IF ONLY THERE WERE GOING TO BE ONE.

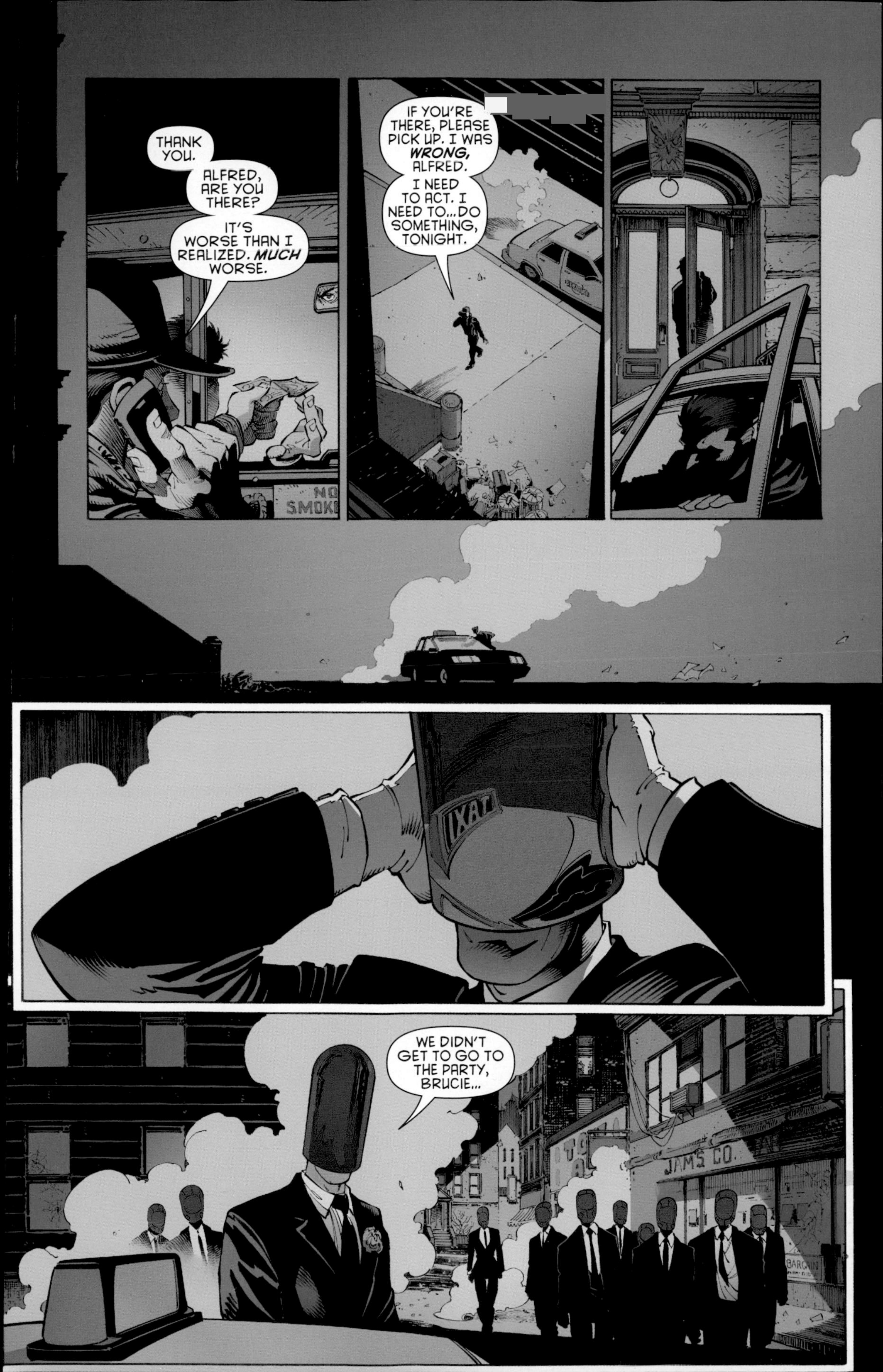
THANK YOU.
ALFRED, ARE YOU THERE?
IT'S WORSE THAN I REALIZED. **MUCH** WORSE.
IF YOU'RE THERE, PLEASE PICK UP. I WAS **WRONG,** ALFRED.
I NEED TO ACT. I NEED TO... DO SOMETHING, TONIGHT.
WE DIDN'T GET TO GO TO THE PARTY, BRUCIE...
JAMS CO.

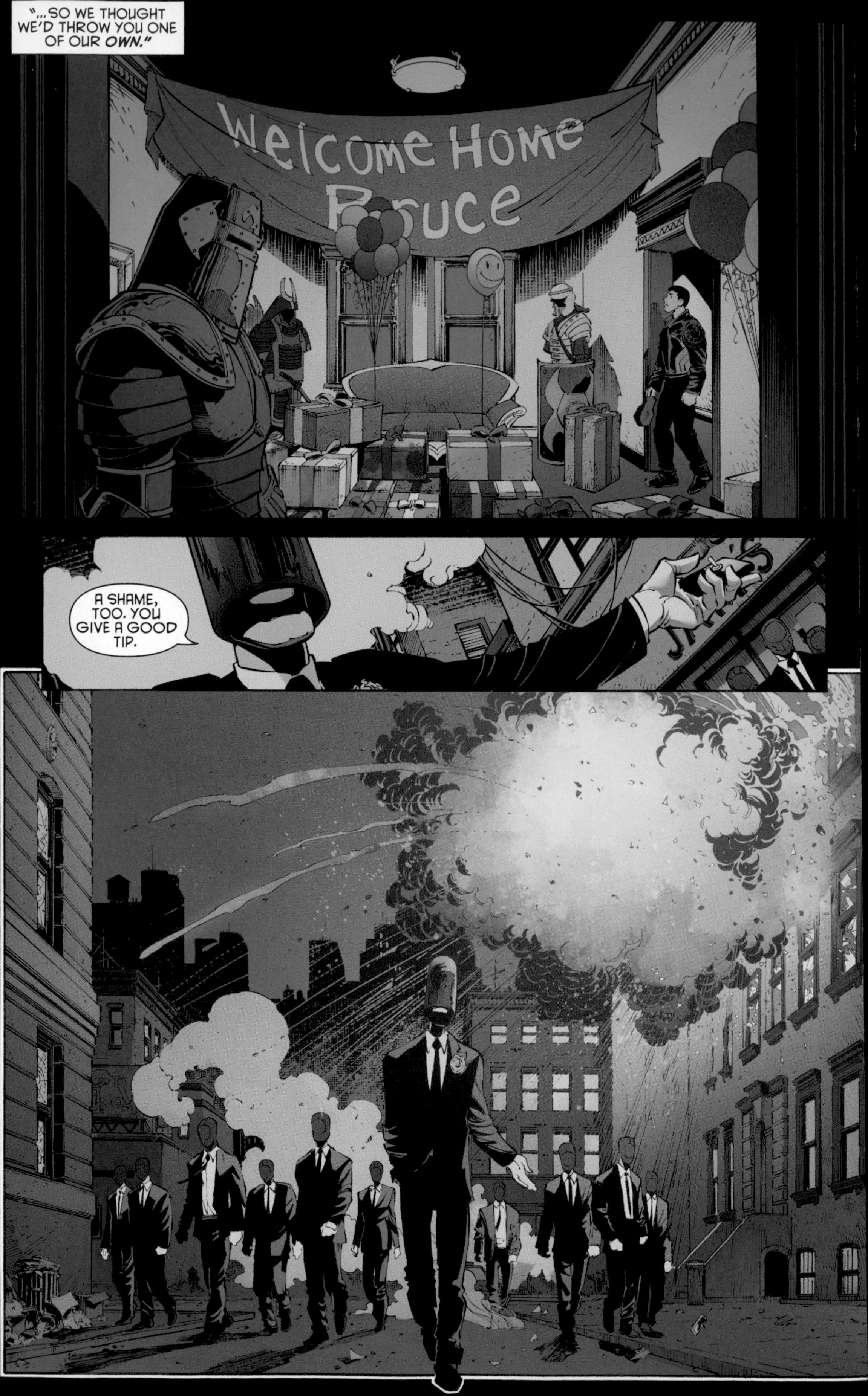
"...SO WE THOUGHT WE'D THROW YOU ONE OF OUR *OWN*."
Welcome Home Bruce
A SHAME, TOO. YOU GIVE A GOOD TIP.

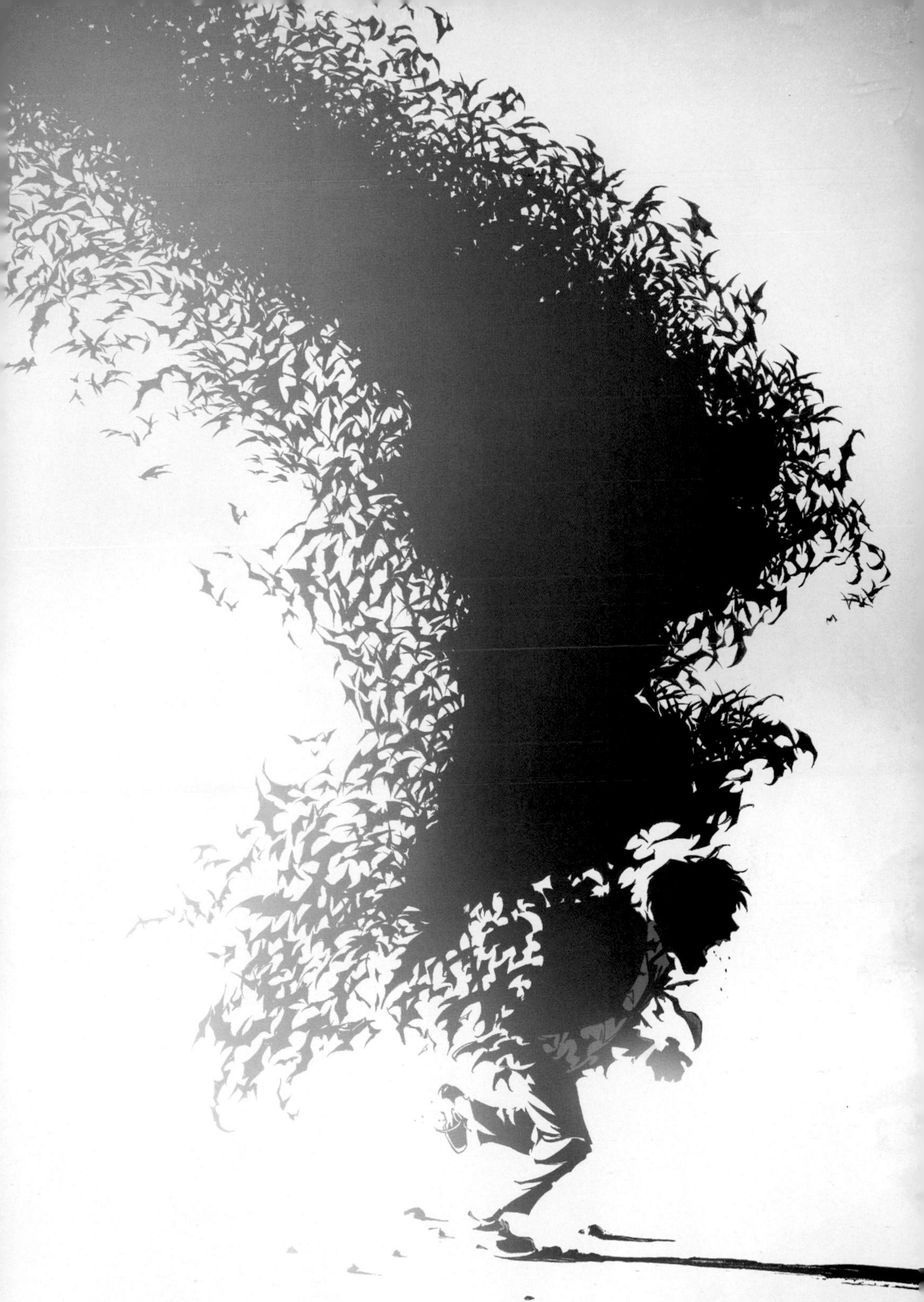

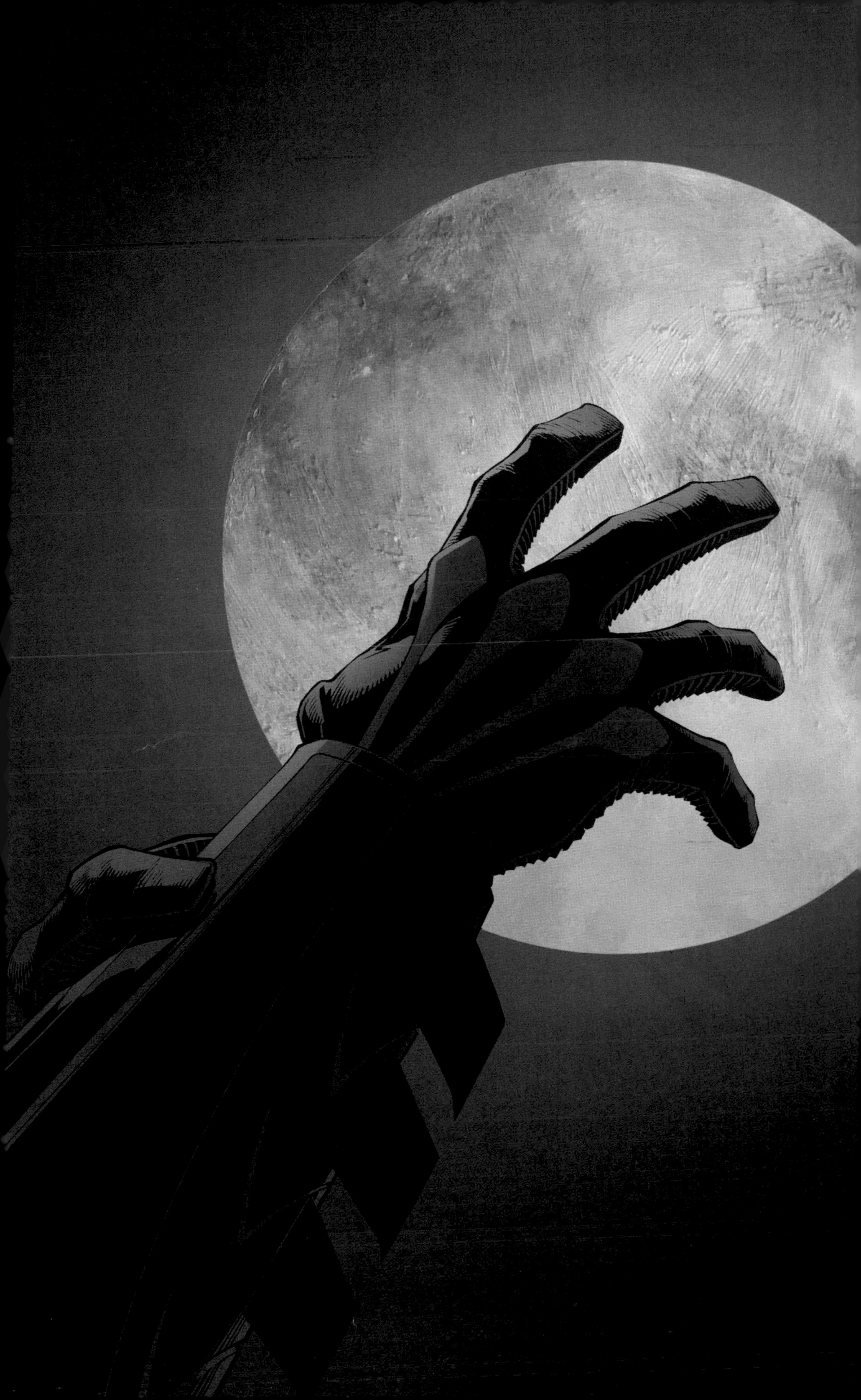

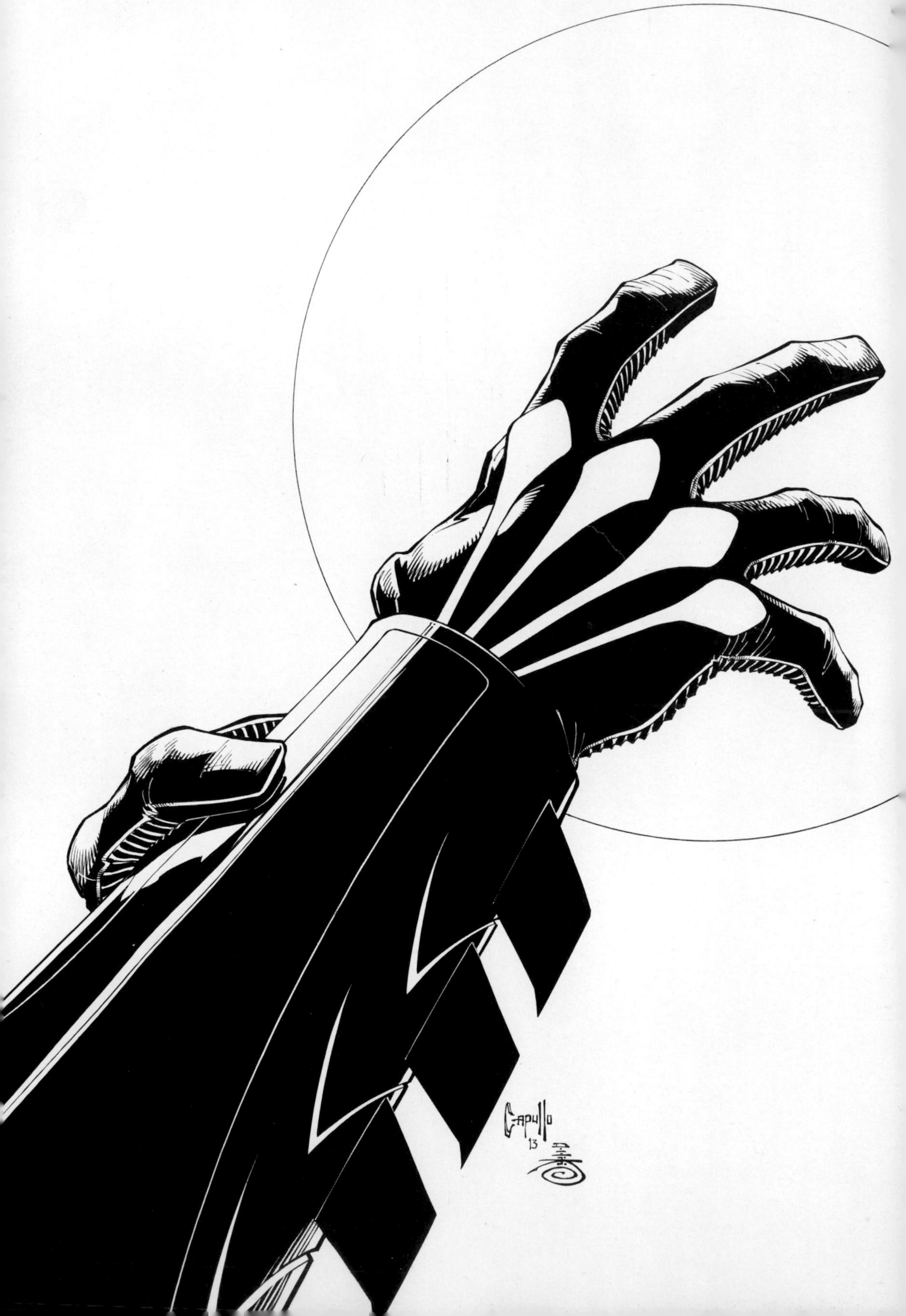
Capullo
13

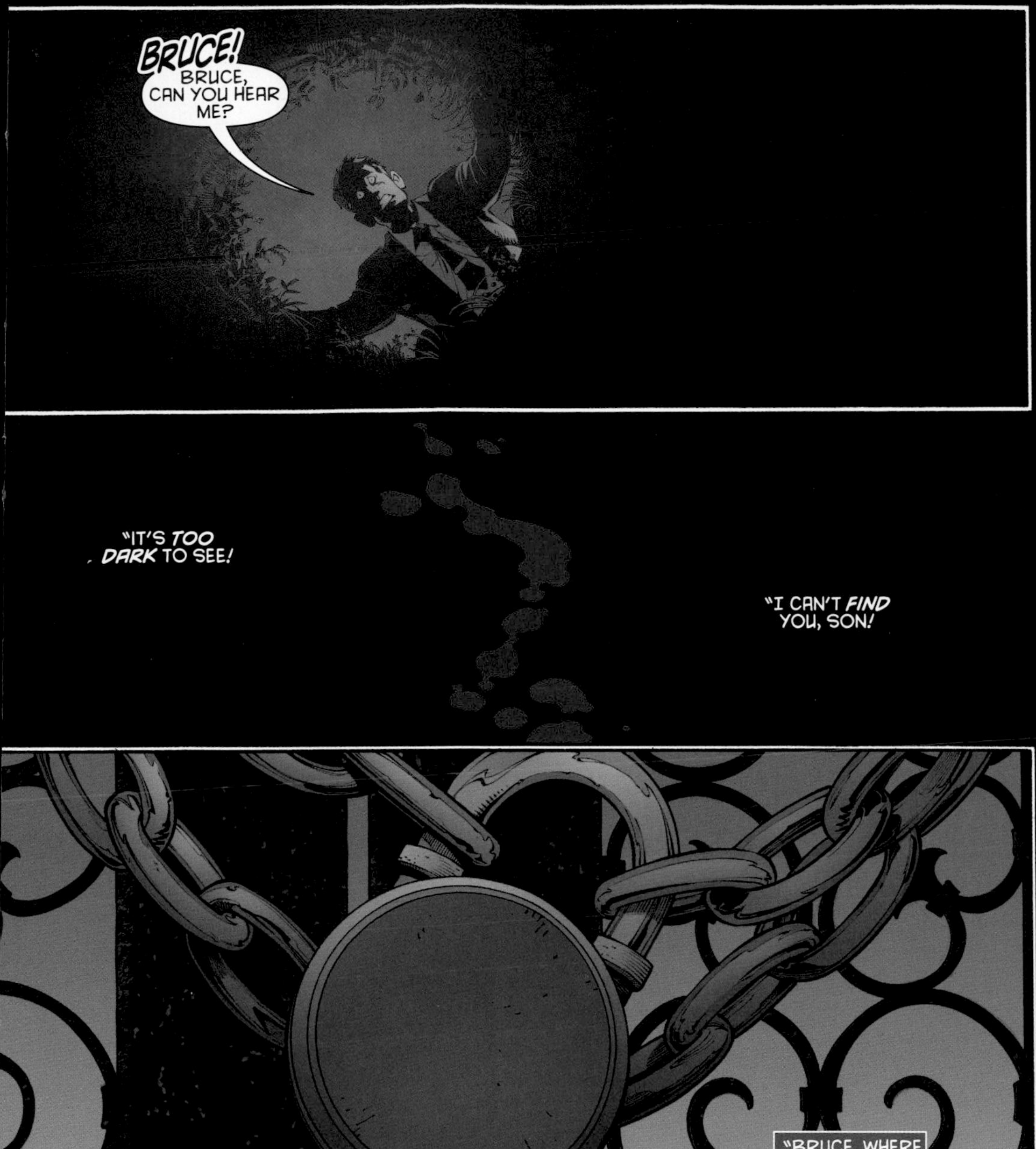
BRUCE! BRUCE, CAN YOU HEAR ME?
"IT'S TOO DARK TO SEE!
"I CAN'T FIND YOU, SON!
"BRUCE, WHERE ARE YOU?!"

ZERO YEAR

SECRET CITY: PART THREE

SCOTT SNYDER WRITER
GREG CAPULLO PENCILLER
DANNY MIKI INKER
FCO PLASCENCIA – COLORIST • **NICK NAPOLITANO** – LETTERER
CAPULLO, MIKI & PLASCENCIA – COVER

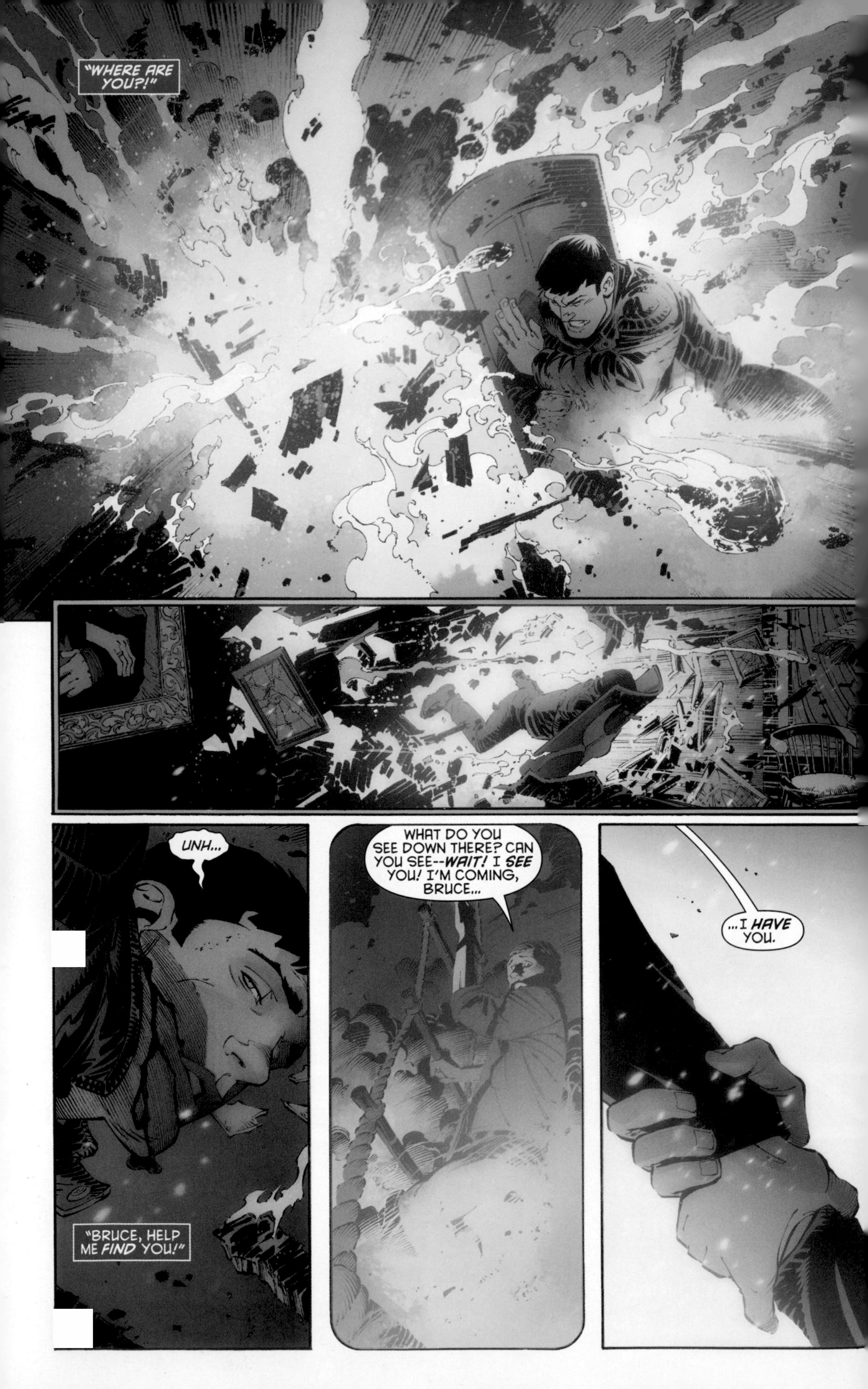
"WHERE ARE YOU?!"
UNH...
"BRUCE, HELP ME FIND YOU!"
WHAT DO YOU SEE DOWN THERE? CAN YOU SEE--WAIT! I SEE YOU! I'M COMING, BRUCE...
...I HAVE YOU.

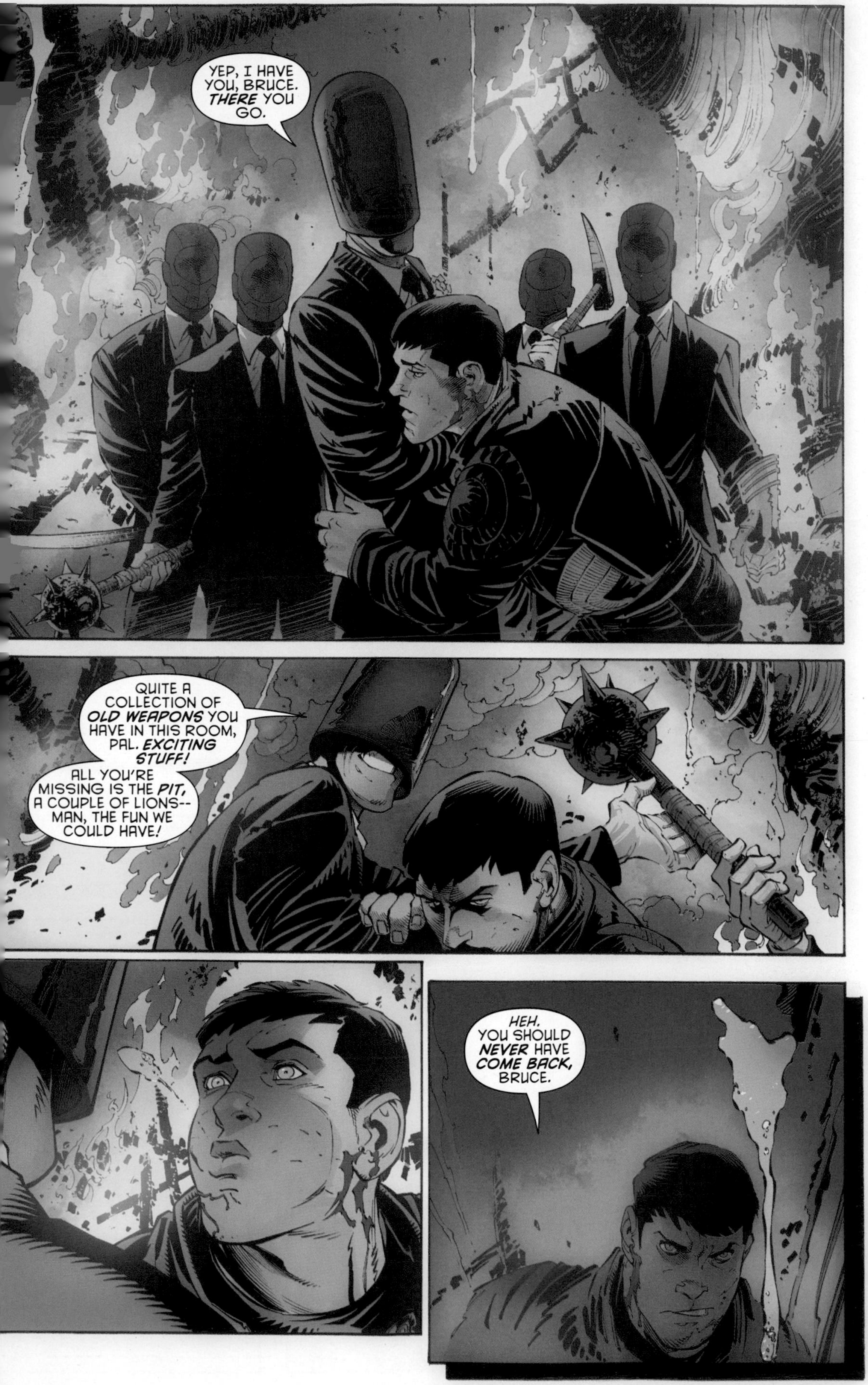
YEP, I HAVE YOU, BRUCE. THERE YOU GO.
QUITE A COLLECTION OF OLD WEAPONS YOU HAVE IN THIS ROOM, PAL. EXCITING STUFF!
ALL YOU'RE MISSING IS THE PIT, A COUPLE OF LIONS-- MAN, THE FUN WE COULD HAVE!
HEH. YOU SHOULD NEVER HAVE COME BACK, BRUCE.

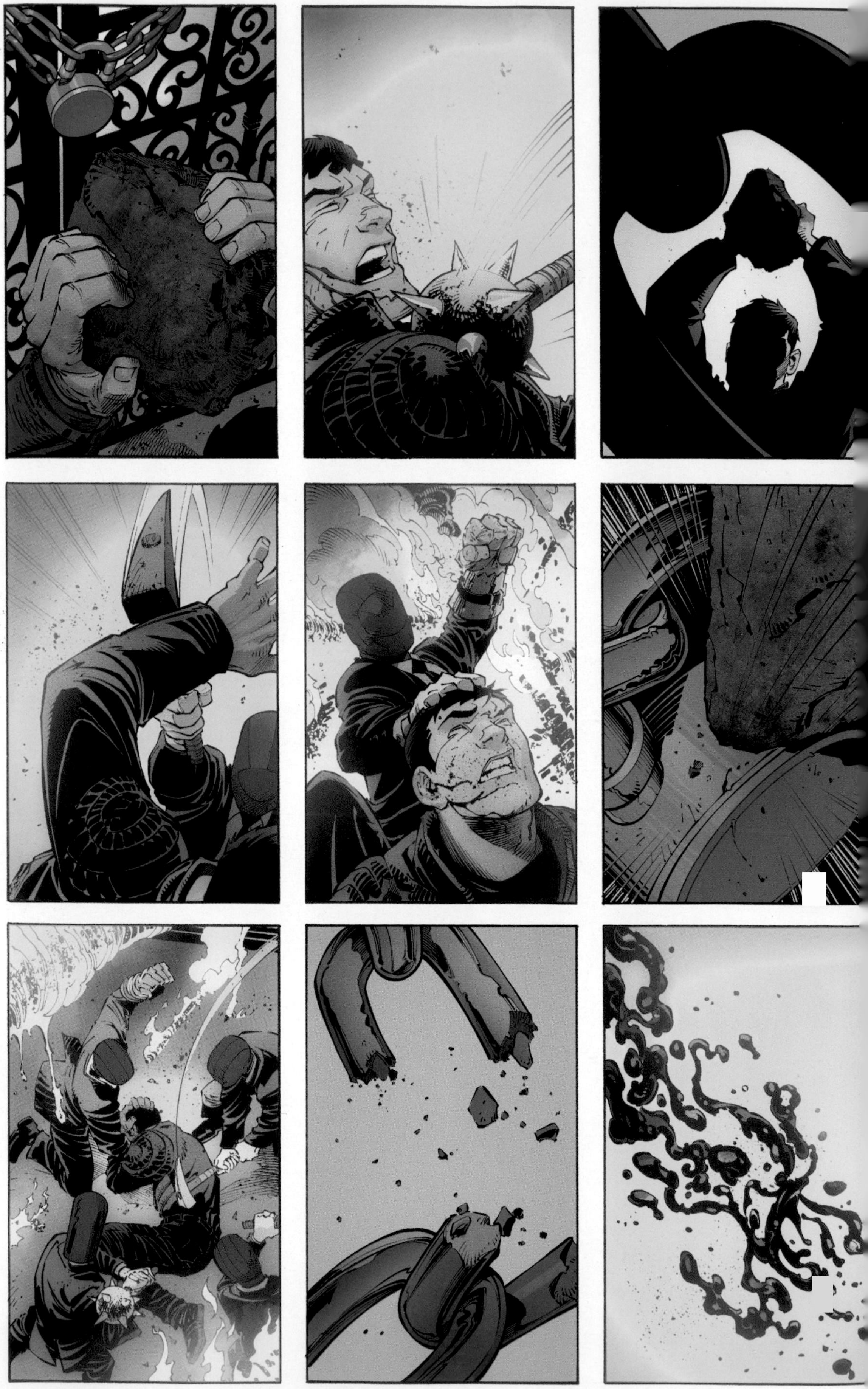

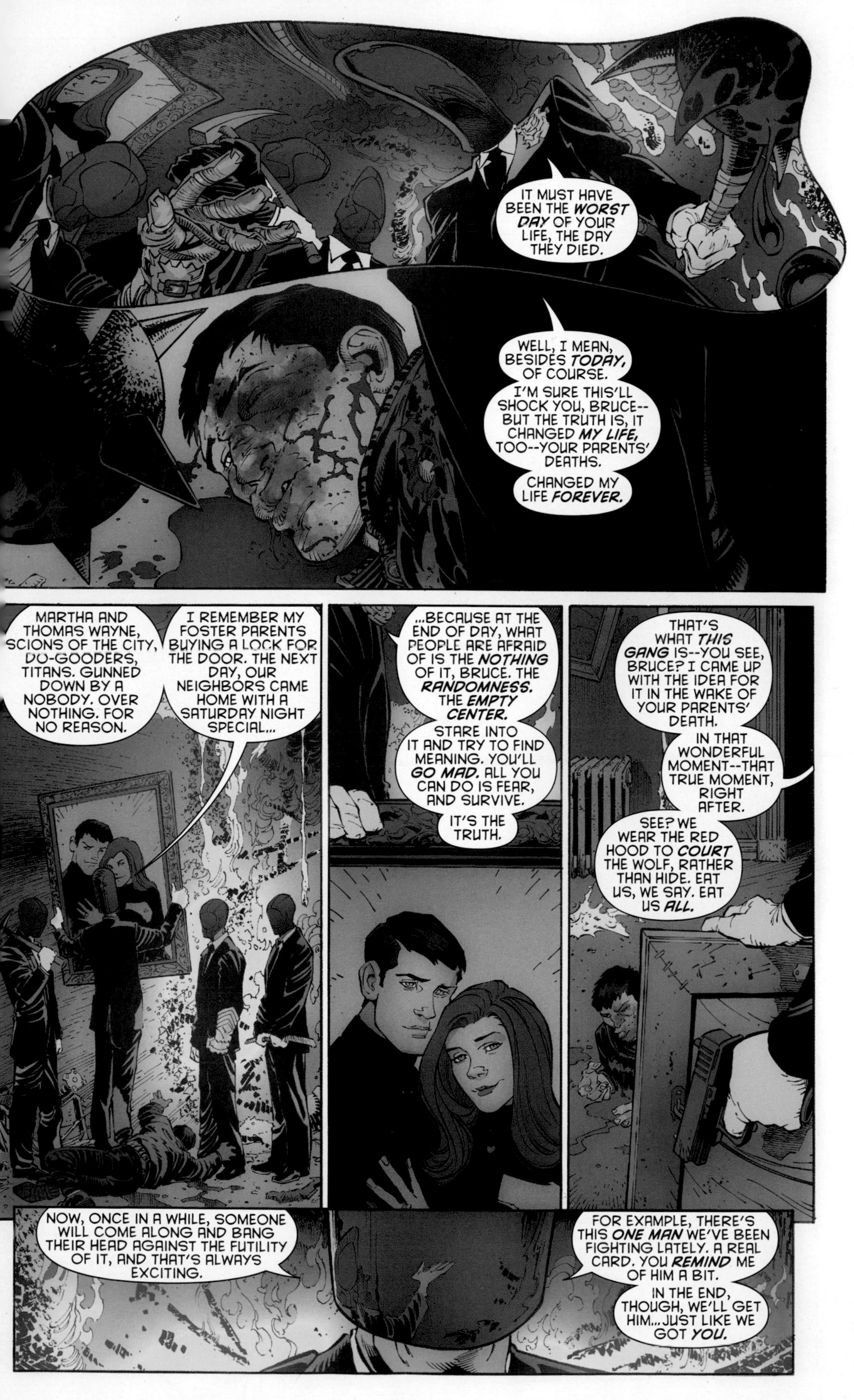
IT MUST HAVE BEEN THE WORST DAY OF YOUR LIFE, THE DAY THEY DIED.
WELL, I MEAN, BESIDES TODAY, OF COURSE.
I'M SURE THIS'LL SHOCK YOU, BRUCE-- BUT THE TRUTH IS, IT CHANGED MY LIFE, TOO--YOUR PARENTS' DEATHS.
CHANGED MY LIFE FOREVER.
MARTHA AND THOMAS WAYNE, SCIONS OF THE CITY, DO-GOODERS, TITANS. GUNNED DOWN BY A NOBODY. OVER NOTHING. FOR NO REASON.
I REMEMBER MY FOSTER PARENTS BUYING A LOCK FOR THE DOOR. THE NEXT DAY, OUR NEIGHBORS CAME HOME WITH A SATURDAY NIGHT SPECIAL...
...BECAUSE AT THE END OF DAY, WHAT PEOPLE ARE AFRAID OF IS THE NOTHING OF IT, BRUCE. THE RANDOMNESS. THE EMPTY CENTER.
STARE INTO IT AND TRY TO FIND MEANING. YOU'LL GO MAD. ALL YOU CAN DO IS FEAR, AND SURVIVE.
IT'S THE TRUTH.
THAT'S WHAT THIS GANG IS--YOU SEE, BRUCE? I CAME UP WITH THE IDEA FOR IT IN THE WAKE OF YOUR PARENTS' DEATH.
IN THAT WONDERFUL MOMENT--THAT TRUE MOMENT, RIGHT AFTER.
SEE? WE WEAR THE RED HOOD TO COURT THE WOLF, RATHER THAN HIDE. EAT US, WE SAY. EAT US ALL.
NOW, ONCE IN A WHILE, SOMEONE WILL COME ALONG AND BANG THEIR HEAD AGAINST THE FUTILITY OF IT, AND THAT'S ALWAYS EXCITING.
FOR EXAMPLE, THERE'S THIS ONE MAN WE'VE BEEN FIGHTING LATELY. A REAL CARD. YOU REMIND ME OF HIM A BIT.
IN THE END, THOUGH, WE'LL GET HIM...JUST LIKE WE GOT YOU.

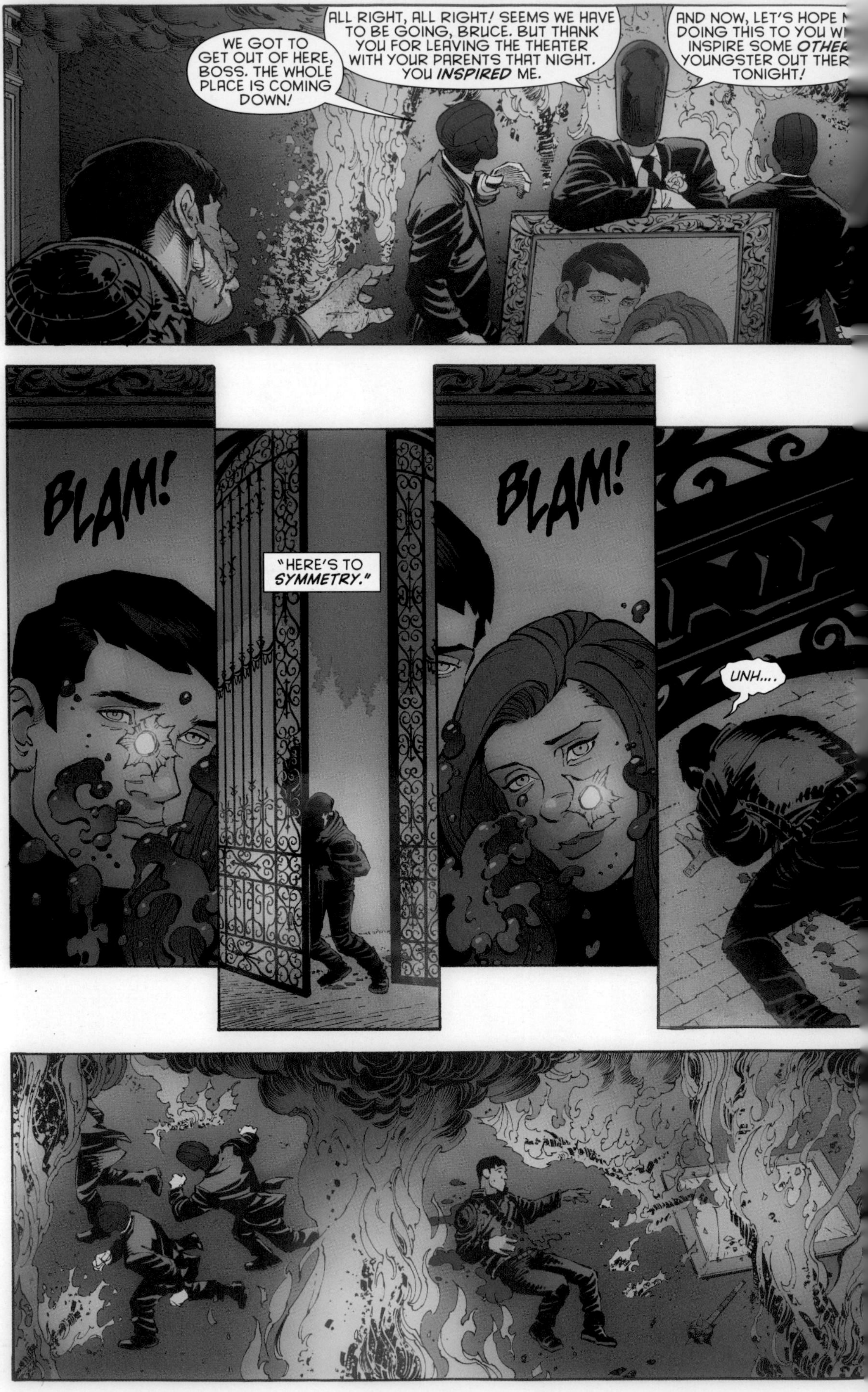
WE GOT TO GET OUT OF HERE, BOSS. THE WHOLE PLACE IS COMING DOWN!
ALL RIGHT, ALL RIGHT! SEEMS WE HAVE TO BE GOING, BRUCE. BUT THANK YOU FOR LEAVING THE THEATER WITH YOUR PARENTS THAT NIGHT. YOU INSPIRED ME.
AND NOW, LET'S HOPE
BLAM!
"HERE'S TO SYMMETRY."
BLAM!
UNH....

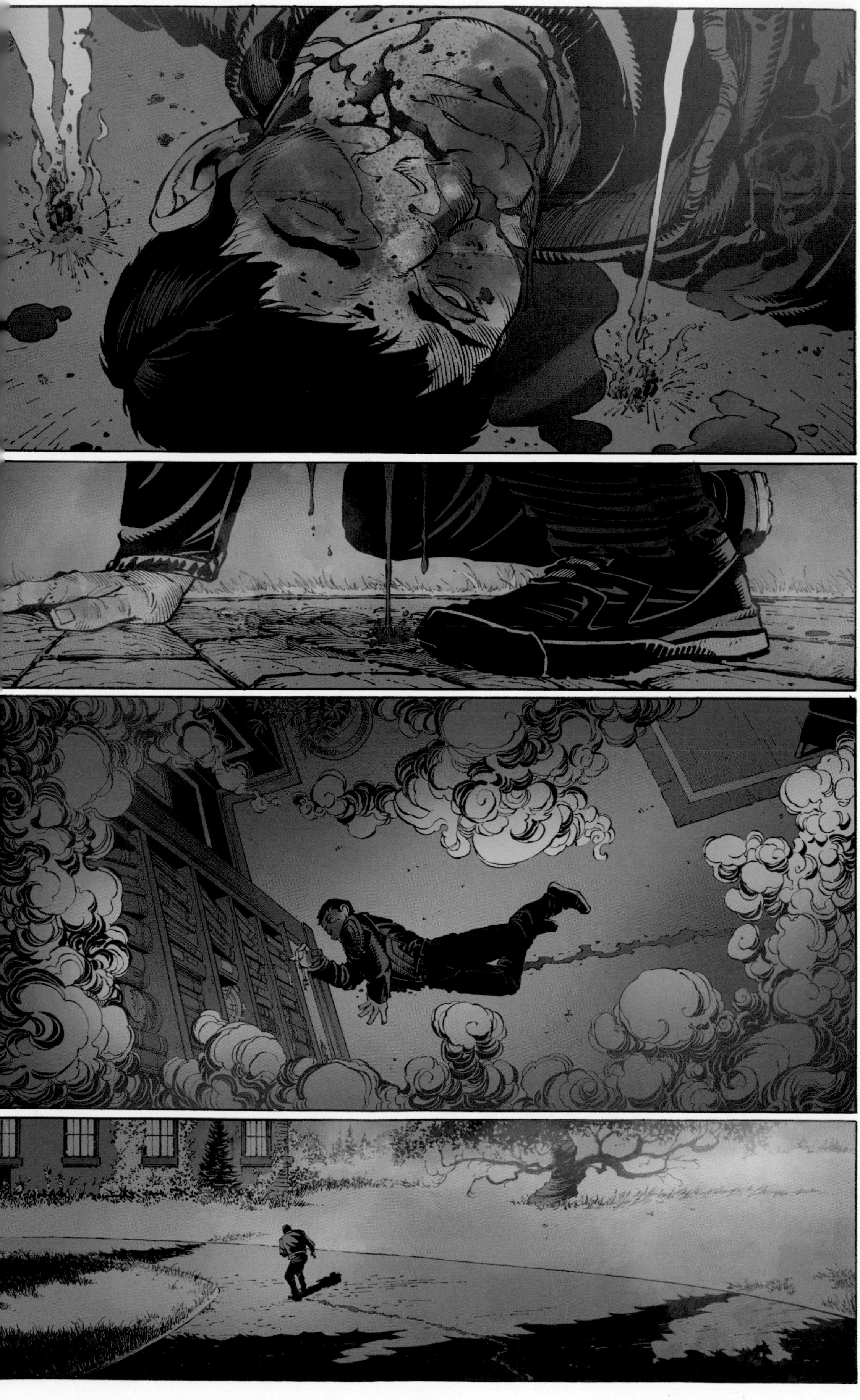

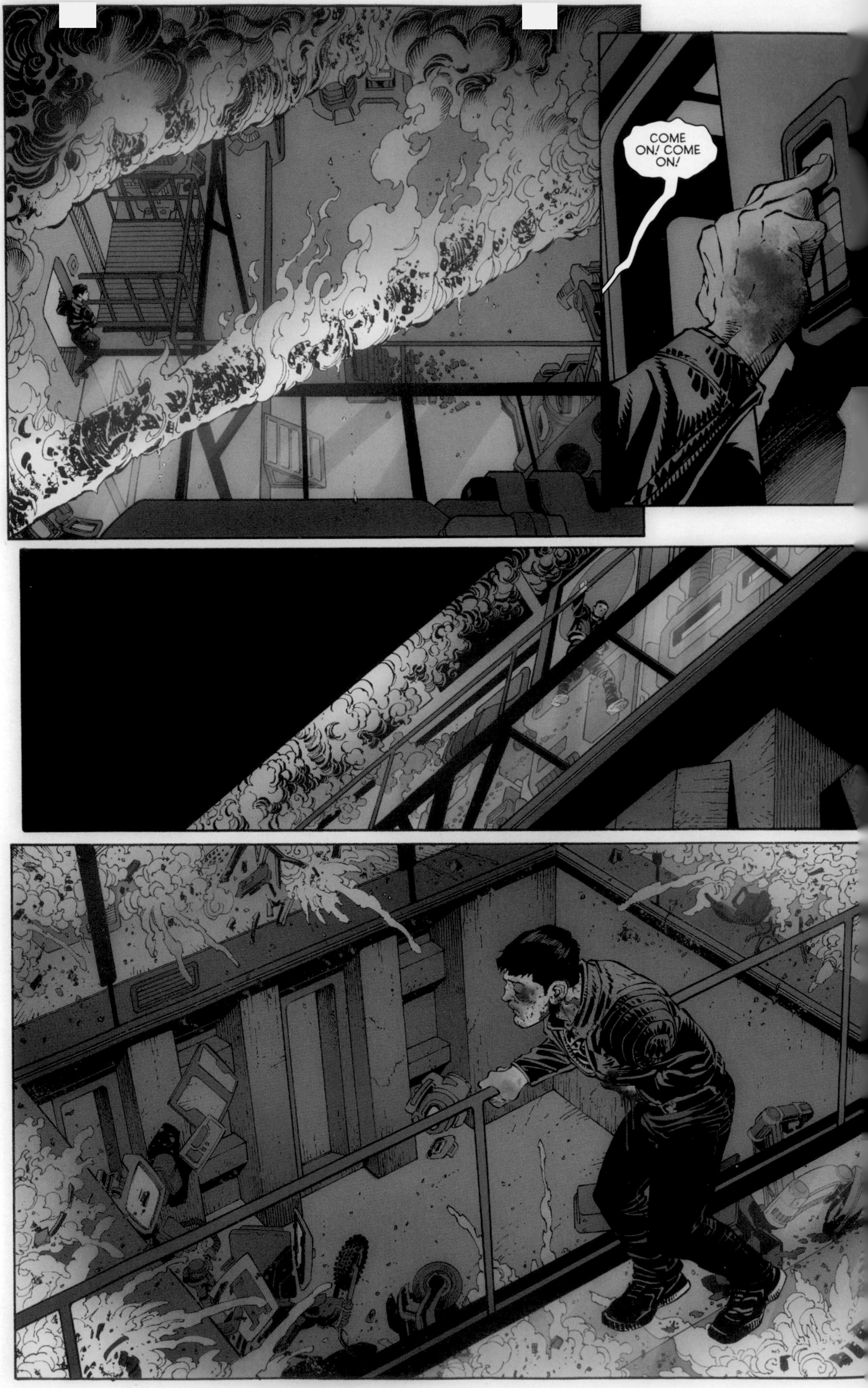
COME ON! COME ON!

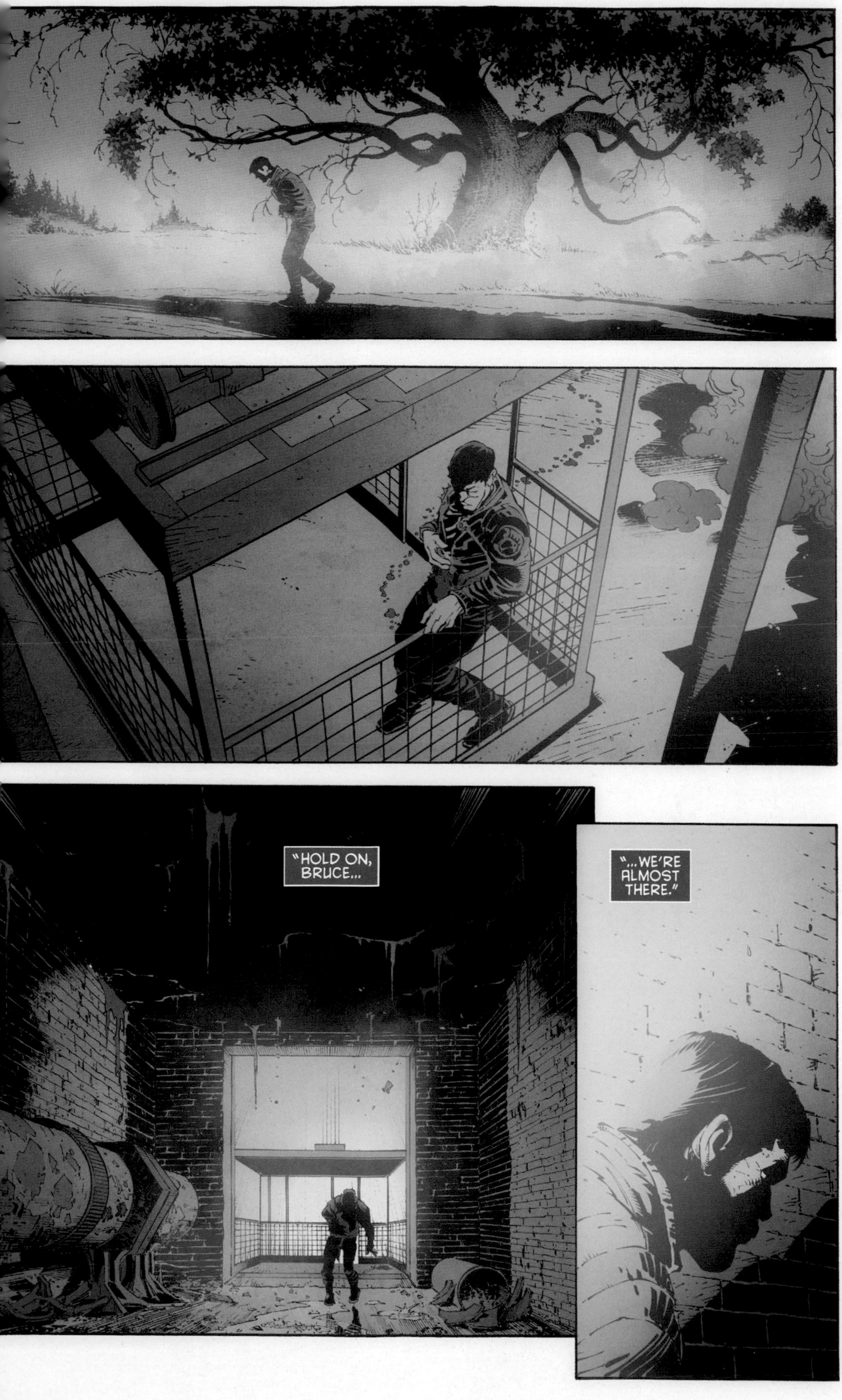
"HOLD ON, BRUCE...
"...WE'RE ALMOST THERE."

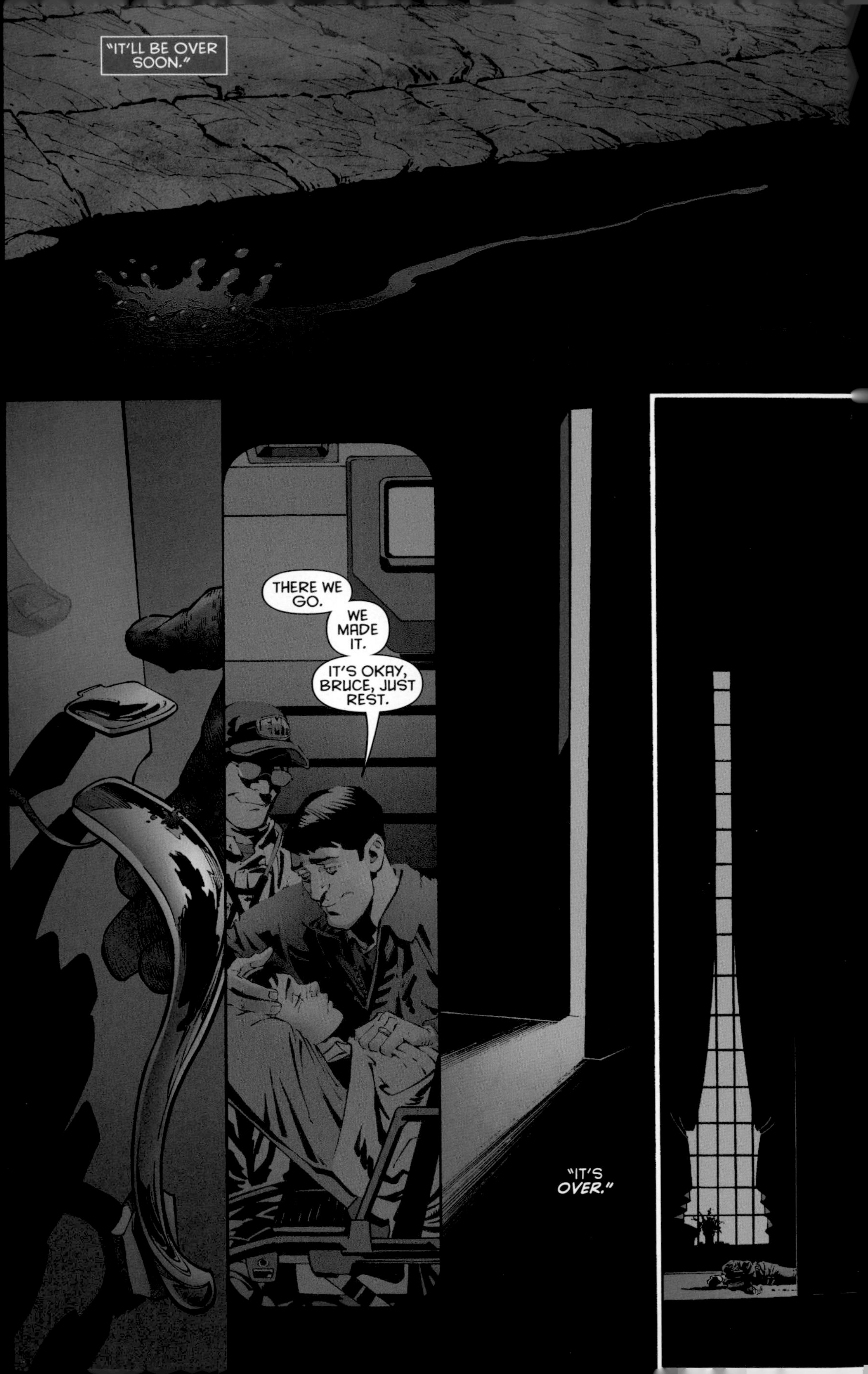
"IT'LL BE OVER SOON."
THERE WE GO.
WE MADE IT.
IT'S OKAY, BRUCE, JUST REST.
"IT'S OVER."

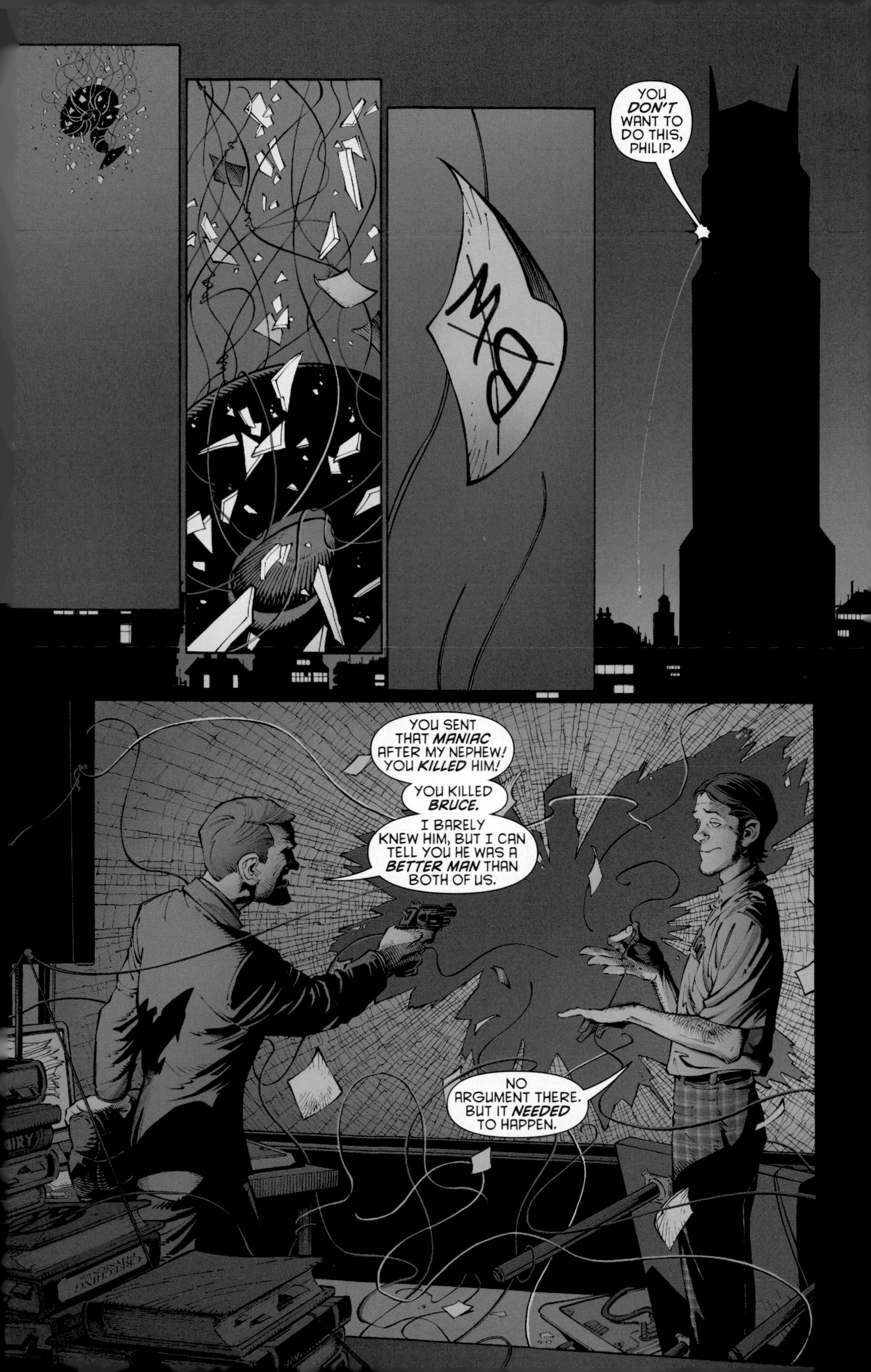
YOU DON'T WANT TO DO THIS, PHILIP.
YOU SENT THAT MANIAC AFTER MY NEPHEW! YOU KILLED HIM!
YOU KILLED BRUCE.
I BARELY KNEW HIM, BUT I CAN TELL YOU HE WAS A BETTER MAN THAN BOTH OF US.
NO ARGUMENT THERE. BUT IT NEEDED TO HAPPEN.

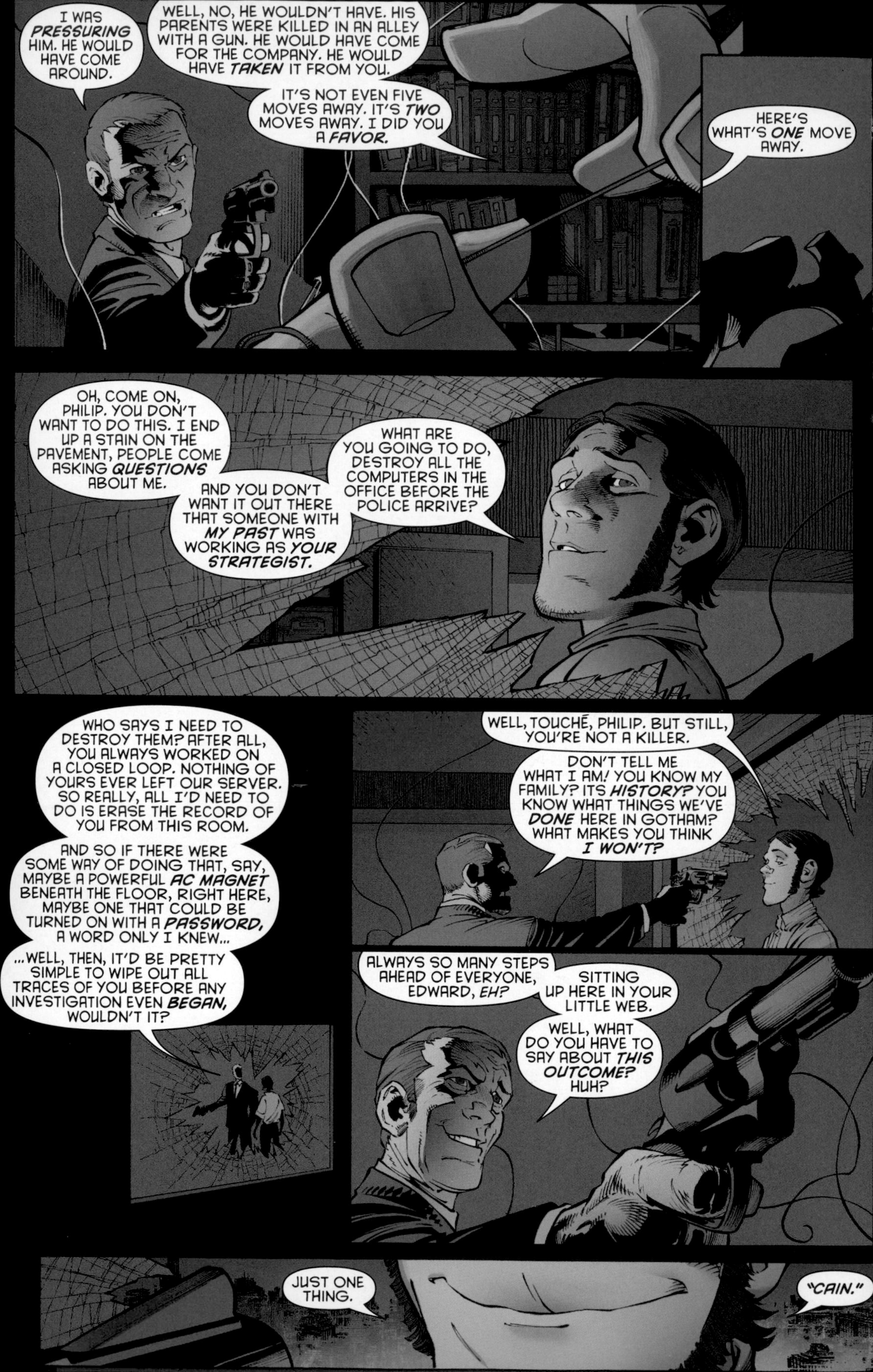
I WAS PRESSURING HIM. HE WOULD HAVE COME AROUND.
WELL, NO, HE WOULDN'T HAVE. HIS PARENTS WERE KILLED IN AN ALLEY WITH A GUN. HE WOULD HAVE COME FOR THE COMPANY. HE WOULD HAVE TAKEN IT FROM YOU.
IT'S NOT EVEN FIVE MOVES AWAY. IT'S TWO MOVES AWAY. I DID YOU A FAVOR.
HERE'S WHAT'S ONE MOVE AWAY.
OH, COME ON, PHILIP. YOU DON'T WANT TO DO THIS. I END UP A STAIN ON THE PAVEMENT, PEOPLE COME ASKING QUESTIONS ABOUT ME.
AND YOU DON'T WANT IT OUT THERE THAT SOMEONE WITH MY PAST WAS WORKING AS YOUR STRATEGIST.
WHAT ARE YOU GOING TO DO, DESTROY ALL THE COMPUTERS IN THE OFFICE BEFORE THE POLICE ARRIVE?
WHO SAYS I NEED TO DESTROY THEM? AFTER ALL, YOU ALWAYS WORKED ON A CLOSED LOOP. NOTHING OF YOURS EVER LEFT OUR SERVER. SO REALLY, ALL I'D NEED TO DO IS ERASE THE RECORD OF YOU FROM THIS ROOM.
AND SO IF THERE WERE SOME WAY OF DOING THAT, SAY, MAYBE A POWERFUL AC MAGNET BENEATH THE FLOOR, RIGHT HERE, MAYBE ONE THAT COULD BE TURNED ON WITH A PASSWORD, A WORD ONLY I KNEW...
...WELL, THEN, IT'D BE PRETTY SIMPLE TO WIPE OUT ALL TRACES OF YOU BEFORE ANY INVESTIGATION EVEN BEGAN, WOULDN'T IT?
WELL, TOUCHÉ, PHILIP. BUT STILL, YOU'RE NOT A KILLER.
DON'T TELL ME WHAT I AM! YOU KNOW MY FAMILY? ITS HISTORY? YOU KNOW WHAT THINGS WE'VE DONE HERE IN GOTHAM? WHAT MAKES YOU THINK I WON'T?
ALWAYS SO MANY STEPS AHEAD OF EVERYONE, EDWARD, EH?
SITTING UP HERE IN YOUR LITTLE WEB.
WELL, WHAT DO YOU HAVE TO SAY ABOUT THIS OUTCOME? HUH?
JUST ONE THING.
"CAIN."

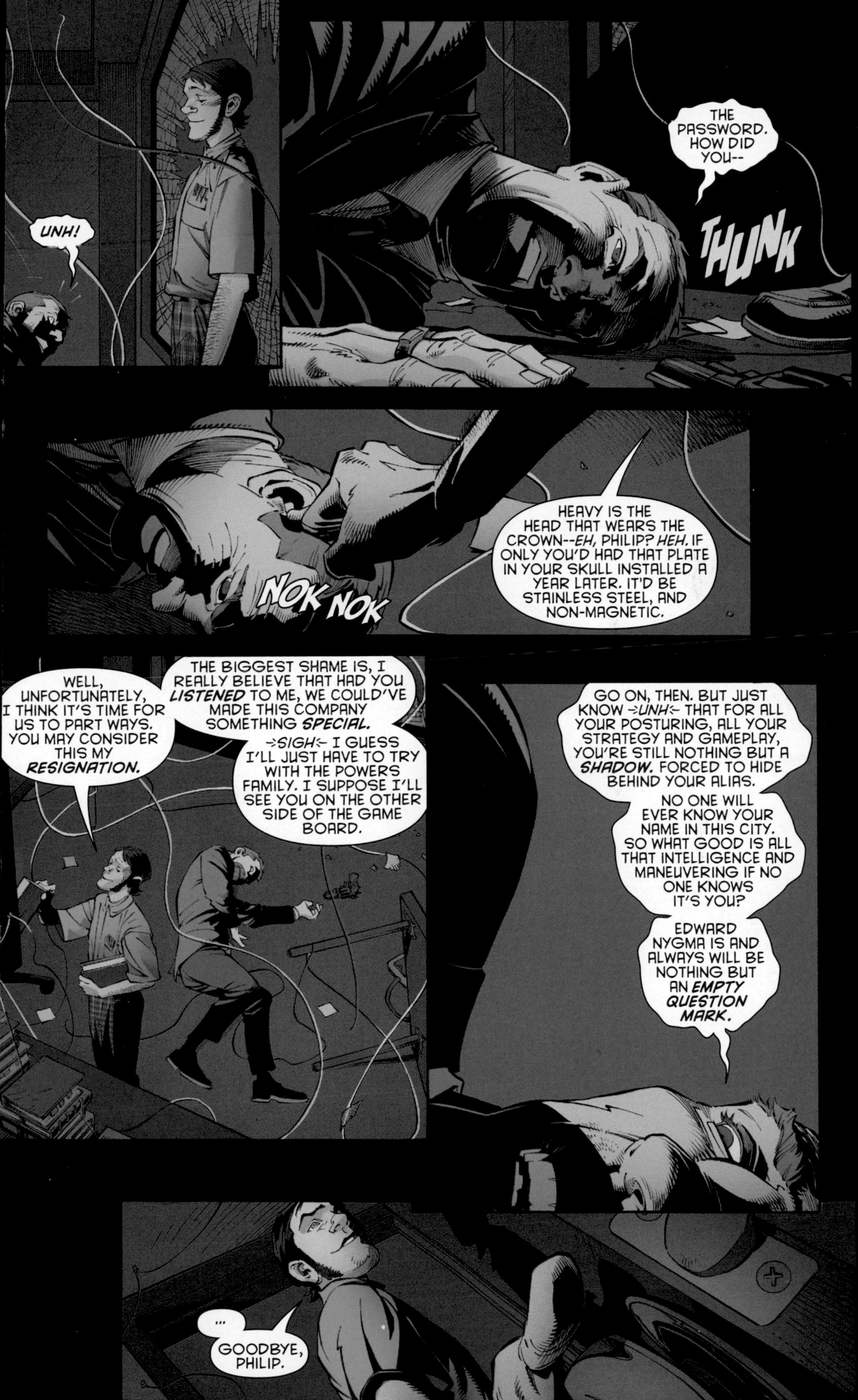
THE PASSWORD. HOW DID YOU--
UNH!
THUNK
HEAVY IS THE HEAD THAT WEARS THE CROWN--EH, PHILIP? HEH. IF ONLY YOU'D HAD THAT PLATE IN YOUR SKULL INSTALLED A YEAR LATER. IT'D BE STAINLESS STEEL, AND NON-MAGNETIC.
NOK NOK
WELL, UNFORTUNATELY, I THINK IT'S TIME FOR US TO PART WAYS. YOU MAY CONSIDER THIS MY RESIGNATION.
THE BIGGEST SHAME IS, I REALLY BELIEVE THAT HAD YOU LISTENED TO ME, WE COULD'VE MADE THIS COMPANY SOMETHING SPECIAL.
⇒SIGH⇐ I GUESS I'LL JUST HAVE TO TRY WITH THE POWERS FAMILY. I SUPPOSE I'LL SEE YOU ON THE OTHER SIDE OF THE GAME BOARD.
GO ON, THEN. BUT JUST KNOW ⇒UNH⇐ THAT FOR ALL YOUR POSTURING, ALL YOUR STRATEGY AND GAMEPLAY, YOU'RE STILL NOTHING BUT A SHADOW. FORCED TO HIDE BEHIND YOUR ALIAS.
NO ONE WILL EVER KNOW YOUR NAME IN THIS CITY. SO WHAT GOOD IS ALL THAT INTELLIGENCE AND MANEUVERING IF NO ONE KNOWS IT'S YOU?
EDWARD NYGMA IS AND ALWAYS WILL BE NOTHING BUT AN EMPTY QUESTION MARK.
... GOODBYE, PHILIP.

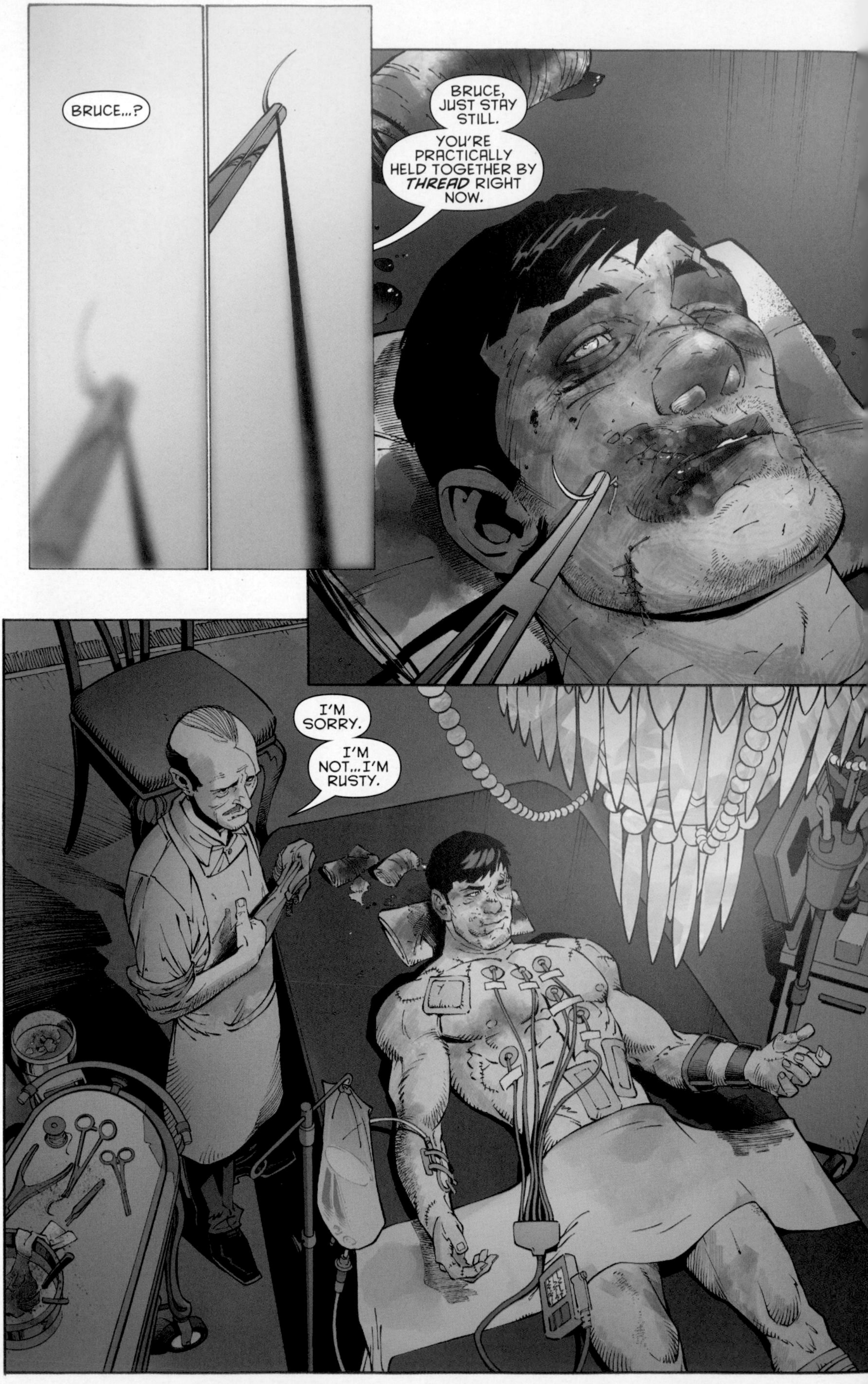
BRUCE...?
BRUCE, JUST STAY STILL.
YOU'RE PRACTICALLY HELD TOGETHER BY *THREAD* RIGHT NOW.
I'M SORRY.
I'M NOT...I'M RUSTY.

YOU NEED TO REST, BRUCE. THE BLOWS YOU TOOK TO THE SKULL...AT LEAST WAIT UNTIL THE SWELLING RECEDES AND YOU'RE CLEAR HEADED.

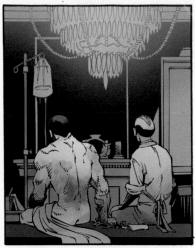

I JUST WANTED TO BE HOME, ALFRED. YOU DIDN'T...YOU DIDN'T HAVE TO *DO* THIS.

YOU KNOW, WHEN IT HAPPENED...WHEN YOUR PARENTS WERE *SHOT*, I REMEMBER BEING AT THE HOSPITAL WHERE THEY WERE TAKEN AFTERWARDS.

I REMEMBER SPEAKING WITH THE DOCTOR. AND HE TOLD ME...HE TOLD ME THAT EVEN IF THEY'D BEEN SHOT IN THE HOSPITAL, IN THE CARDIAC WARD, THE *SEVERITY* OF THE WOUNDS WOULD HAVE BEEN *LETHAL*.

THE THING IS, I WAS ON THE BATTLEFIELD, BRUCE, AND I WAS GOOD. THERE WERE TIMES WHEN I WAS SURE...NO, WHEN *EVERYONE* WAS SURE THAT SOMEONE WAS *DONE FOR* AND...AND I WAS ABLE TO...

...WHAT I'M TRYING TO SAY IS THAT WE MIGHT DISAGREE, WE MIGHT FIGHT. BUT NO MATTER WHAT...NO MATTER *WHAT*, I'LL ALWAYS BE HERE TO PATCH YOU UP.

THAT MUCH I PROMISE.

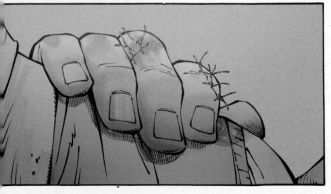

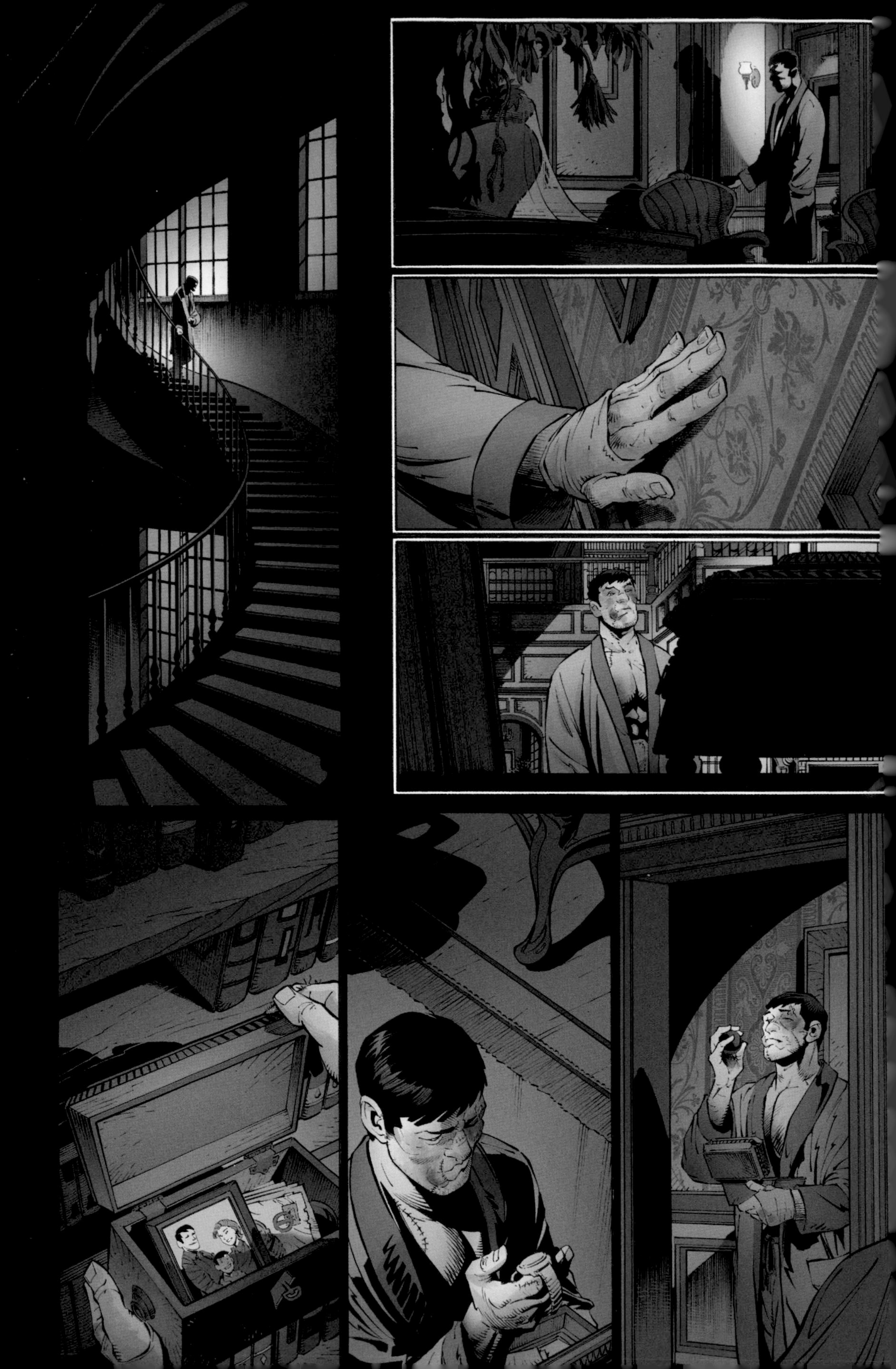

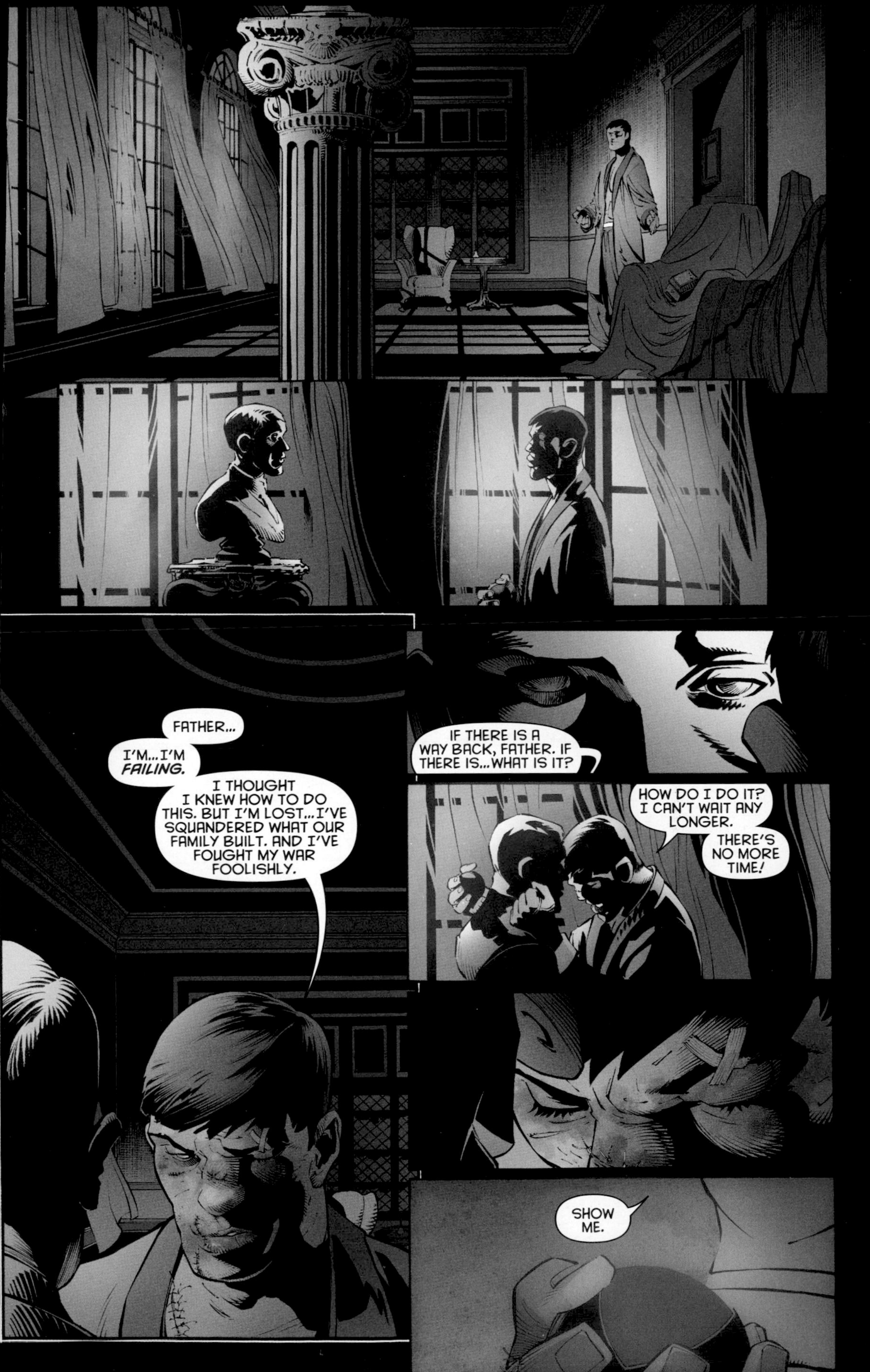
FATHER...
I'M...I'M FAILING.
I THOUGHT I KNEW HOW TO DO THIS. BUT I'M LOST...I'VE SQUANDERED WHAT OUR FAMILY BUILT. AND I'VE FOUGHT MY WAR FOOLISHLY.
IF THERE IS A WAY BACK, FATHER. IF THERE IS...WHAT IS IT?
HOW DO I DO IT? I CAN'T WAIT ANY LONGER.
THERE'S NO MORE TIME!
SHOW ME.

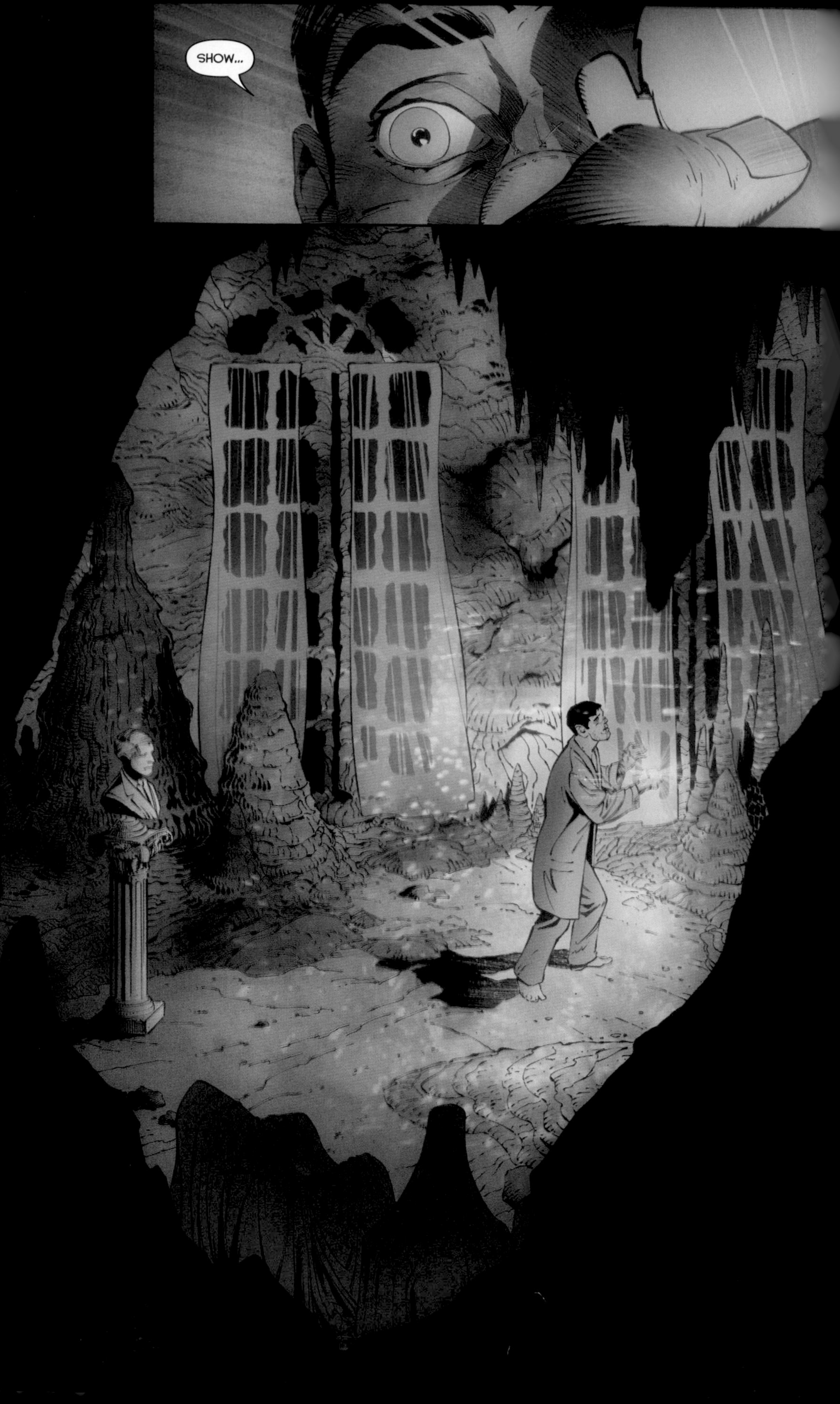
SHOW...

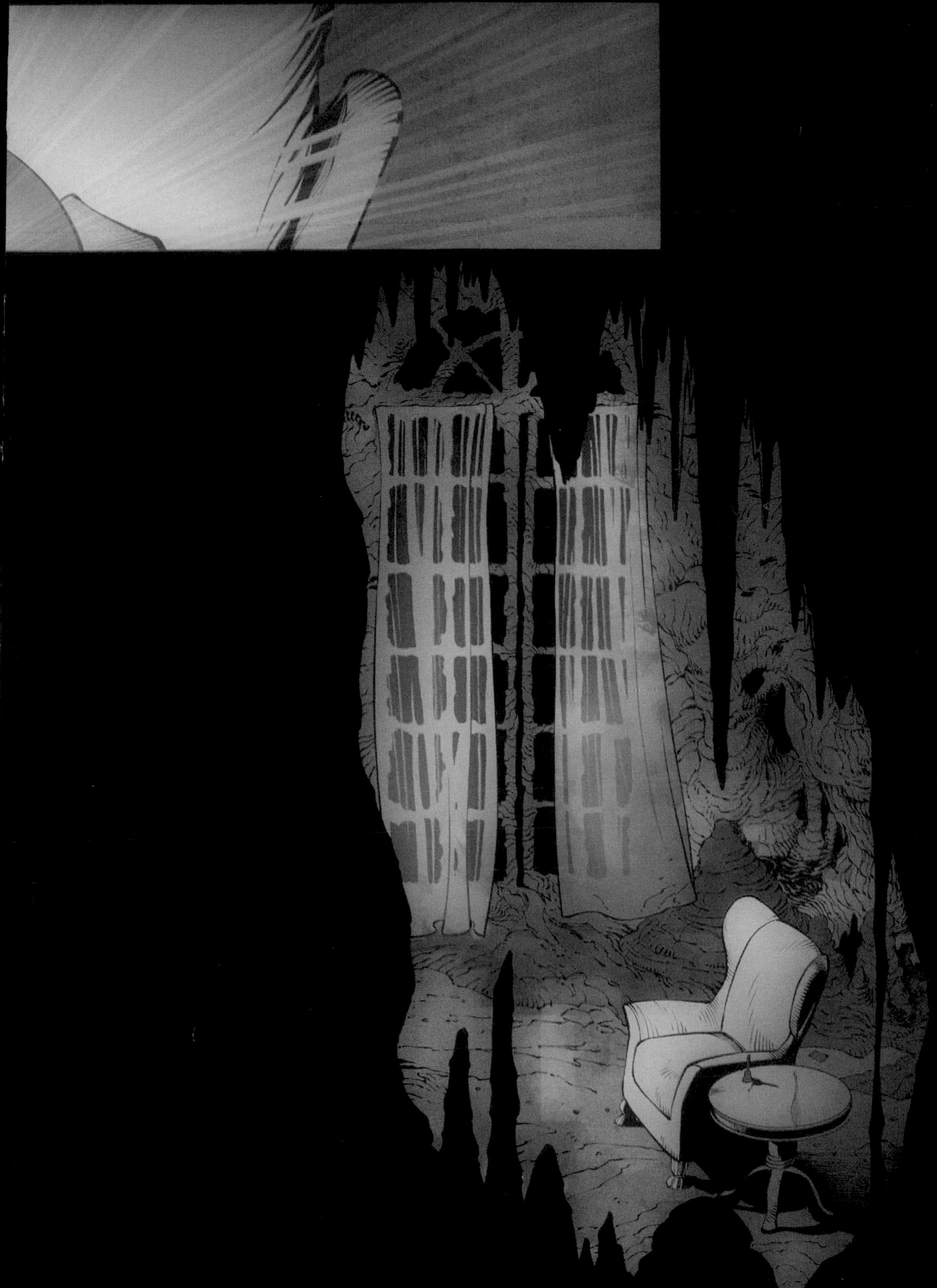

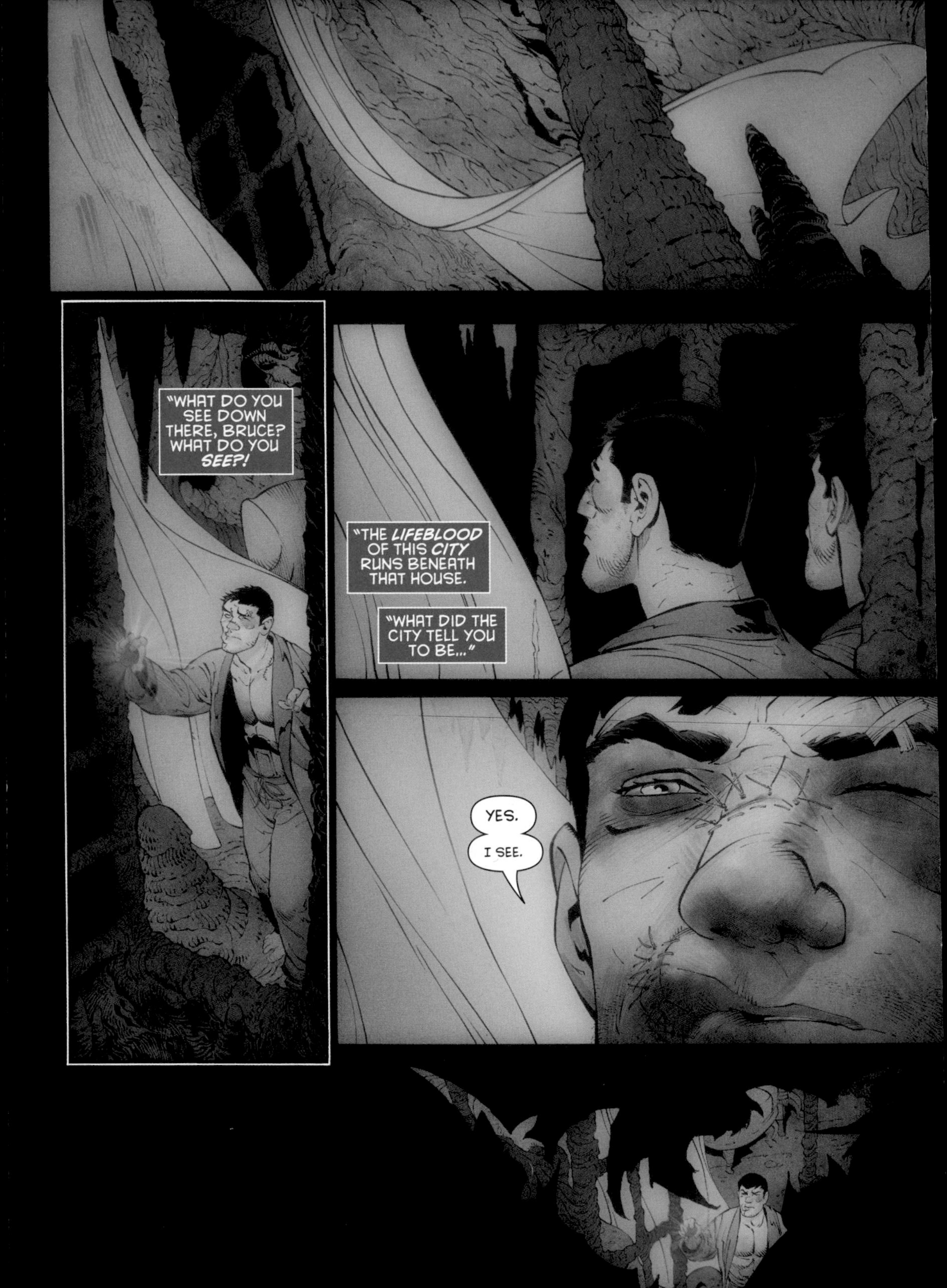
"WHAT DO YOU SEE DOWN THERE, BRUCE? WHAT DO YOU *SEE?!*
"THE *LIFEBLOOD* OF THIS *CITY* RUNS BENEATH THAT HOUSE.
"WHAT DID THE CITY TELL YOU TO BE..."
YES.
I SEE.

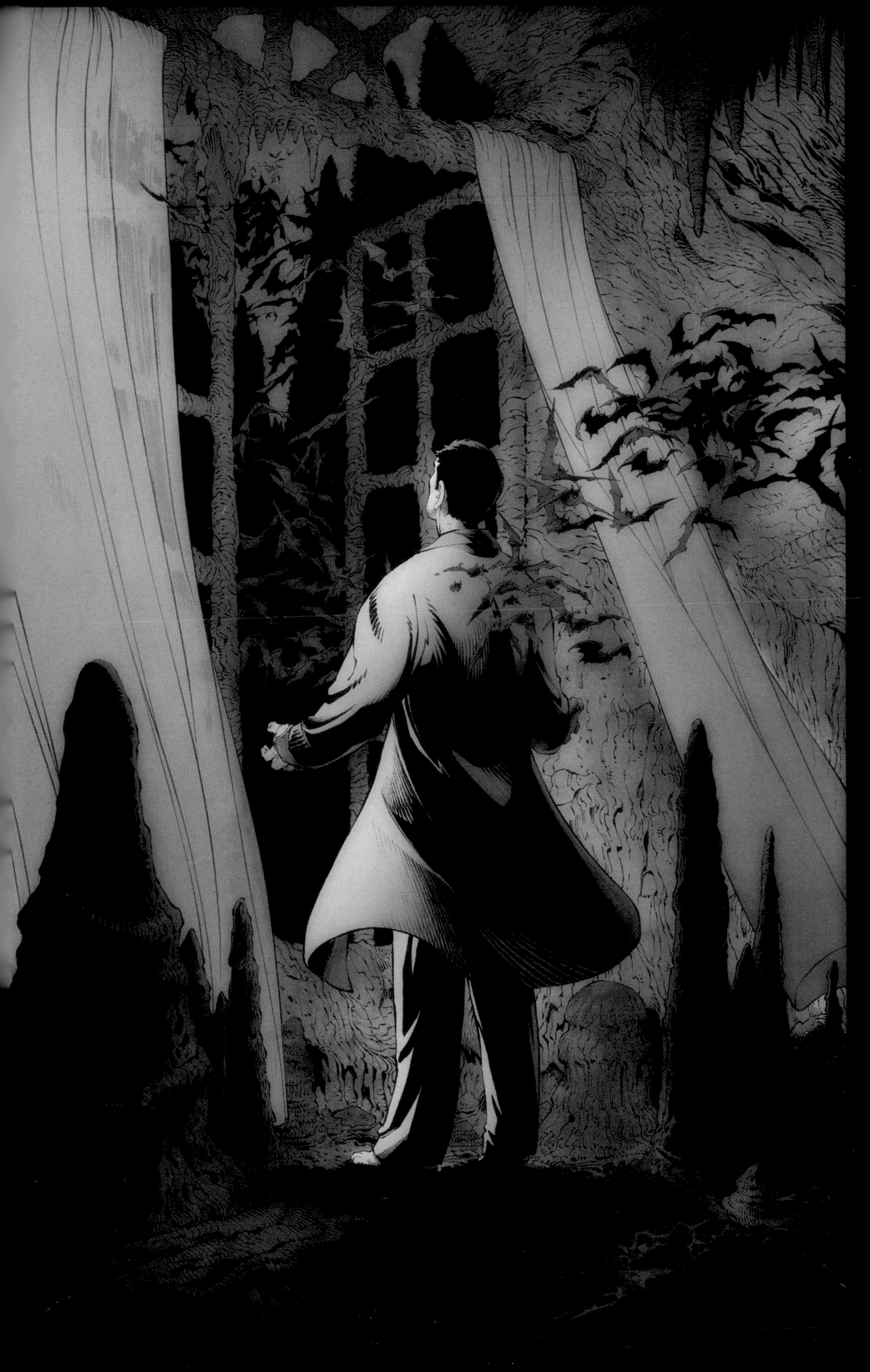

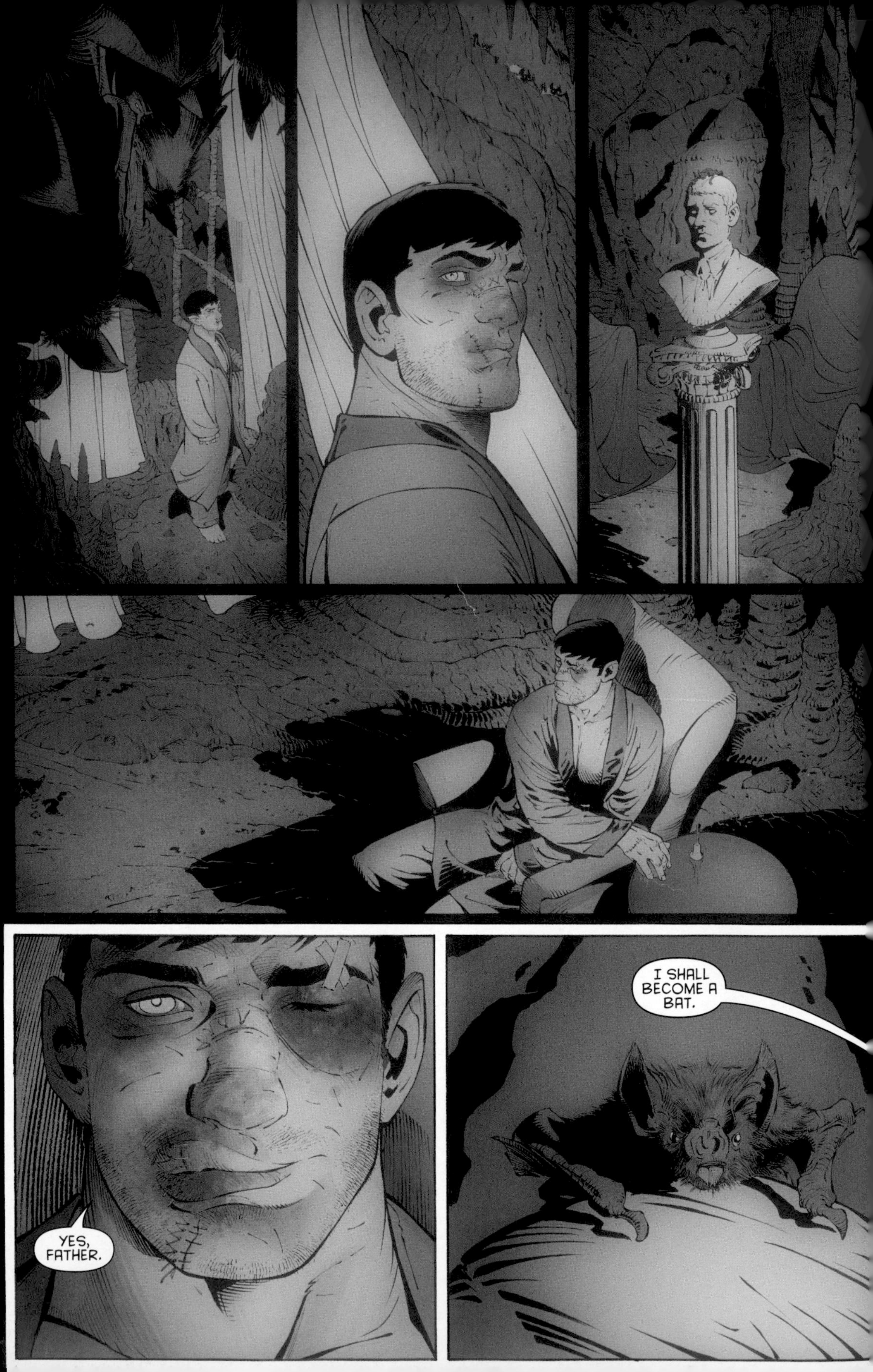
YES, FATHER.
I SHALL BECOME A BAT.

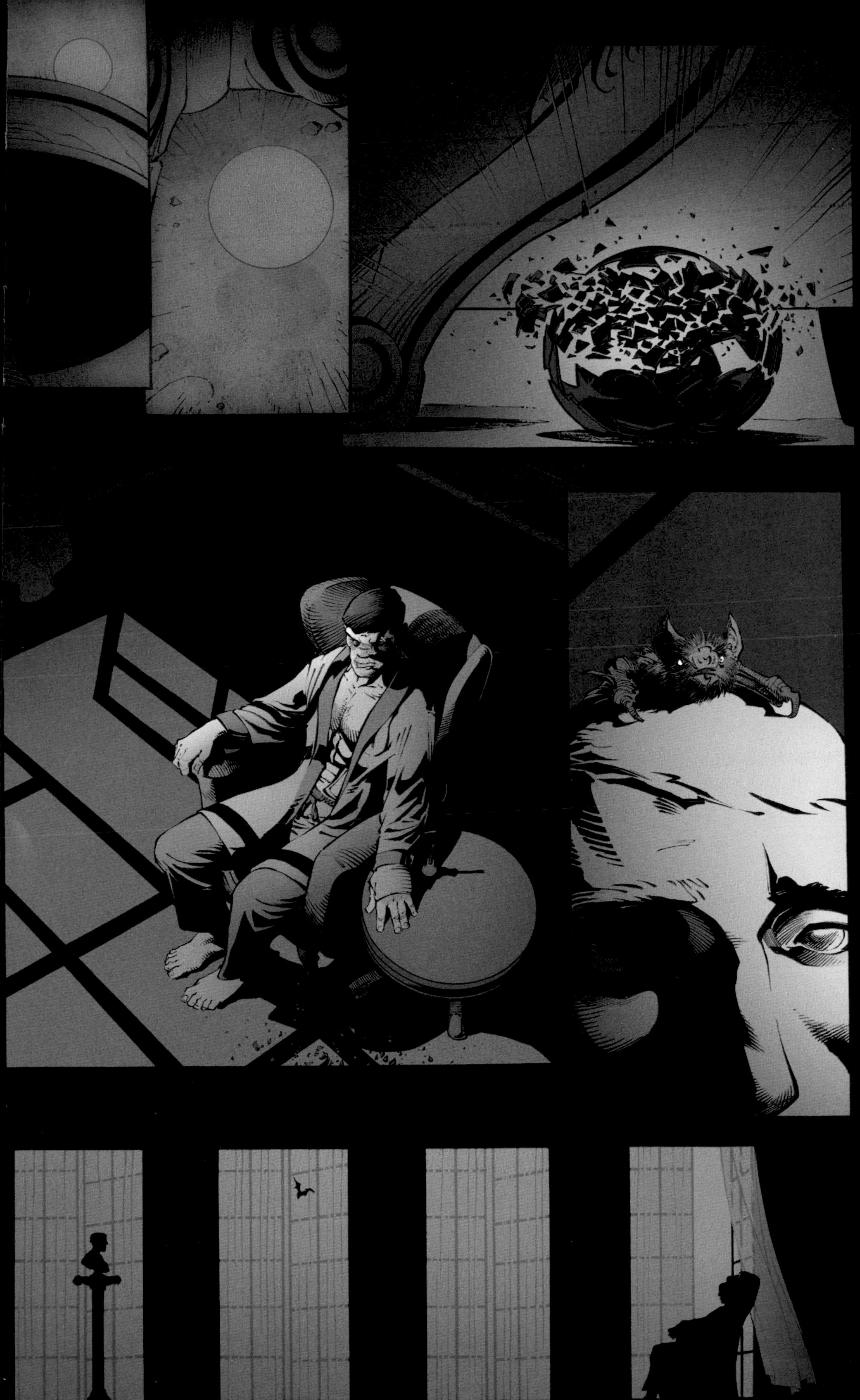

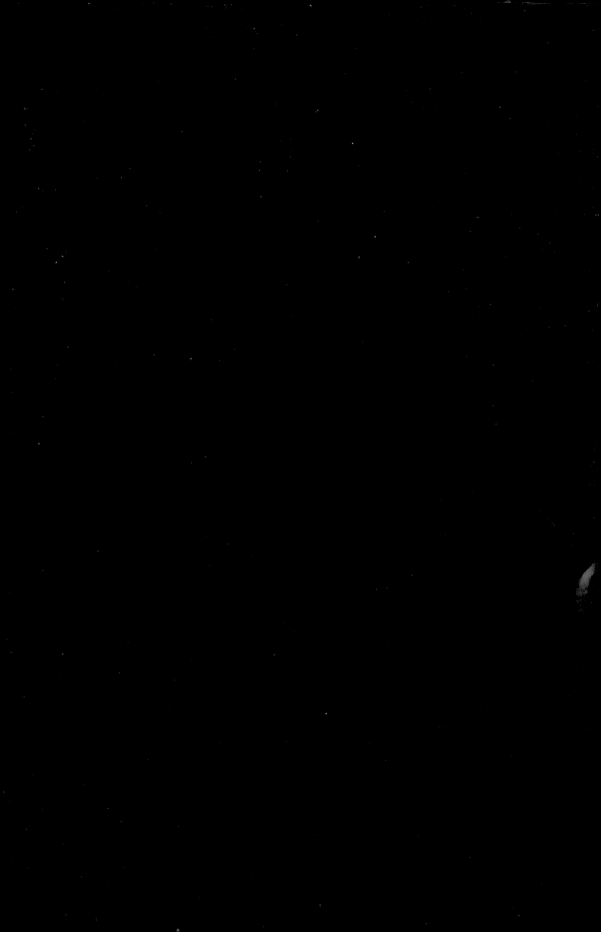

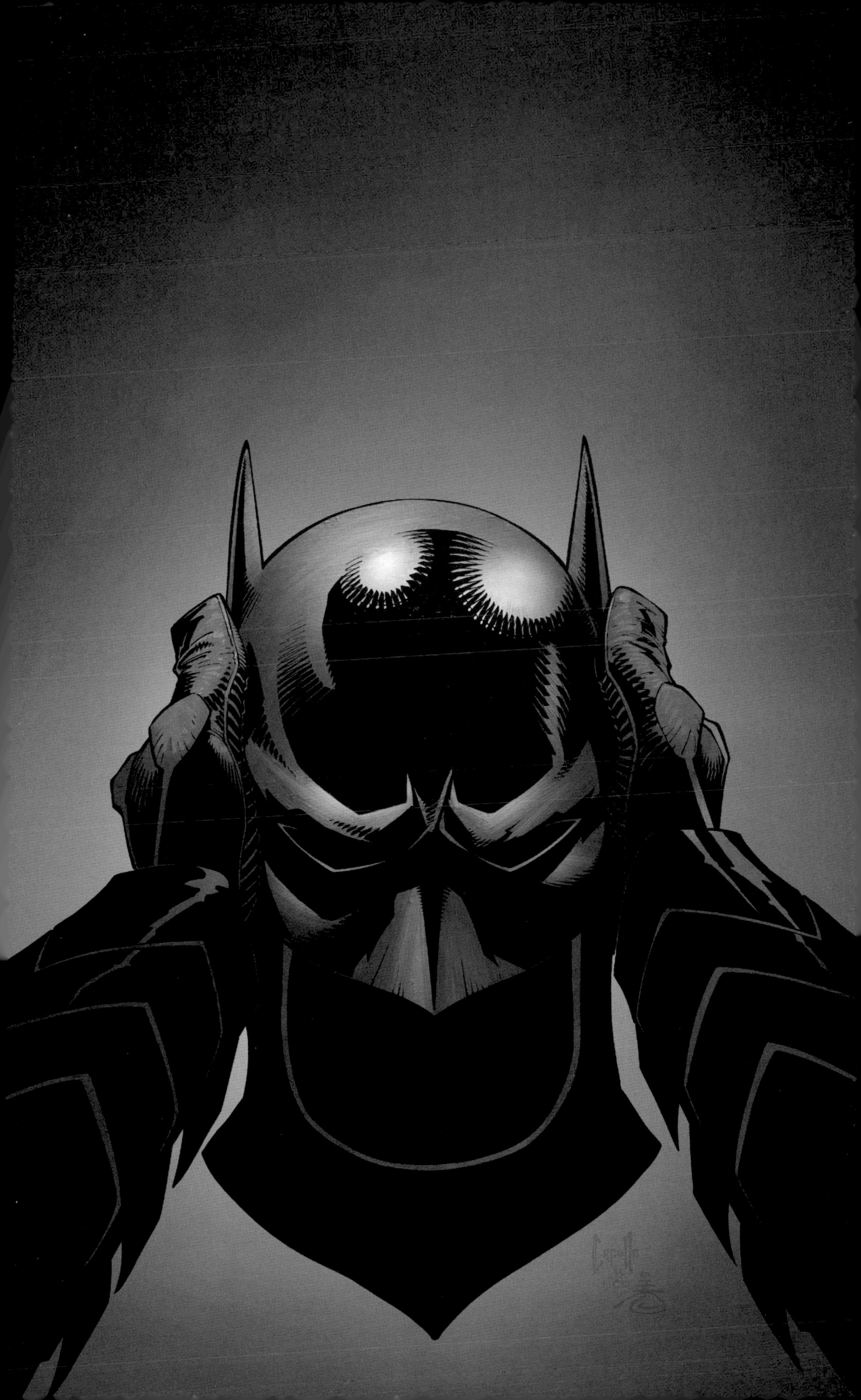

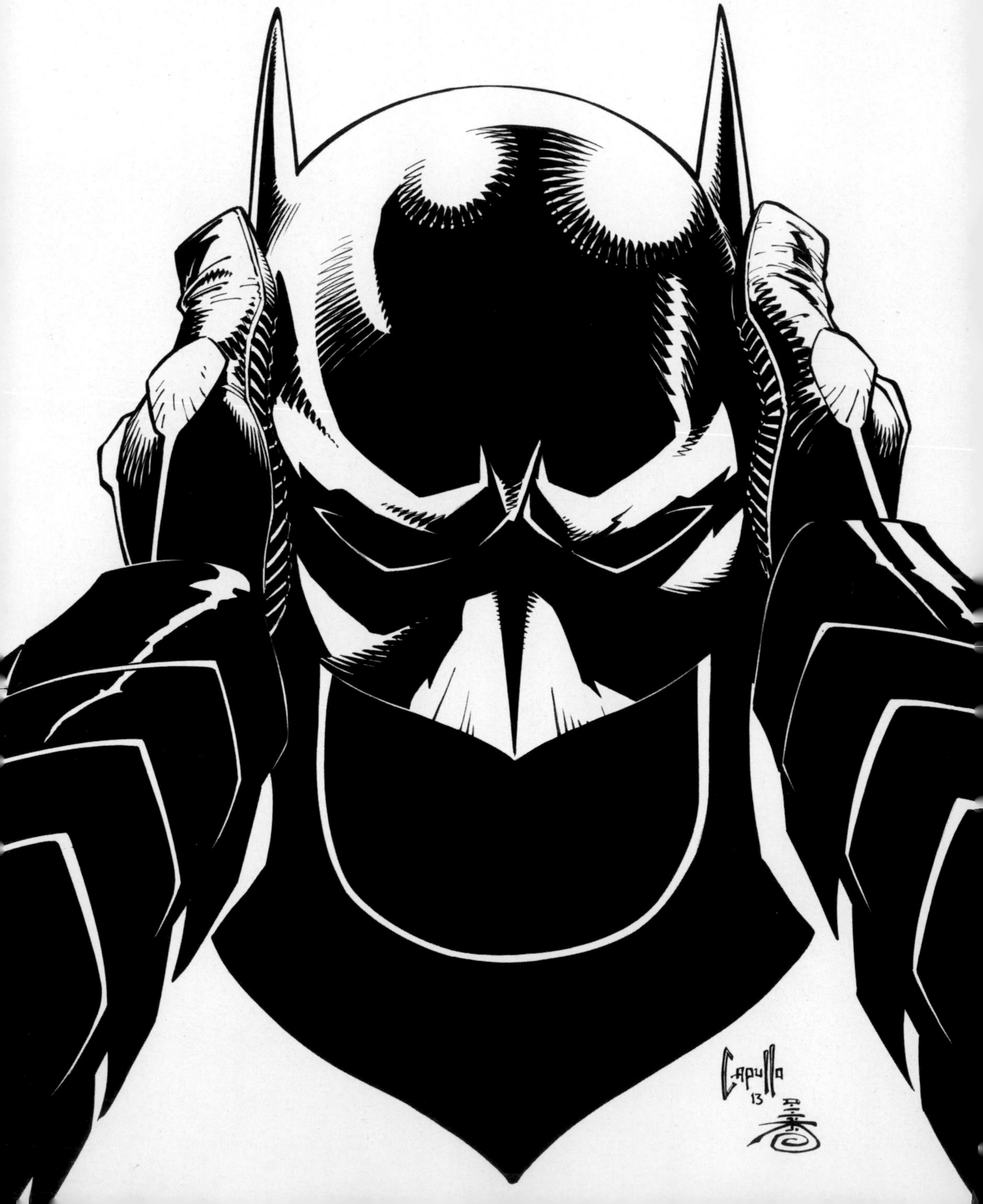
Capullo
13

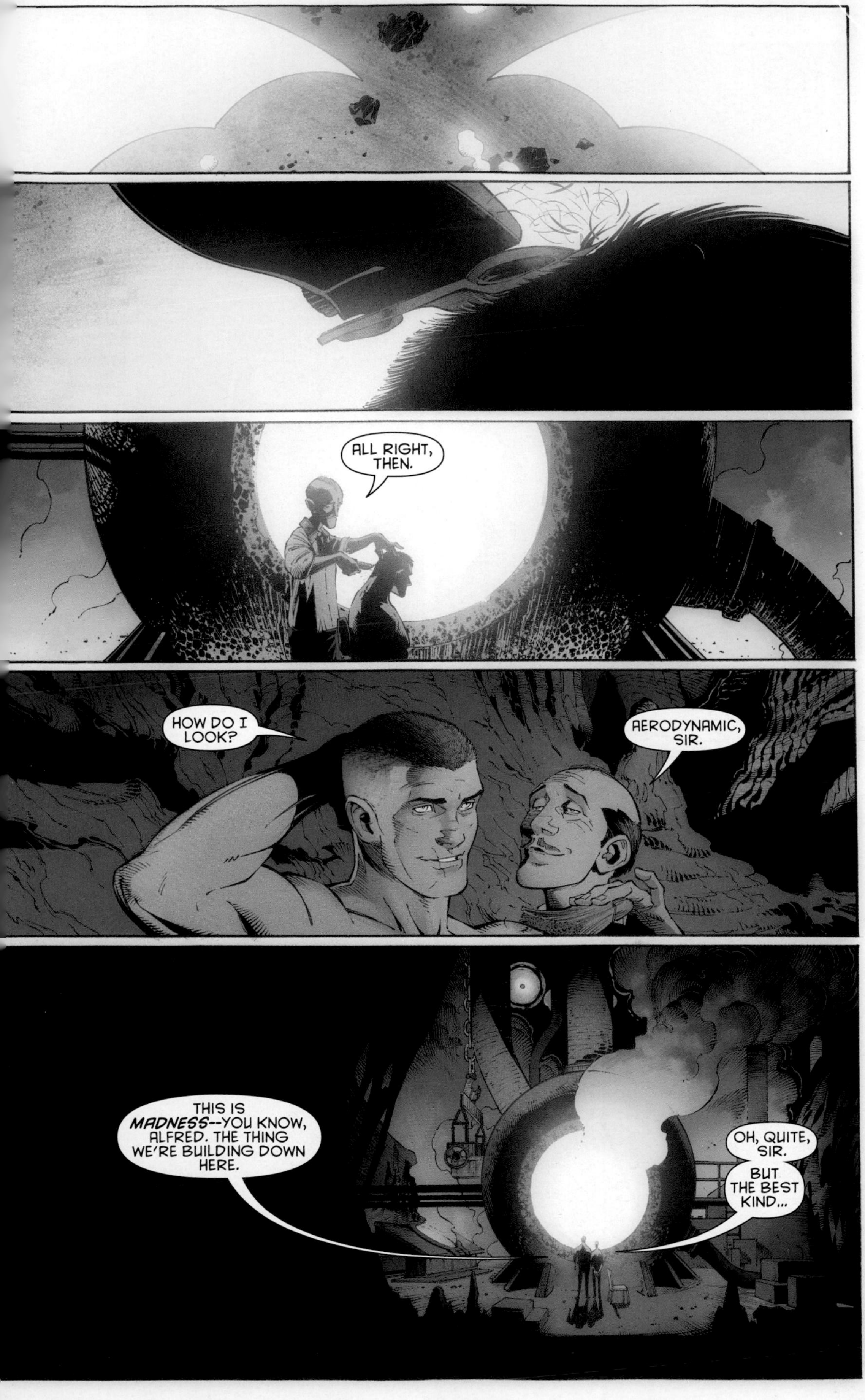
ALL RIGHT, THEN.
HOW DO I LOOK?
AERODYNAMIC, SIR.
THIS IS MADNESS--YOU KNOW, ALFRED. THE THING WE'RE BUILDING DOWN HERE.
OH, QUITE, SIR.
BUT THE BEST KIND...

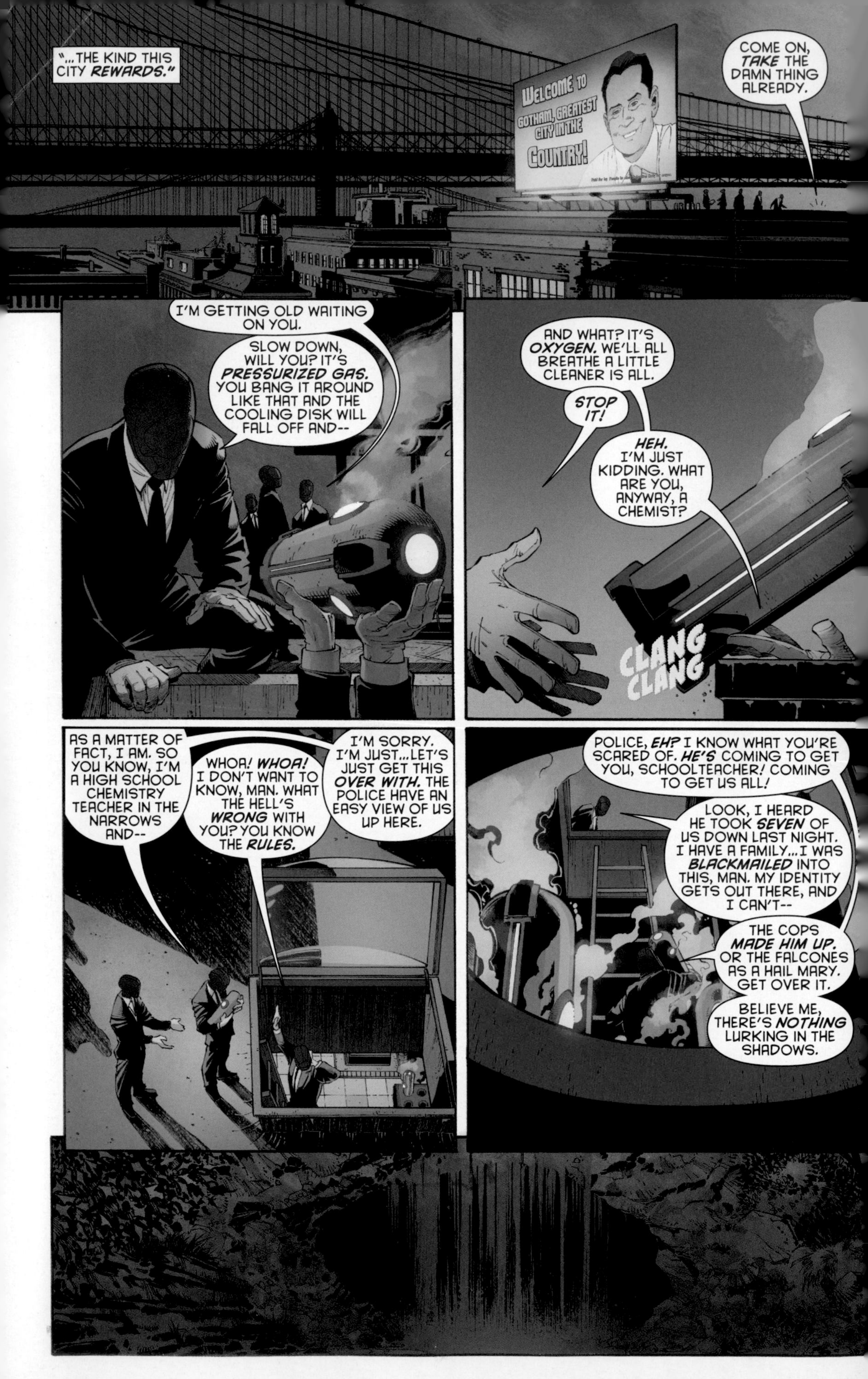
"...THE KIND THIS CITY REWARDS."
WELCOME TO GOTHAM, GREATEST CITY IN THE COUNTRY!
COME ON, TAKE THE DAMN THING ALREADY.
I'M GETTING OLD WAITING ON YOU.
SLOW DOWN, WILL YOU? IT'S PRESSURIZED GAS. YOU BANG IT AROUND LIKE THAT AND THE COOLING DISK WILL FALL OFF AND--
AND WHAT? IT'S OXYGEN. WE'LL ALL BREATHE A LITTLE CLEANER IS ALL.
STOP IT!
HEH. I'M JUST KIDDING. WHAT ARE YOU, ANYWAY, A CHEMIST?
CLANG CLANG
AS A MATTER OF FACT, I AM. SO YOU KNOW, I'M A HIGH SCHOOL CHEMISTRY TEACHER IN THE NARROWS AND--
WHOA! WHOA! I DON'T WANT TO KNOW, MAN. WHAT THE HELL'S WRONG WITH YOU? YOU KNOW THE RULES.
I'M SORRY. I'M JUST...LET'S JUST GET THIS OVER WITH. THE POLICE HAVE AN EASY VIEW OF US UP HERE.
POLICE, EH? I KNOW WHAT YOU'RE SCARED OF. HE'S COMING TO GET YOU, SCHOOLTEACHER! COMING TO GET US ALL!
LOOK, I HEARD HE TOOK SEVEN OF US DOWN LAST NIGHT. I HAVE A FAMILY...I WAS BLACKMAILED INTO THIS, MAN. MY IDENTITY GETS OUT THERE, AND I CAN'T--
THE COPS MADE HIM UP. OR THE FALCONES AS A HAIL MARY. GET OVER IT.
BELIEVE ME, THERE'S NOTHING LURKING IN THE SHADOWS.

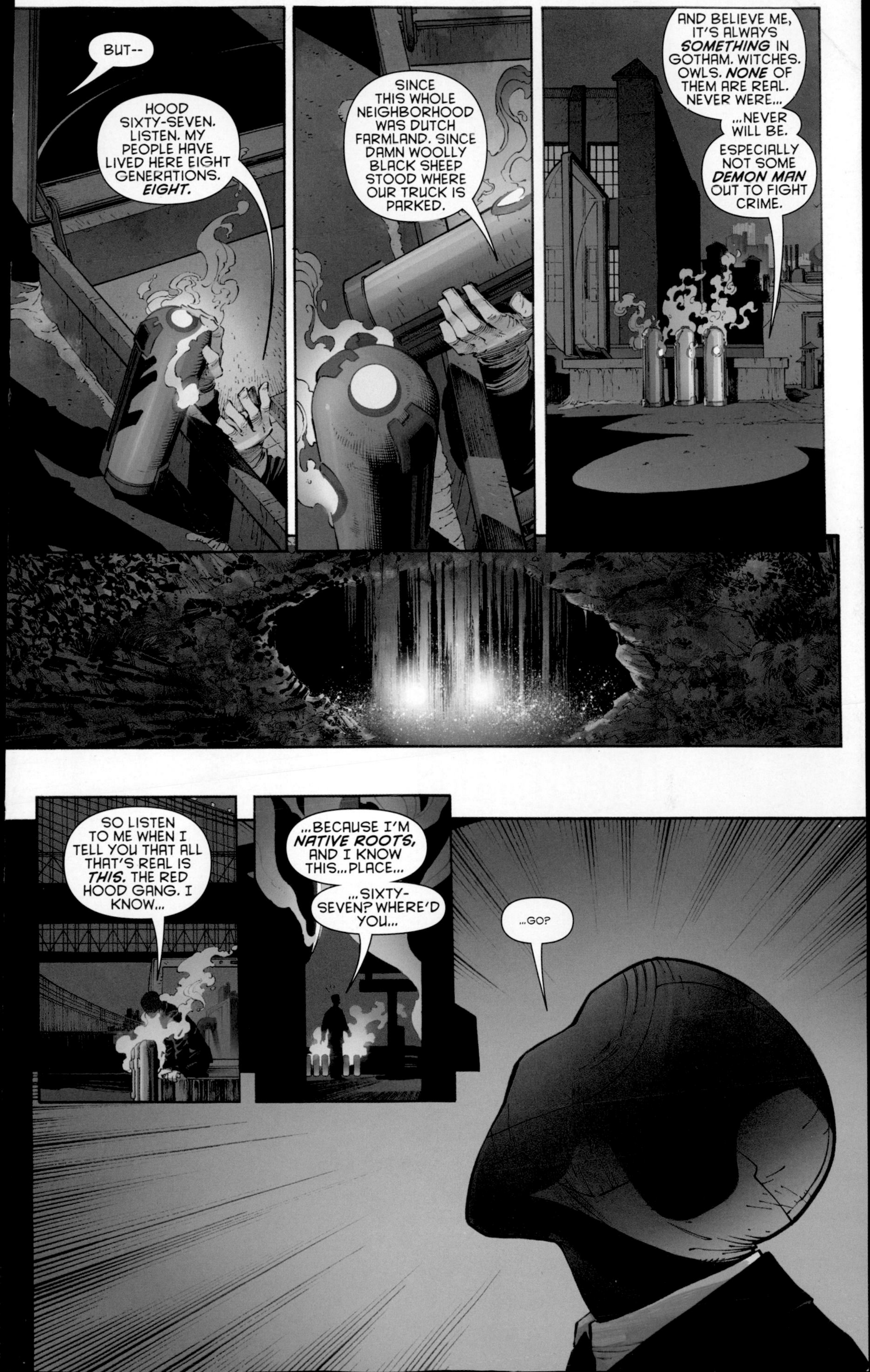
BUT--
HOOD SIXTY-SEVEN. LISTEN. MY PEOPLE HAVE LIVED HERE EIGHT GENERATIONS. EIGHT.
SINCE THIS WHOLE NEIGHBORHOOD WAS DUTCH FARMLAND. SINCE DAMN WOOLLY BLACK SHEEP STOOD WHERE OUR TRUCK IS PARKED.
AND BELIEVE ME, IT'S ALWAYS SOMETHING IN GOTHAM. WITCHES. OWLS. NONE OF THEM ARE REAL. NEVER WERE...
...NEVER WILL BE.
ESPECIALLY NOT SOME DEMON MAN OUT TO FIGHT CRIME.
SO LISTEN TO ME WHEN I TELL YOU THAT ALL THAT'S REAL IS THIS. THE RED HOOD GANG. I KNOW...
...BECAUSE I'M NATIVE ROOTS, AND I KNOW THIS...PLACE...
...SIXTY-SEVEN? WHERE'D YOU...
...GO?

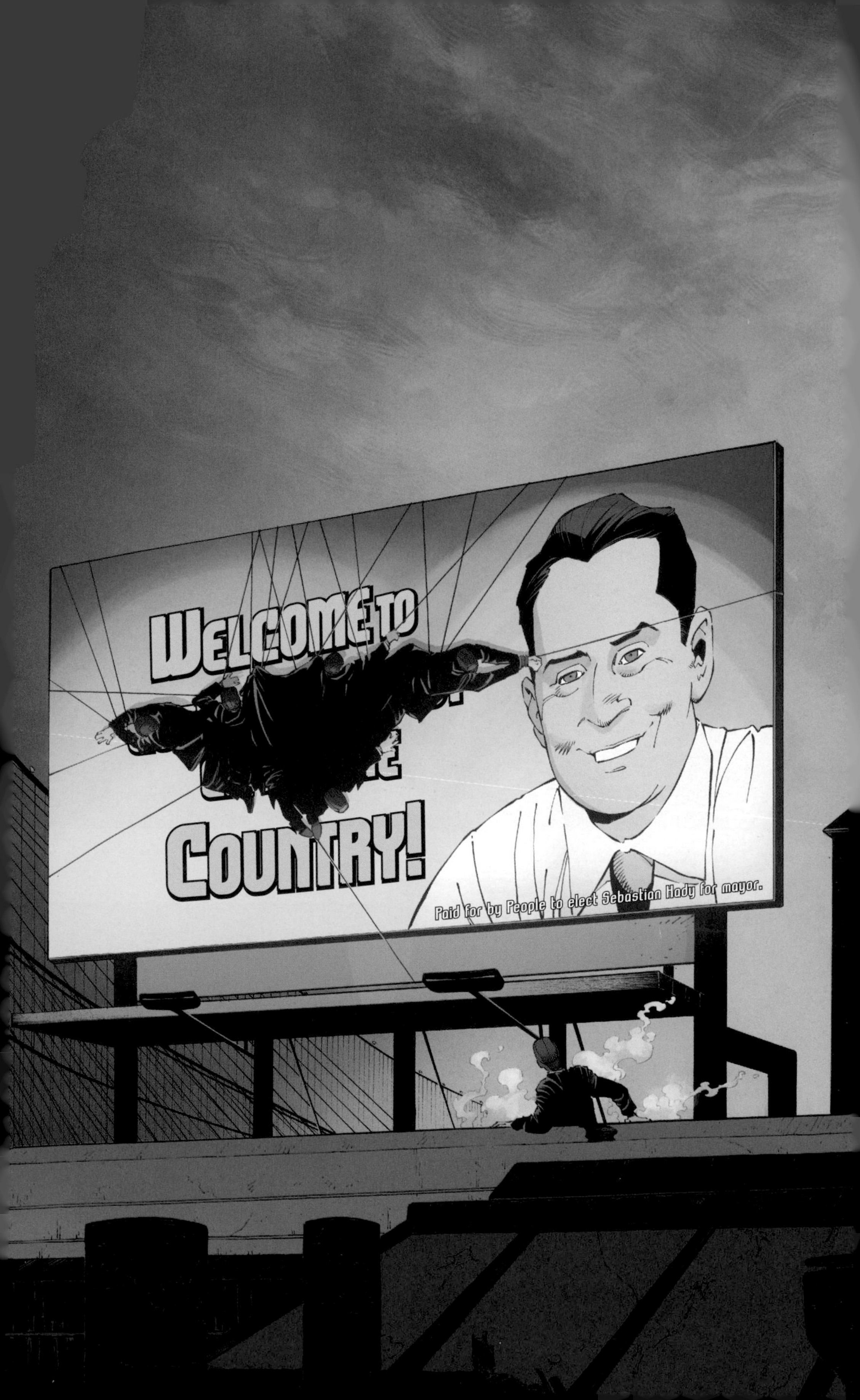
WELCOME TO
COUNTRY!
Paid for by People to elect Sebastian Hady for mayor.

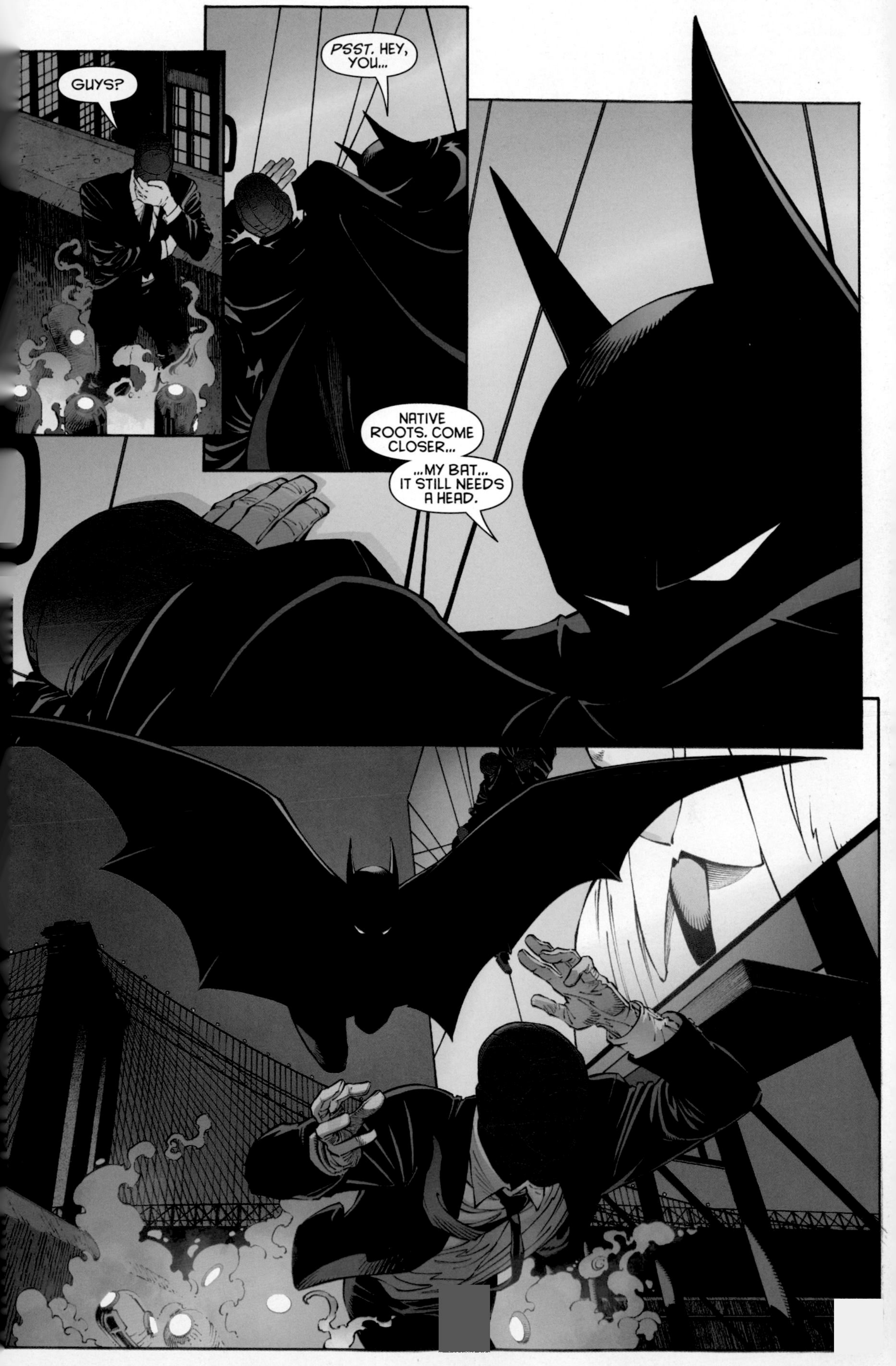
GUYS?
PSST. HEY, YOU...
NATIVE ROOTS. COME CLOSER...
...MY BAT... IT STILL NEEDS A HEAD.

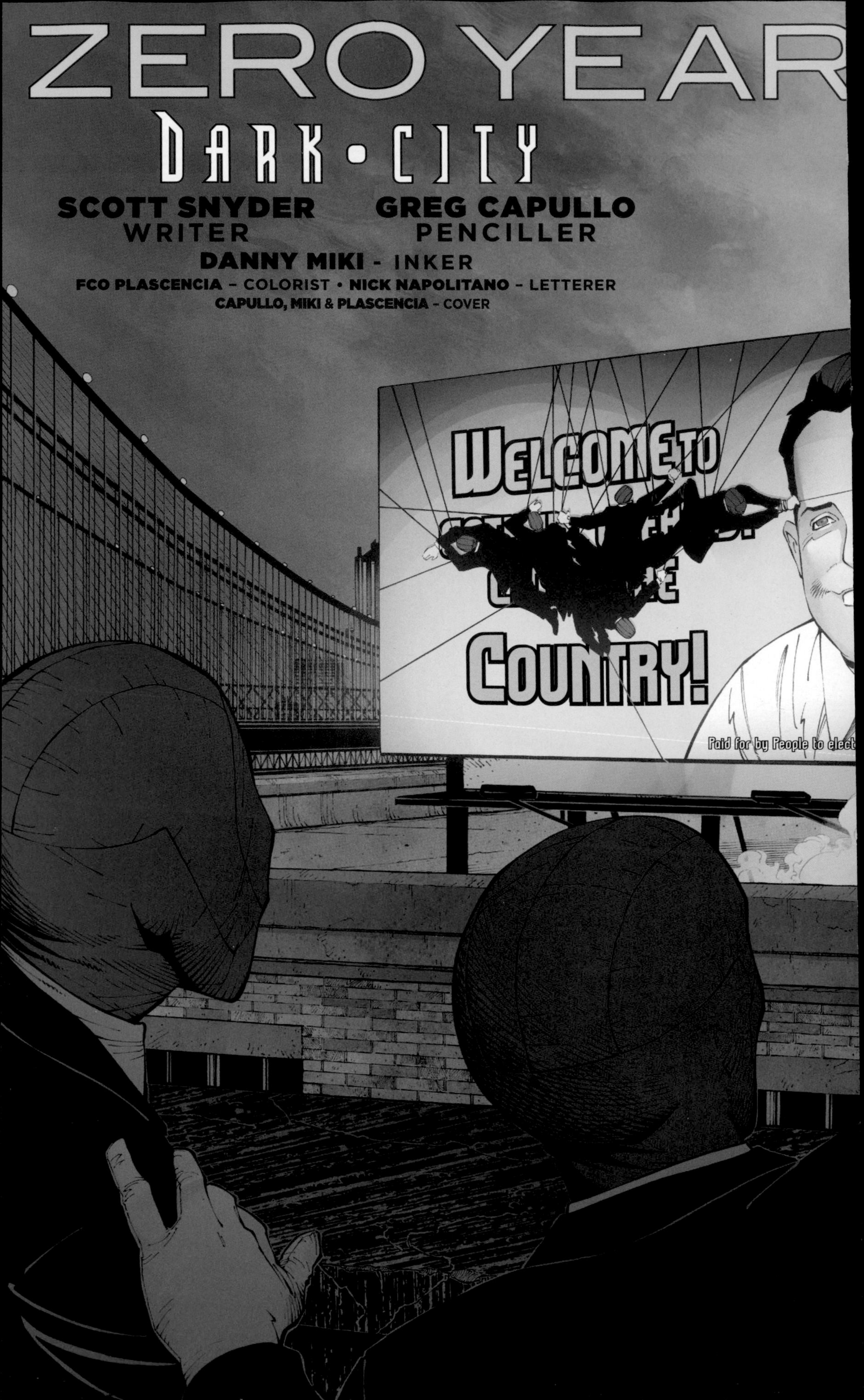
ZERO YEAR
DARK • CITY
SCOTT SNYDER WRITER
GREG CAPULLO PENCILLER
DANNY MIKI - INKER
FCO PLASCENCIA - COLORIST • NICK NAPOLITANO - LETTERER
CAPULLO, MIKI & PLASCENCIA - COVER
WELCOME TO
COUNTRY!
Paid for by People to elect

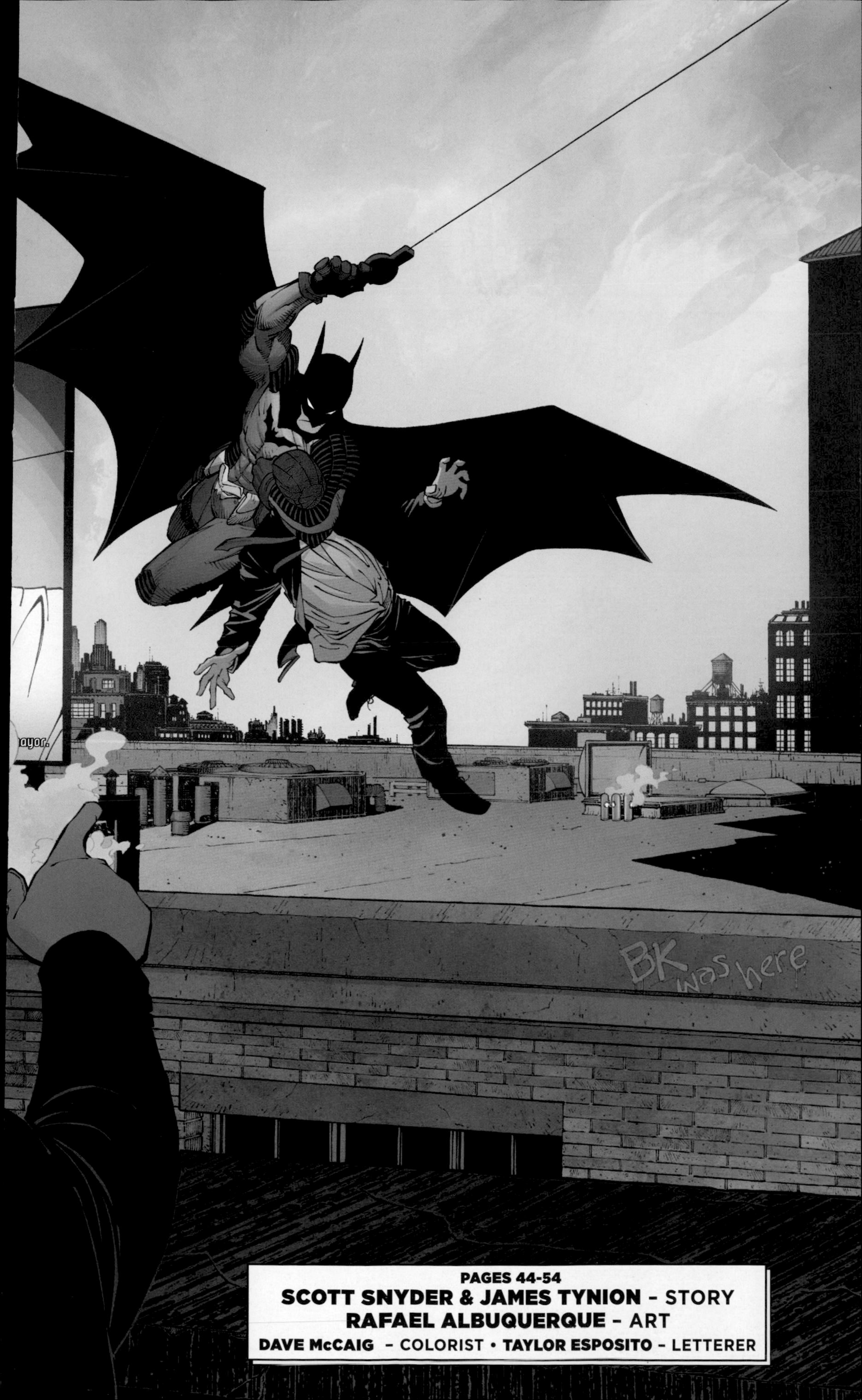
BK was here
PAGES 44-54
SCOTT SNYDER & JAMES TYNION - STORY
RAFAEL ALBUQUERQUE - ART
DAVE McCAIG - COLORIST • TAYLOR ESPOSITO - LETTERER

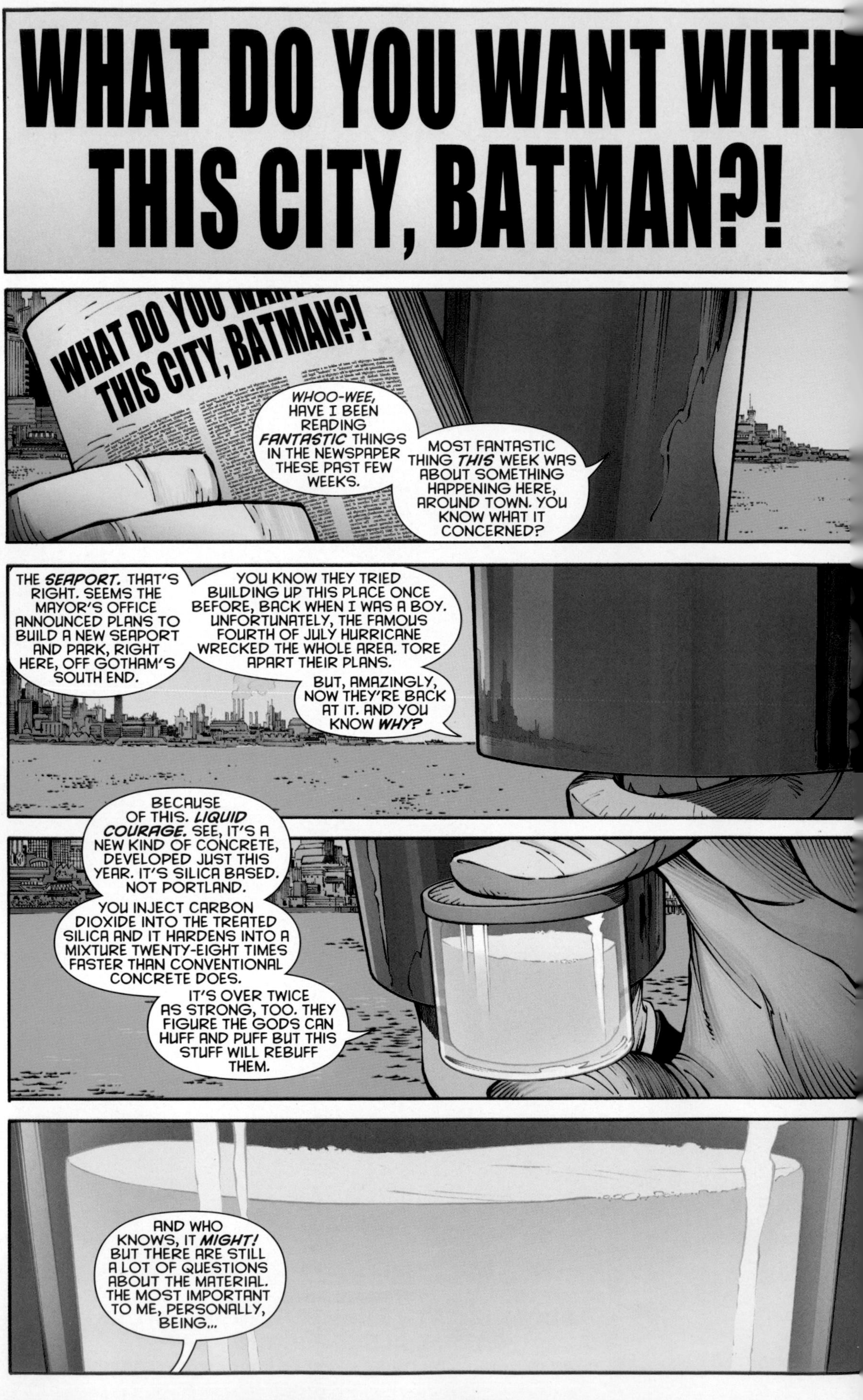
WHAT DO YOU WANT WITH THIS CITY, BATMAN?!
WHAT DO YOU WANT WITH THIS CITY, BATMAN?!
WHOO-WEE, HAVE I BEEN READING FANTASTIC THINGS IN THE NEWSPAPER THESE PAST FEW WEEKS.
MOST FANTASTIC THING THIS WEEK WAS ABOUT SOMETHING HAPPENING HERE, AROUND TOWN. YOU KNOW WHAT IT CONCERNED?
THE SEAPORT. THAT'S RIGHT. SEEMS THE MAYOR'S OFFICE ANNOUNCED PLANS TO BUILD A NEW SEAPORT AND PARK, RIGHT HERE, OFF GOTHAM'S SOUTH END.
YOU KNOW THEY TRIED BUILDING UP THIS PLACE ONCE BEFORE, BACK WHEN I WAS A BOY. UNFORTUNATELY, THE FAMOUS FOURTH OF JULY HURRICANE WRECKED THE WHOLE AREA. TORE APART THEIR PLANS.
BUT, AMAZINGLY, NOW THEY'RE BACK AT IT. AND YOU KNOW WHY?
BECAUSE OF THIS. LIQUID COURAGE. SEE, IT'S A NEW KIND OF CONCRETE, DEVELOPED JUST THIS YEAR. IT'S SILICA BASED. NOT PORTLAND.
YOU INJECT CARBON DIOXIDE INTO THE TREATED SILICA AND IT HARDENS INTO A MIXTURE TWENTY-EIGHT TIMES FASTER THAN CONVENTIONAL CONCRETE DOES.
IT'S OVER TWICE AS STRONG, TOO. THEY FIGURE THE GODS CAN HUFF AND PUFF BUT THIS STUFF WILL REBUFF THEM.
AND WHO KNOWS, IT MIGHT! BUT THERE ARE STILL A LOT OF QUESTIONS ABOUT THE MATERIAL. THE MOST IMPORTANT TO ME, PERSONALLY, BEING...

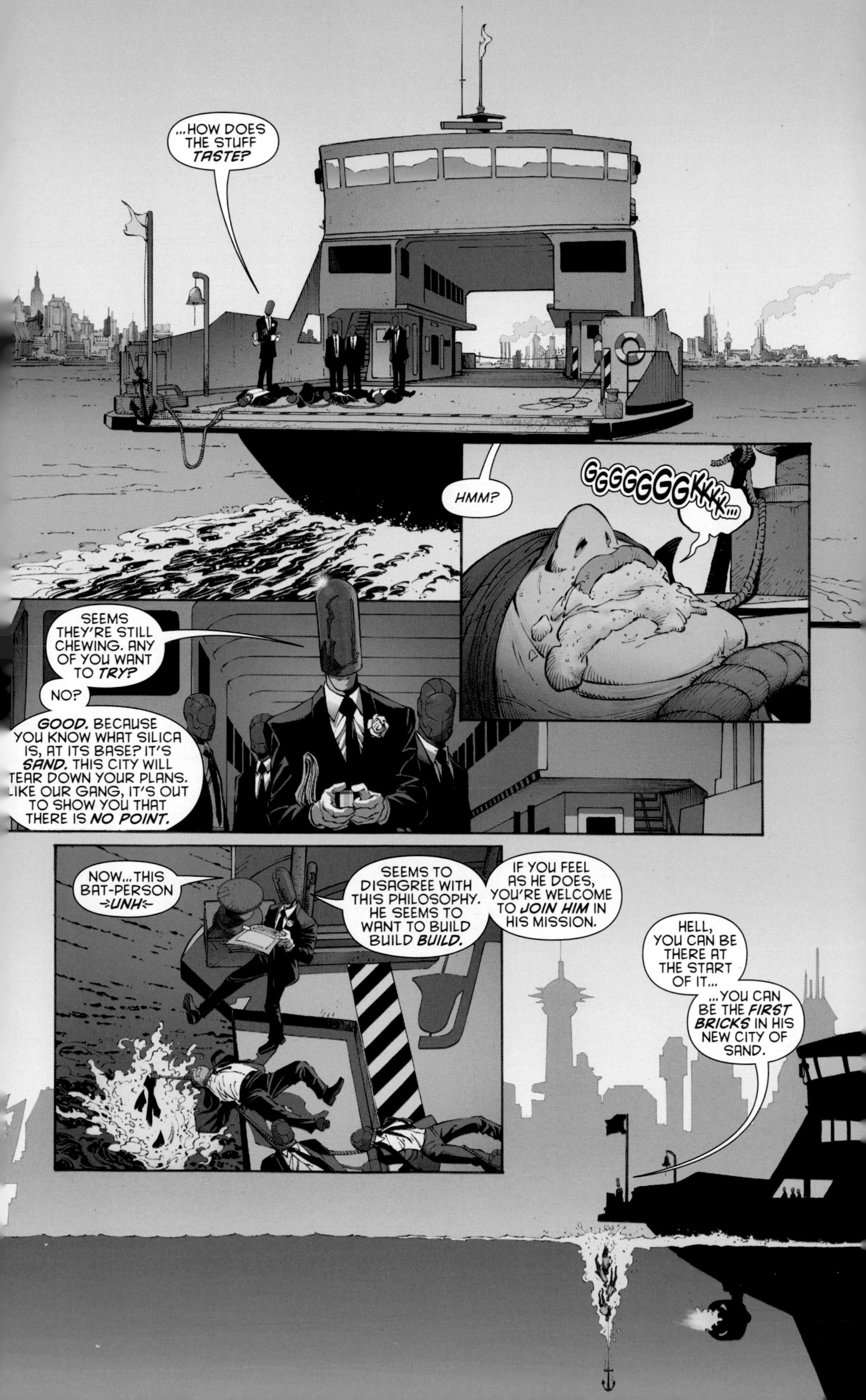
...HOW DOES THE STUFF TASTE?
HMM?
GGGGGGGKKKK...
SEEMS THEY'RE STILL CHEWING. ANY OF YOU WANT TO TRY?
NO?
GOOD. BECAUSE YOU KNOW WHAT SILICA IS, AT ITS BASE? IT'S SAND. THIS CITY WILL TEAR DOWN YOUR PLANS. LIKE OUR GANG, IT'S OUT TO SHOW YOU THAT THERE IS NO POINT.
NOW... THIS BAT-PERSON -UNH-
SEEMS TO DISAGREE WITH THIS PHILOSOPHY. HE SEEMS TO WANT TO BUILD BUILD BUILD.
IF YOU FEEL AS HE DOES, YOU'RE WELCOME TO JOIN HIM IN HIS MISSION.
HELL, YOU CAN BE THERE AT THE START OF IT...
...YOU CAN BE THE FIRST BRICKS IN HIS NEW CITY OF SAND.

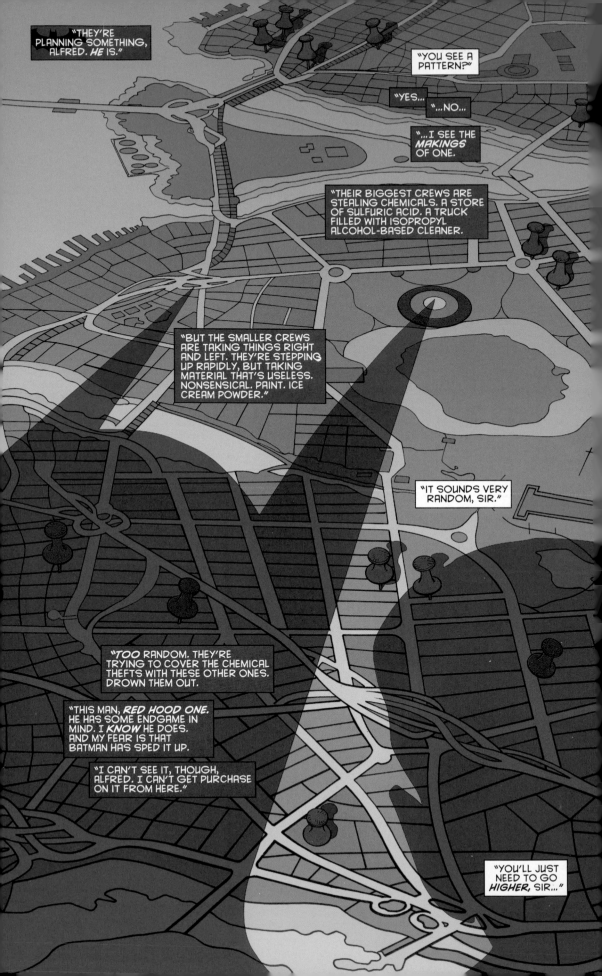

"THEY'RE PLANNING SOMETHING, ALFRED. *HE* IS."

"YOU SEE A PATTERN?"

"YES...

"...NO...

"...I SEE THE *MAKINGS* OF ONE.

"THEIR BIGGEST CREWS ARE STEALING CHEMICALS. A STORE OF SULFURIC ACID. A TRUCK FILLED WITH ISOPROPYL ALCOHOL-BASED CLEANER.

"BUT THE SMALLER CREWS ARE TAKING THINGS RIGHT AND LEFT. THEY'RE STEPPING UP RAPIDLY, BUT TAKING MATERIAL THAT'S USELESS. NONSENSICAL. PAINT. ICE CREAM POWDER."

"IT SOUNDS VERY RANDOM, SIR."

"*TOO* RANDOM. THEY'RE TRYING TO COVER THE CHEMICAL THEFTS WITH THESE OTHER ONES. DROWN THEM OUT.

"THIS MAN, *RED HOOD ONE.* HE HAS SOME ENDGAME IN MIND. I *KNOW* HE DOES. AND MY FEAR IS THAT BATMAN HAS SPED IT UP.

"I CAN'T SEE IT, THOUGH, ALFRED. I CAN'T GET PURCHASE ON IT FROM HERE."

"YOU'LL JUST NEED TO GO *HIGHER,* SIR..."

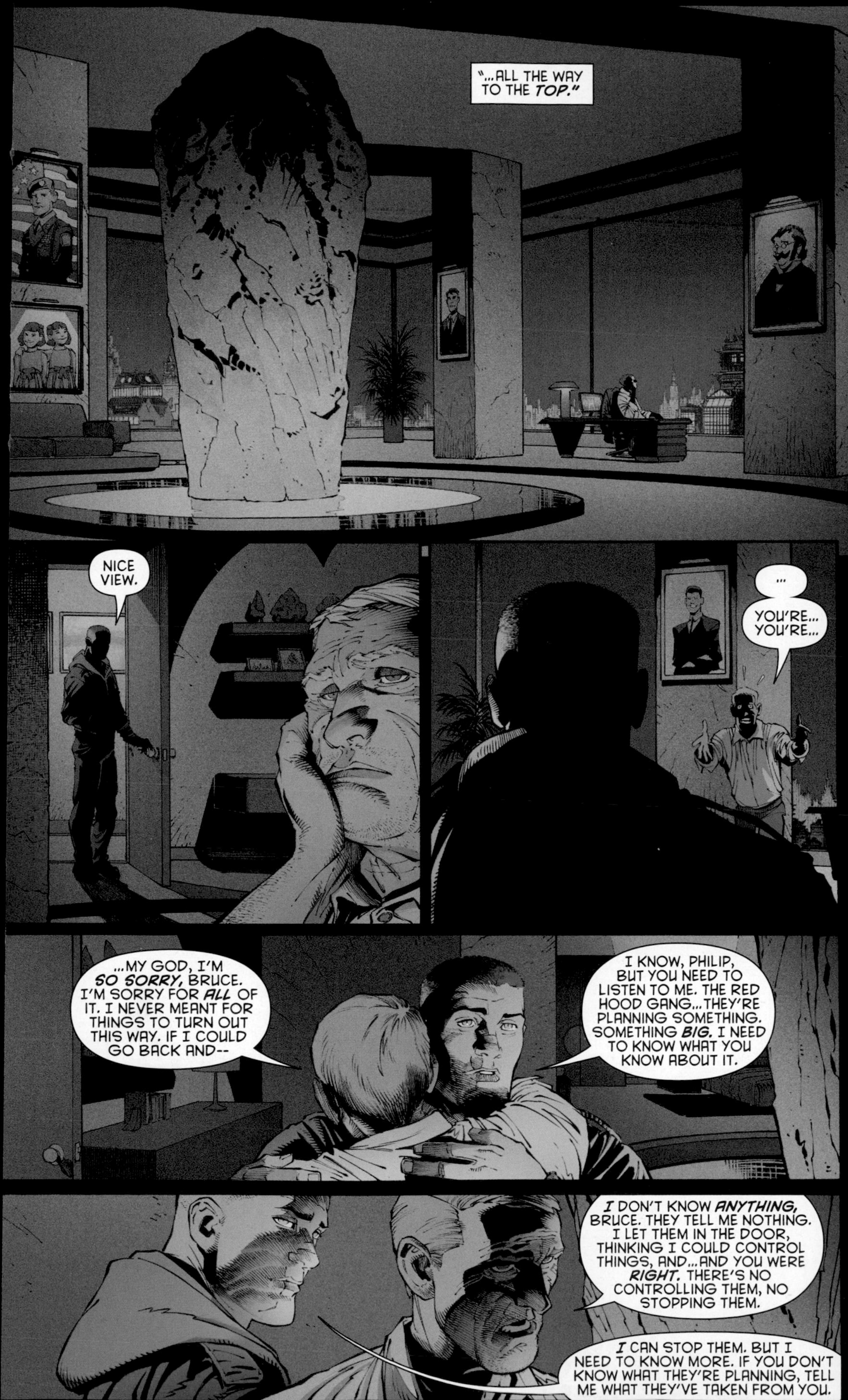
"...ALL THE WAY TO THE TOP."
NICE VIEW.
...
YOU'RE... YOU'RE...
...MY GOD, I'M SO SORRY, BRUCE. I'M SORRY FOR ALL OF IT. I NEVER MEANT FOR THINGS TO TURN OUT THIS WAY. IF I COULD GO BACK AND--
I KNOW, PHILIP, BUT YOU NEED TO LISTEN TO ME. THE RED HOOD GANG... THEY'RE PLANNING SOMETHING. SOMETHING BIG. I NEED TO KNOW WHAT YOU KNOW ABOUT IT.
I DON'T KNOW ANYTHING, BRUCE. THEY TELL ME NOTHING. I LET THEM IN THE DOOR, THINKING I COULD CONTROL THINGS, AND... AND YOU WERE RIGHT. THERE'S NO CONTROLLING THEM, NO STOPPING THEM.
I CAN STOP THEM. BUT I NEED TO KNOW MORE. IF YOU DON'T KNOW WHAT THEY'RE PLANNING, TELL ME WHAT THEY'VE TAKEN FROM YOU.

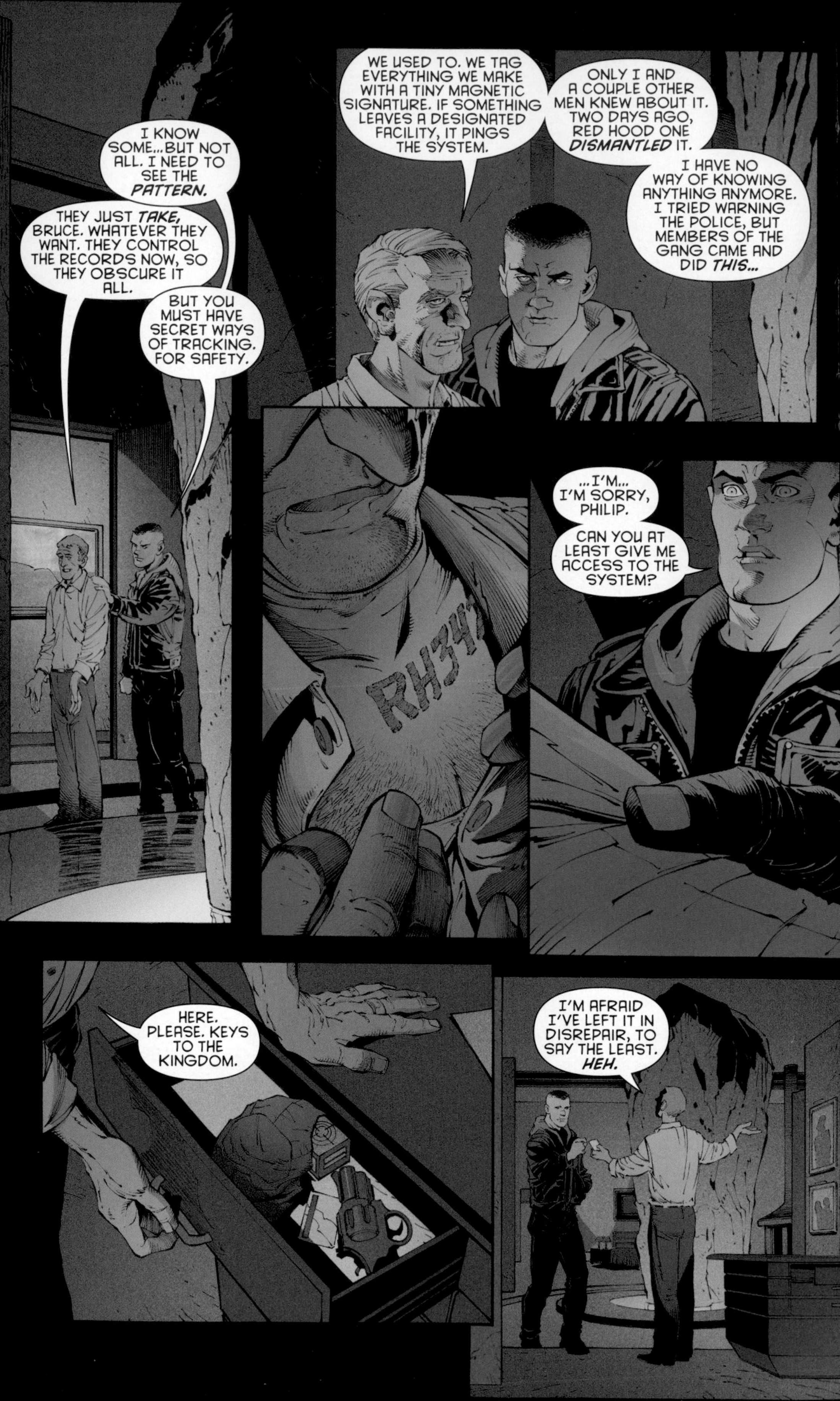
I KNOW SOME...BUT NOT ALL. I NEED TO SEE THE PATTERN.
THEY JUST TAKE, BRUCE. WHATEVER THEY WANT. THEY CONTROL THE RECORDS NOW, SO THEY OBSCURE IT ALL.
BUT YOU MUST HAVE SECRET WAYS OF TRACKING. FOR SAFETY.
WE USED TO. WE TAG EVERYTHING WE MAKE WITH A TINY MAGNETIC SIGNATURE. IF SOMETHING LEAVES A DESIGNATED FACILITY, IT PINGS THE SYSTEM.
ONLY I AND A COUPLE OTHER MEN KNEW ABOUT IT. TWO DAYS AGO, RED HOOD ONE DISMANTLED IT.
I HAVE NO WAY OF KNOWING ANYTHING ANYMORE. I TRIED WARNING THE POLICE, BUT MEMBERS OF THE GANG CAME AND DID THIS...
...I'M... I'M SORRY, PHILIP.
CAN YOU AT LEAST GIVE ME ACCESS TO THE SYSTEM?
HERE. PLEASE. KEYS TO THE KINGDOM.
I'M AFRAID I'VE LEFT IT IN DISREPAIR, TO SAY THE LEAST. HEH.

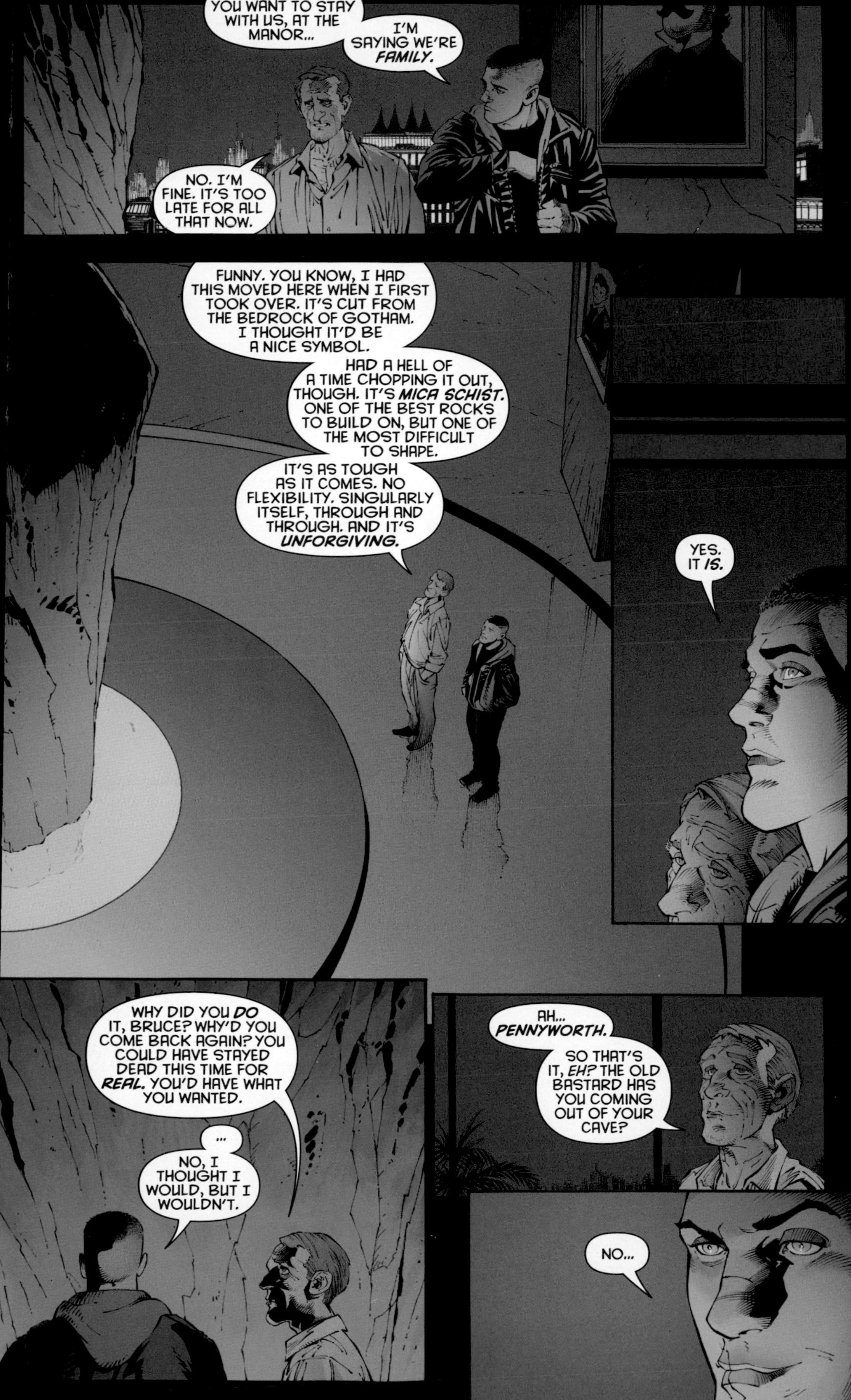
PHILIP, LOOK, IF YOU WANT TO STAY WITH US, AT THE MANOR...
I'M SAYING WE'RE *FAMILY.*
NO. I'M FINE. IT'S TOO LATE FOR ALL THAT NOW.
FUNNY. YOU KNOW, I HAD THIS MOVED HERE WHEN I FIRST TOOK OVER. IT'S CUT FROM THE BEDROCK OF GOTHAM. I THOUGHT IT'D BE A NICE SYMBOL.
HAD A HELL OF A TIME CHOPPING IT OUT, THOUGH. IT'S *MICA SCHIST.* ONE OF THE BEST ROCKS TO BUILD ON, BUT ONE OF THE MOST DIFFICULT TO SHAPE.
IT'S AS TOUGH AS IT COMES. NO FLEXIBILITY. SINGULARLY ITSELF, THROUGH AND THROUGH. AND IT'S *UNFORGIVING.*
YES. IT *IS.*
WHY DID YOU *DO* IT, BRUCE? WHY'D YOU COME BACK AGAIN? YOU COULD HAVE STAYED DEAD THIS TIME FOR *REAL.* YOU'D HAVE WHAT YOU WANTED.
...
NO, I THOUGHT I WOULD, BUT I WOULDN'T.
AH... *PENNYWORTH.*
SO THAT'S IT, *EH?* THE OLD BASTARD HAS YOU COMING OUT OF YOUR CAVE?
NO...

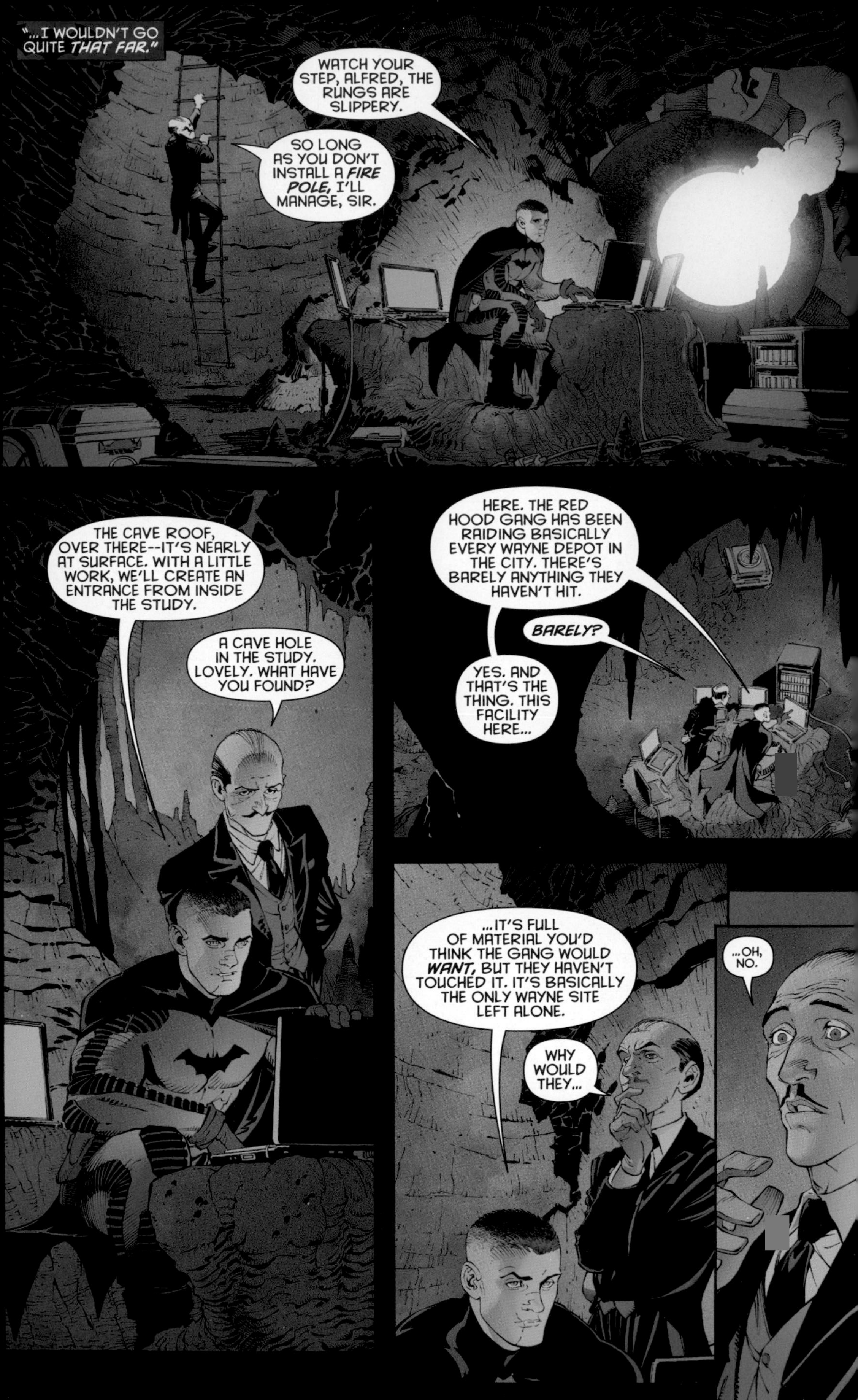
"...I WOULDN'T GO QUITE *THAT FAR.*"
WATCH YOUR STEP, ALFRED, THE RUNGS ARE SLIPPERY.
SO LONG AS YOU DON'T INSTALL A *FIRE POLE,* I'LL MANAGE, SIR.
THE CAVE ROOF, OVER THERE--IT'S NEARLY AT SURFACE. WITH A LITTLE WORK, WE'LL CREATE AN ENTRANCE FROM INSIDE THE STUDY.
A CAVE HOLE IN THE STUDY. LOVELY. WHAT HAVE YOU FOUND?
HERE. THE RED HOOD GANG HAS BEEN RAIDING BASICALLY EVERY WAYNE DEPOT IN THE CITY. THERE'S BARELY ANYTHING THEY HAVEN'T HIT.
BARELY?
YES. AND THAT'S THE THING. THIS FACILITY HERE...
...IT'S FULL OF MATERIAL YOU'D THINK THE GANG WOULD *WANT,* BUT THEY HAVEN'T TOUCHED IT. IT'S BASICALLY THE ONLY WAYNE SITE LEFT ALONE.
WHY WOULD THEY...
...OH, NO.

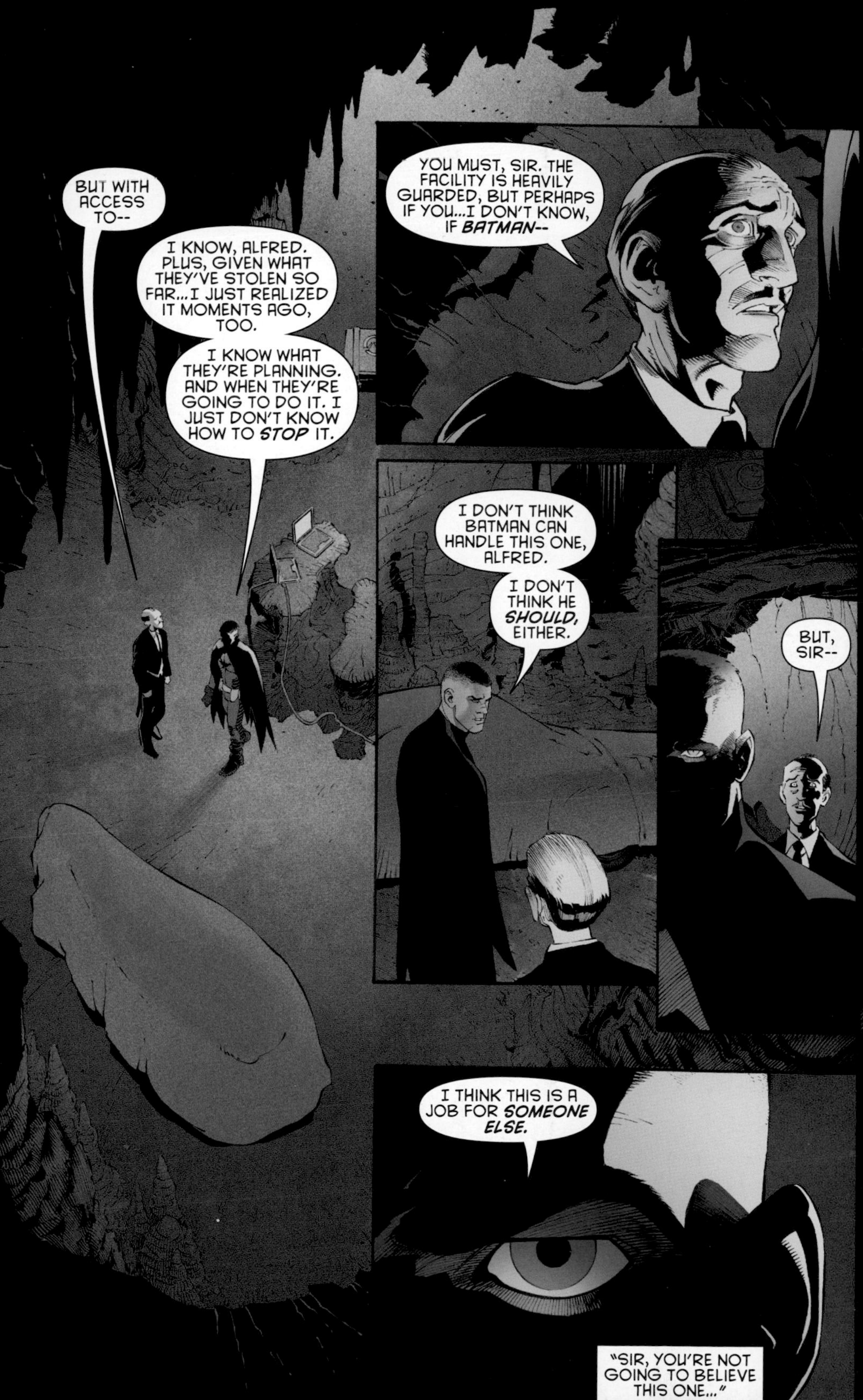
BUT WITH ACCESS TO--
I KNOW, ALFRED. PLUS, GIVEN WHAT THEY'VE STOLEN SO FAR...I JUST REALIZED IT MOMENTS AGO, TOO.
I KNOW WHAT THEY'RE PLANNING. AND WHEN THEY'RE GOING TO DO IT. I JUST DON'T KNOW HOW TO *STOP* IT.
YOU MUST, SIR. THE FACILITY IS HEAVILY GUARDED, BUT PERHAPS IF YOU...I DON'T KNOW, IF *BATMAN*--
I DON'T THINK BATMAN CAN HANDLE THIS ONE, ALFRED.
I DON'T THINK HE *SHOULD,* EITHER.
BUT, SIR--
I THINK THIS IS A JOB FOR *SOMEONE ELSE.*
"SIR, YOU'RE NOT GOING TO BELIEVE THIS ONE..."

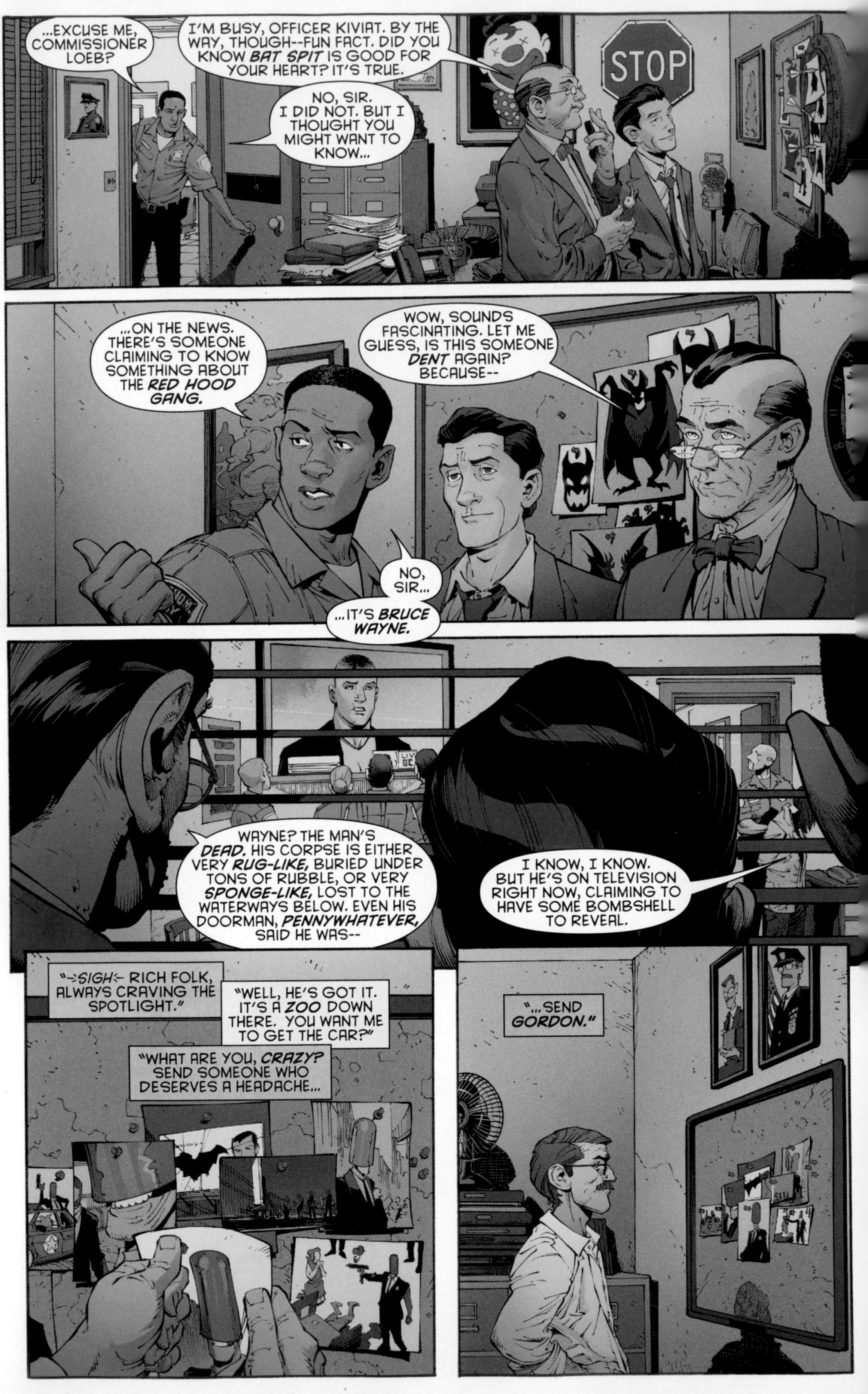

...EXCUSE ME, COMMISSIONER LOEB?
I'M BUSY, OFFICER KIVIAT. BY THE WAY, THOUGH--FUN FACT. DID YOU KNOW BAT SPIT IS GOOD FOR YOUR HEART? IT'S TRUE.
NO, SIR. I DID NOT. BUT I THOUGHT YOU MIGHT WANT TO KNOW...
STOP
...ON THE NEWS. THERE'S SOMEONE CLAIMING TO KNOW SOMETHING ABOUT THE RED HOOD GANG.
WOW, SOUNDS FASCINATING. LET ME GUESS, IS THIS SOMEONE DENT AGAIN? BECAUSE--
NO, SIR...
...IT'S BRUCE WAYNE.
WAYNE? THE MAN'S DEAD. HIS CORPSE IS EITHER VERY RUG-LIKE, BURIED UNDER TONS OF RUBBLE, OR VERY SPONGE-LIKE, LOST TO THE WATERWAYS BELOW. EVEN HIS DOORMAN, PENNYWHATEVER, SAID HE WAS--
I KNOW, I KNOW. BUT HE'S ON TELEVISION RIGHT NOW, CLAIMING TO HAVE SOME BOMBSHELL TO REVEAL.
"-SIGH- RICH FOLK, ALWAYS CRAVING THE SPOTLIGHT."
"WELL, HE'S GOT IT. IT'S A ZOO DOWN THERE. YOU WANT ME TO GET THE CAR?"
"WHAT ARE YOU, CRAZY? SEND SOMEONE WHO DESERVES A HEADACHE...
"...SEND GORDON."

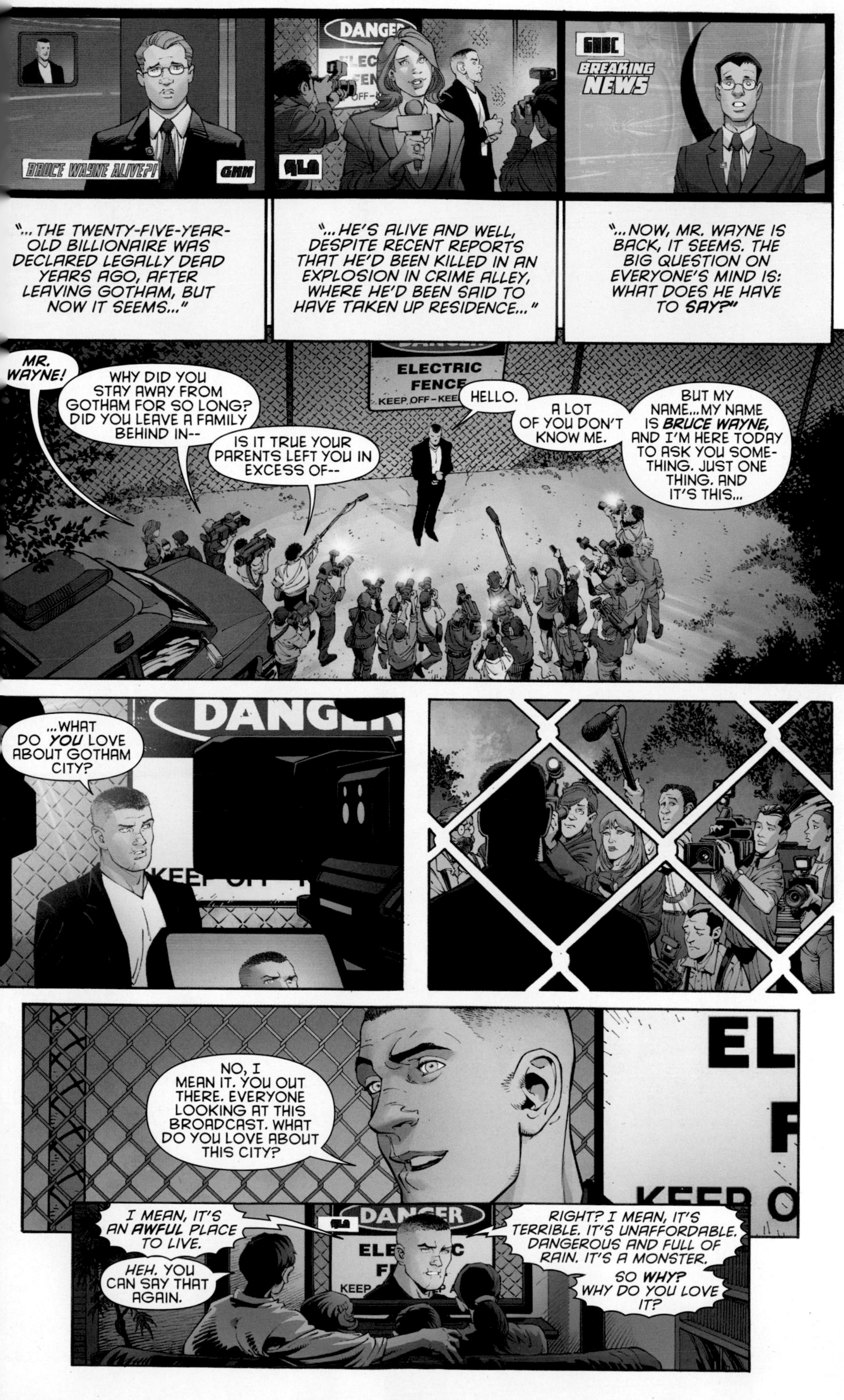
BRUCE WAYNE ALIVE?!
GNN
"...THE TWENTY-FIVE-YEAR-OLD BILLIONAIRE WAS DECLARED LEGALLY DEAD YEARS AGO, AFTER LEAVING GOTHAM, BUT NOW IT SEEMS..."
DANGER
"...HE'S ALIVE AND WELL, DESPITE RECENT REPORTS THAT HE'D BEEN KILLED IN AN EXPLOSION IN CRIME ALLEY, WHERE HE'D BEEN SAID TO HAVE TAKEN UP RESIDENCE..."
GNBC
BREAKING NEWS
"...NOW, MR. WAYNE IS BACK, IT SEEMS. THE BIG QUESTION ON EVERYONE'S MIND IS: WHAT DOES HE HAVE TO SAY?"
MR. WAYNE!
WHY DID YOU STAY AWAY FROM GOTHAM FOR SO LONG? DID YOU LEAVE A FAMILY BEHIND IN--
IS IT TRUE YOUR PARENTS LEFT YOU IN EXCESS OF--
ELECTRIC FENCE
HELLO.
A LOT OF YOU DON'T KNOW ME.
BUT MY NAME...MY NAME IS BRUCE WAYNE, AND I'M HERE TODAY TO ASK YOU SOMETHING. JUST ONE THING. AND IT'S THIS...
DANGER
...WHAT DO YOU LOVE ABOUT GOTHAM CITY?
NO, I MEAN IT. YOU OUT THERE. EVERYONE LOOKING AT THIS BROADCAST. WHAT DO YOU LOVE ABOUT THIS CITY?
I MEAN, IT'S AN AWFUL PLACE TO LIVE.
HEH. YOU CAN SAY THAT AGAIN.
DANGER
RIGHT? I MEAN, IT'S TERRIBLE. IT'S UNAFFORDABLE. DANGEROUS AND FULL OF RAIN. IT'S A MONSTER.
SO WHY? WHY DO YOU LOVE IT?

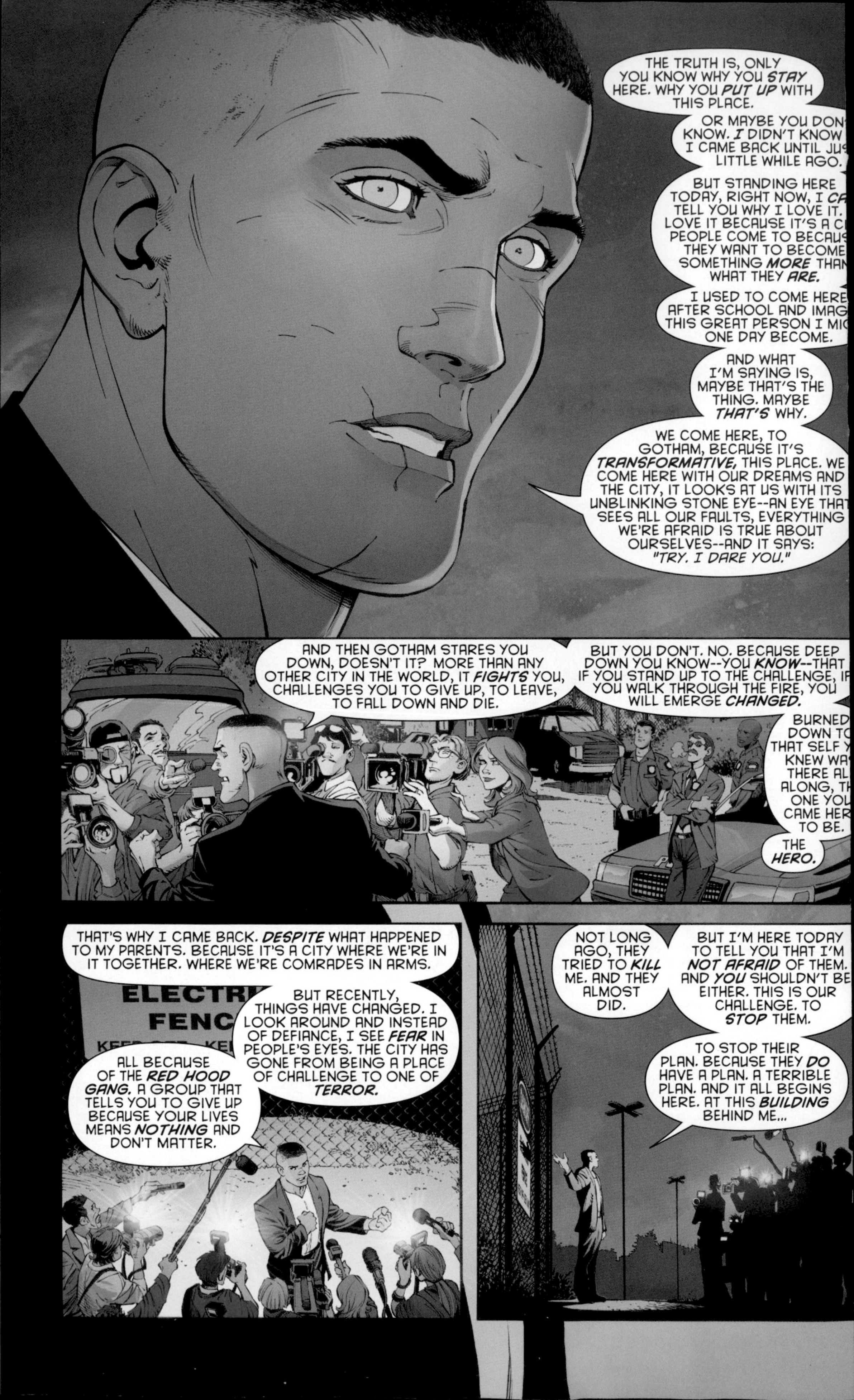
THE TRUTH IS, ONLY YOU KNOW WHY YOU STAY HERE. WHY YOU PUT UP WITH THIS PLACE.
OR MAYBE YOU DON KNOW. I DIDN'T KNOW I CAME BACK UNTIL JUS LITTLE WHILE AGO.
BUT STANDING HERE TODAY, RIGHT NOW, I CA TELL YOU WHY I LOVE IT. LOVE IT BECAUSE IT'S A CI PEOPLE COME TO BECAUS THEY WANT TO BECOME SOMETHING MORE THAN WHAT THEY ARE.
I USED TO COME HERE AFTER SCHOOL AND IMAG THIS GREAT PERSON I MIG ONE DAY BECOME.
AND WHAT I'M SAYING IS, MAYBE THAT'S THE THING. MAYBE THAT'S WHY.
WE COME HERE, TO GOTHAM, BECAUSE IT'S TRANSFORMATIVE, THIS PLACE. WE COME HERE WITH OUR DREAMS AND THE CITY, IT LOOKS AT US WITH ITS UNBLINKING STONE EYE--AN EYE THAT SEES ALL OUR FAULTS, EVERYTHING WE'RE AFRAID IS TRUE ABOUT OURSELVES--AND IT SAYS: "TRY. I DARE YOU."
AND THEN GOTHAM STARES YOU DOWN, DOESN'T IT? MORE THAN ANY OTHER CITY IN THE WORLD, IT FIGHTS YOU, CHALLENGES YOU TO GIVE UP, TO LEAVE, TO FALL DOWN AND DIE.
BUT YOU DON'T. NO. BECAUSE DEEP DOWN YOU KNOW--YOU KNOW--THAT IF YOU STAND UP TO THE CHALLENGE, IF YOU WALK THROUGH THE FIRE, YOU WILL EMERGE CHANGED.
BURNED DOWN TO THAT SELF Y KNEW WA THERE AL ALONG, TH ONE YOU CAME HER TO BE.
THE HERO.
THAT'S WHY I CAME BACK. DESPITE WHAT HAPPENED TO MY PARENTS. BECAUSE IT'S A CITY WHERE WE'RE IN IT TOGETHER. WHERE WE'RE COMRADES IN ARMS.
ELECTRI FENC
BUT RECENTLY, THINGS HAVE CHANGED. I LOOK AROUND AND INSTEAD OF DEFIANCE, I SEE FEAR IN PEOPLE'S EYES. THE CITY HAS GONE FROM BEING A PLACE OF CHALLENGE TO ONE OF TERROR.
ALL BECAUSE OF THE RED HOOD GANG. A GROUP THAT TELLS YOU TO GIVE UP BECAUSE YOUR LIVES MEANS NOTHING AND DON'T MATTER.
NOT LONG AGO, THEY TRIED TO KILL ME. AND THEY ALMOST DID.
BUT I'M HERE TODAY TO TELL YOU THAT I'M NOT AFRAID OF THEM. AND YOU SHOULDN'T BE EITHER. THIS IS OUR CHALLENGE. TO STOP THEM.
TO STOP THEIR PLAN. BECAUSE THEY DO HAVE A PLAN. A TERRIBLE PLAN. AND IT ALL BEGINS HERE. AT THIS BUILDING BEHIND ME...

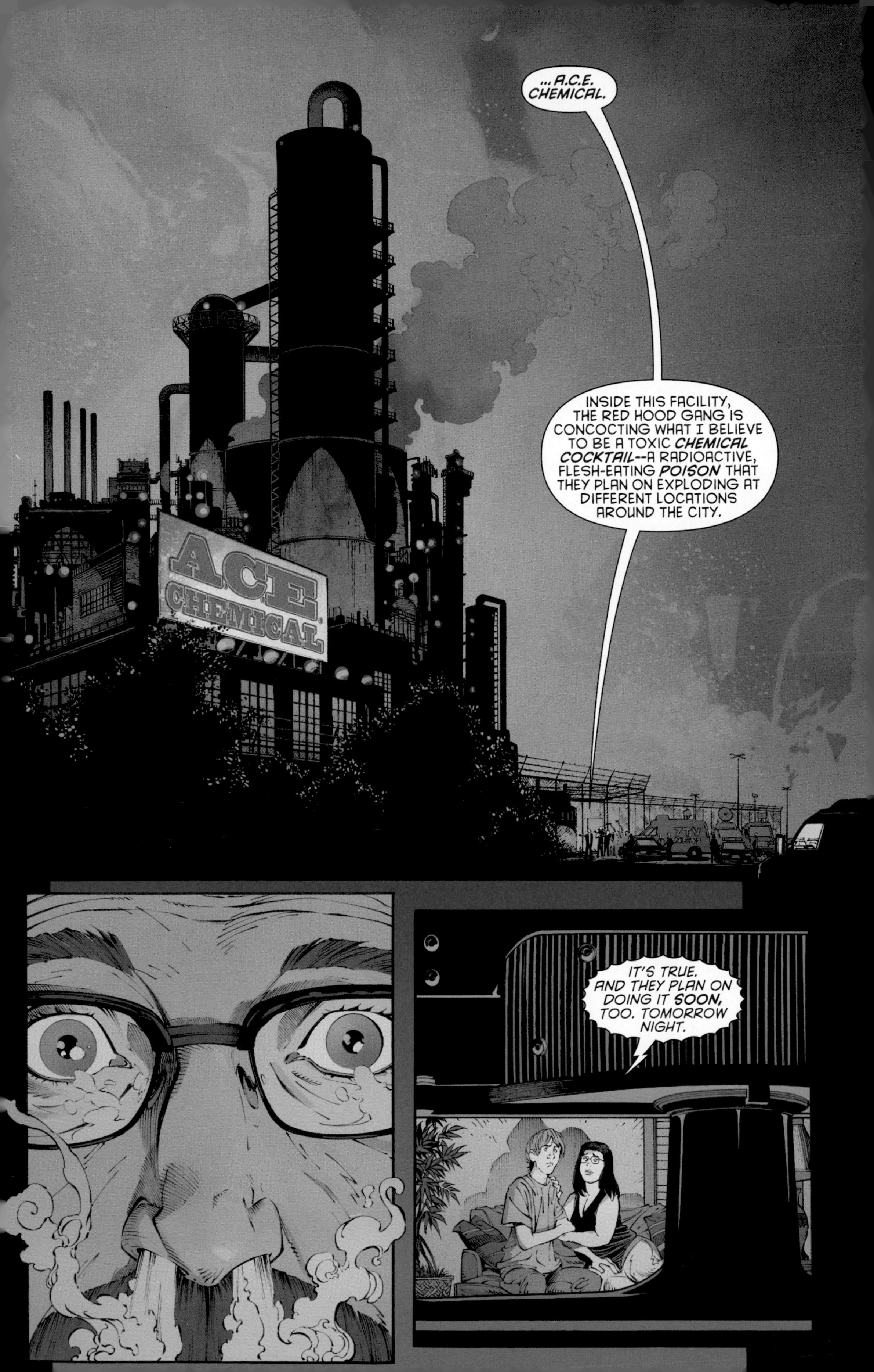
...A.C.E. CHEMICAL.
INSIDE THIS FACILITY, THE RED HOOD GANG IS CONCOCTING WHAT I BELIEVE TO BE A TOXIC CHEMICAL COCKTAIL--A RADIOACTIVE, FLESH-EATING POISON THAT THEY PLAN ON EXPLODING AT DIFFERENT LOCATIONS AROUND THE CITY.
A.C.E. CHEMICAL
IT'S TRUE. AND THEY PLAN ON DOING IT SOON, TOO. TOMORROW NIGHT.

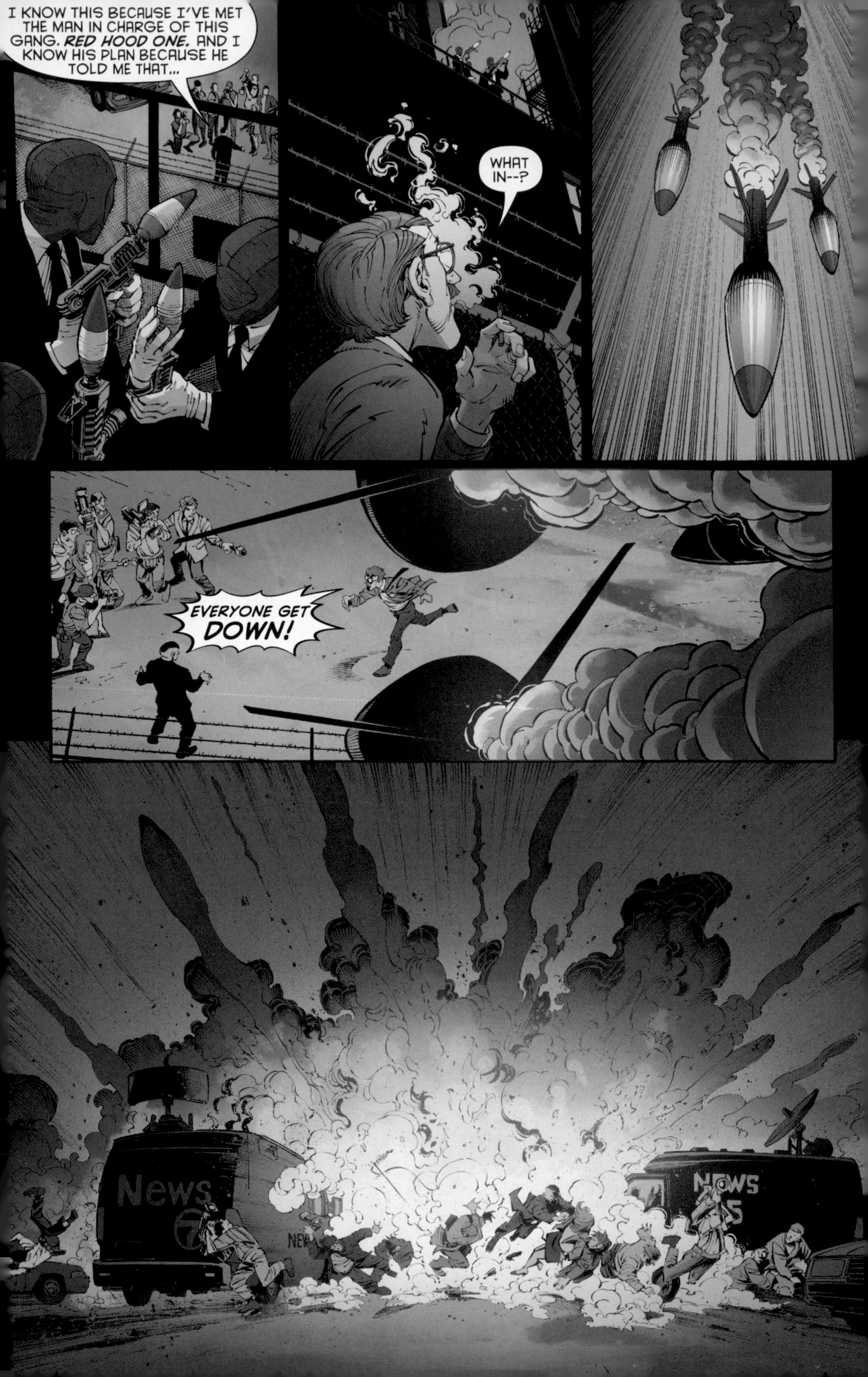
I KNOW THIS BECAUSE I'VE MET THE MAN IN CHARGE OF THIS GANG. ***RED HOOD ONE.*** AND I KNOW HIS PLAN BECAUSE HE TOLD ME THAT...
WHAT IN--?
EVERYONE GET **DOWN!**
News
NEWS 5

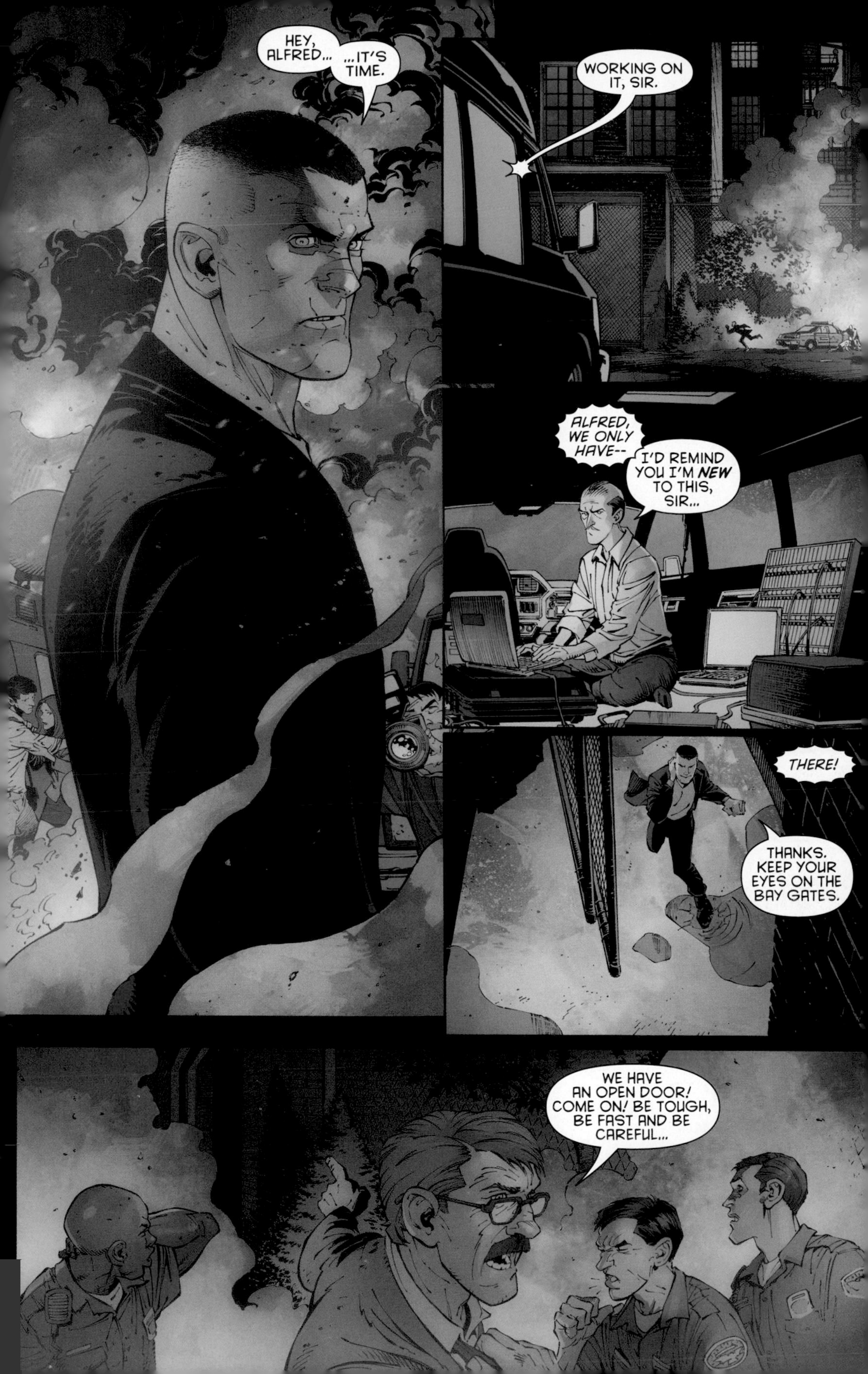
HEY, ALFRED...
...IT'S TIME.
WORKING ON IT, SIR.
ALFRED, WE ONLY HAVE--
I'D REMIND YOU I'M NEW TO THIS, SIR...
THERE!
THANKS. KEEP YOUR EYES ON THE BAY GATES.
WE HAVE AN OPEN DOOR! COME ON! BE TOUGH, BE FAST AND BE CAREFUL...

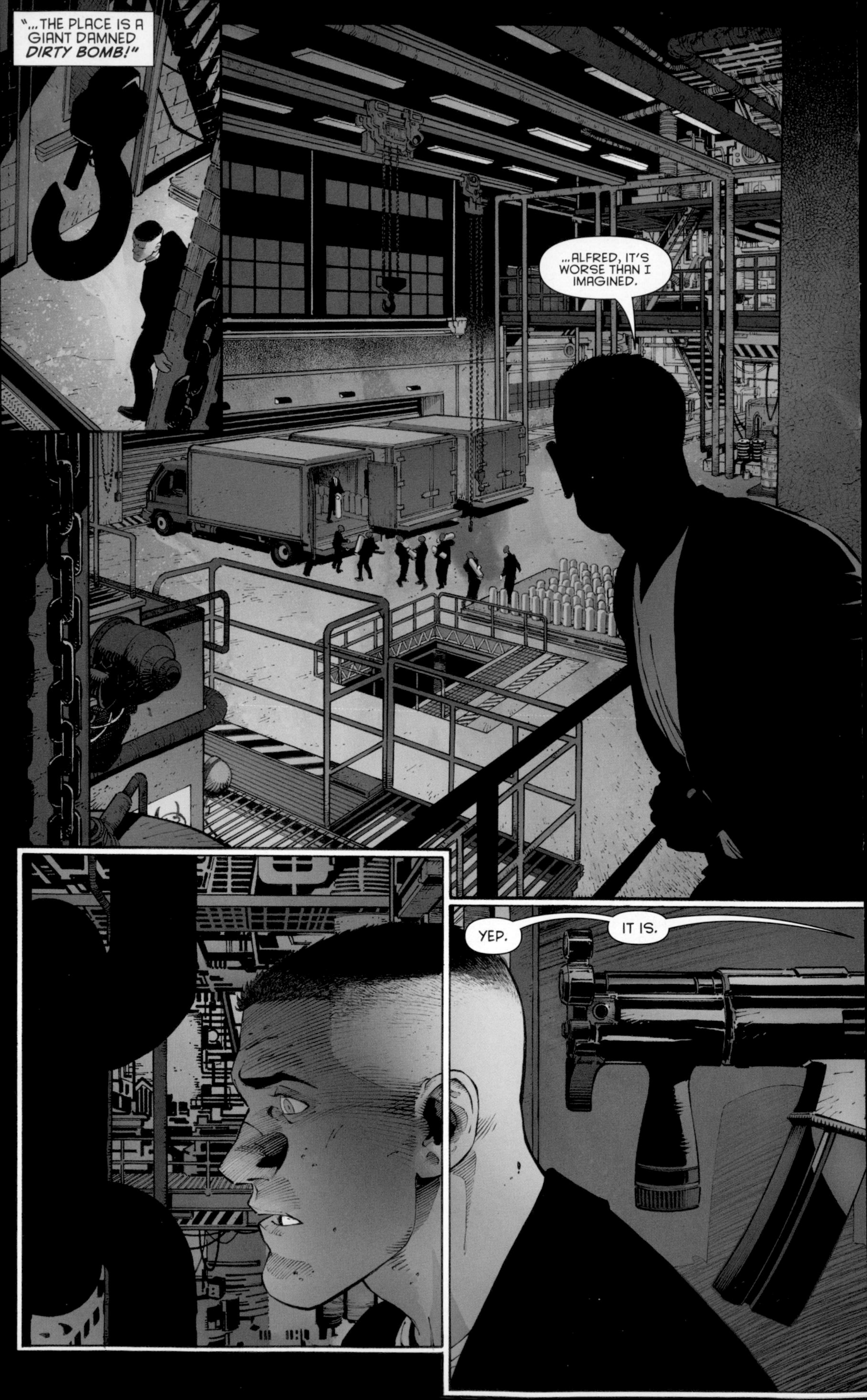
"...THE PLACE IS A GIANT DAMNED *DIRTY BOMB!*"
...ALFRED, IT'S WORSE THAN I IMAGINED.
YEP.
IT IS.

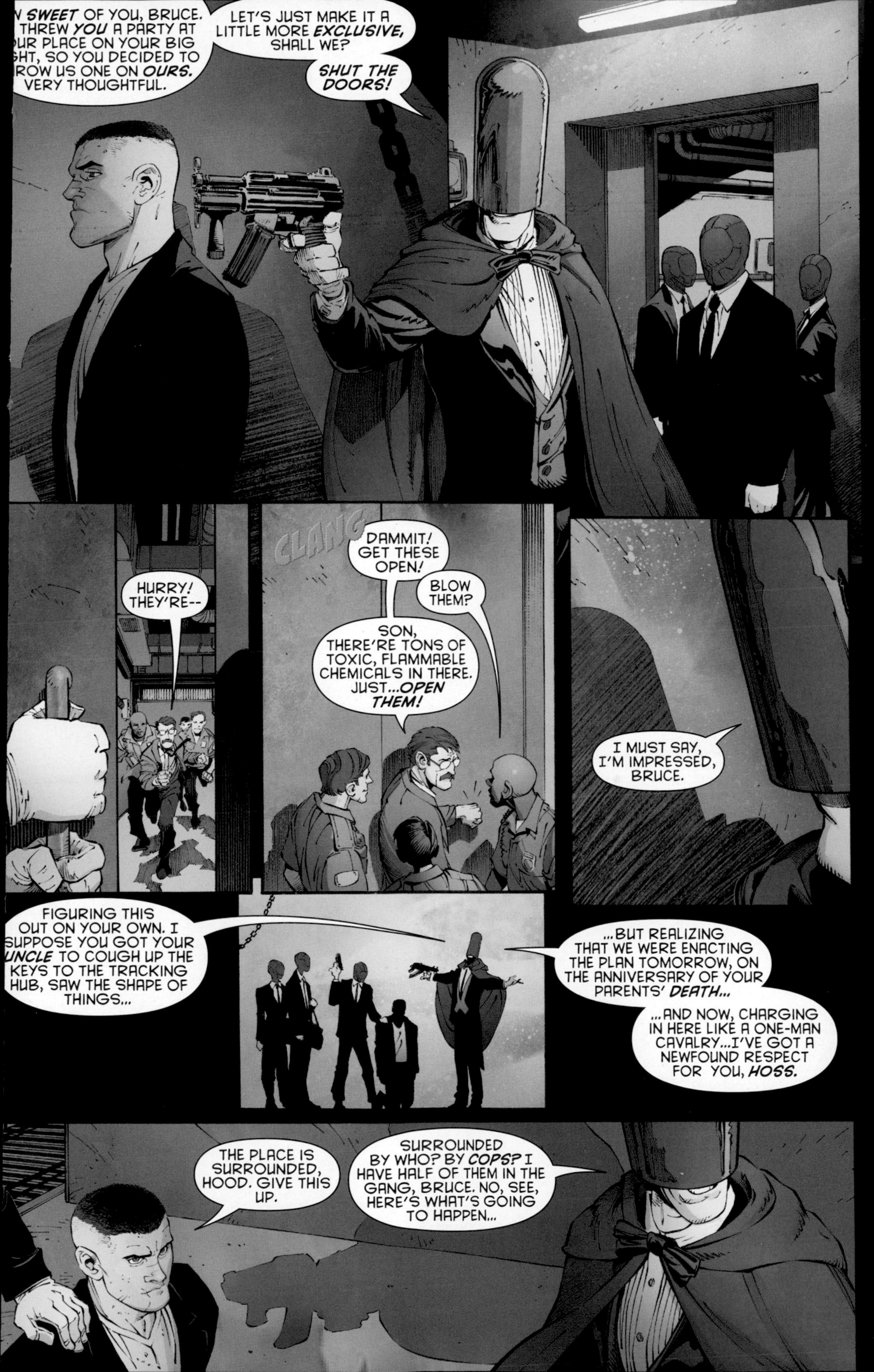

N SWEET OF YOU, BRUCE. THREW YOU A PARTY AT UR PLACE ON YOUR BIG GHT, SO YOU DECIDED TO ROW US ONE ON OURS. VERY THOUGHTFUL.
LET'S JUST MAKE IT A LITTLE MORE EXCLUSIVE, SHALL WE?
SHUT THE DOORS!
HURRY! THEY'RE--
CLANG
DAMMIT! GET THESE OPEN!
BLOW THEM?
SON, THERE'RE TONS OF TOXIC, FLAMMABLE CHEMICALS IN THERE. JUST...OPEN THEM!
I MUST SAY, I'M IMPRESSED, BRUCE.
FIGURING THIS OUT ON YOUR OWN. I SUPPOSE YOU GOT YOUR UNCLE TO COUGH UP THE KEYS TO THE TRACKING HUB, SAW THE SHAPE OF THINGS...
...BUT REALIZING THAT WE WERE ENACTING THE PLAN TOMORROW, ON THE ANNIVERSARY OF YOUR PARENTS' DEATH...
...AND NOW, CHARGING IN HERE LIKE A ONE-MAN CAVALRY...I'VE GOT A NEWFOUND RESPECT FOR YOU, HOSS.
THE PLACE IS SURROUNDED, HOOD. GIVE THIS UP.
SURROUNDED BY WHO? BY COPS? I HAVE HALF OF THEM IN THE GANG, BRUCE. NO, SEE, HERE'S WHAT'S GOING TO HAPPEN...

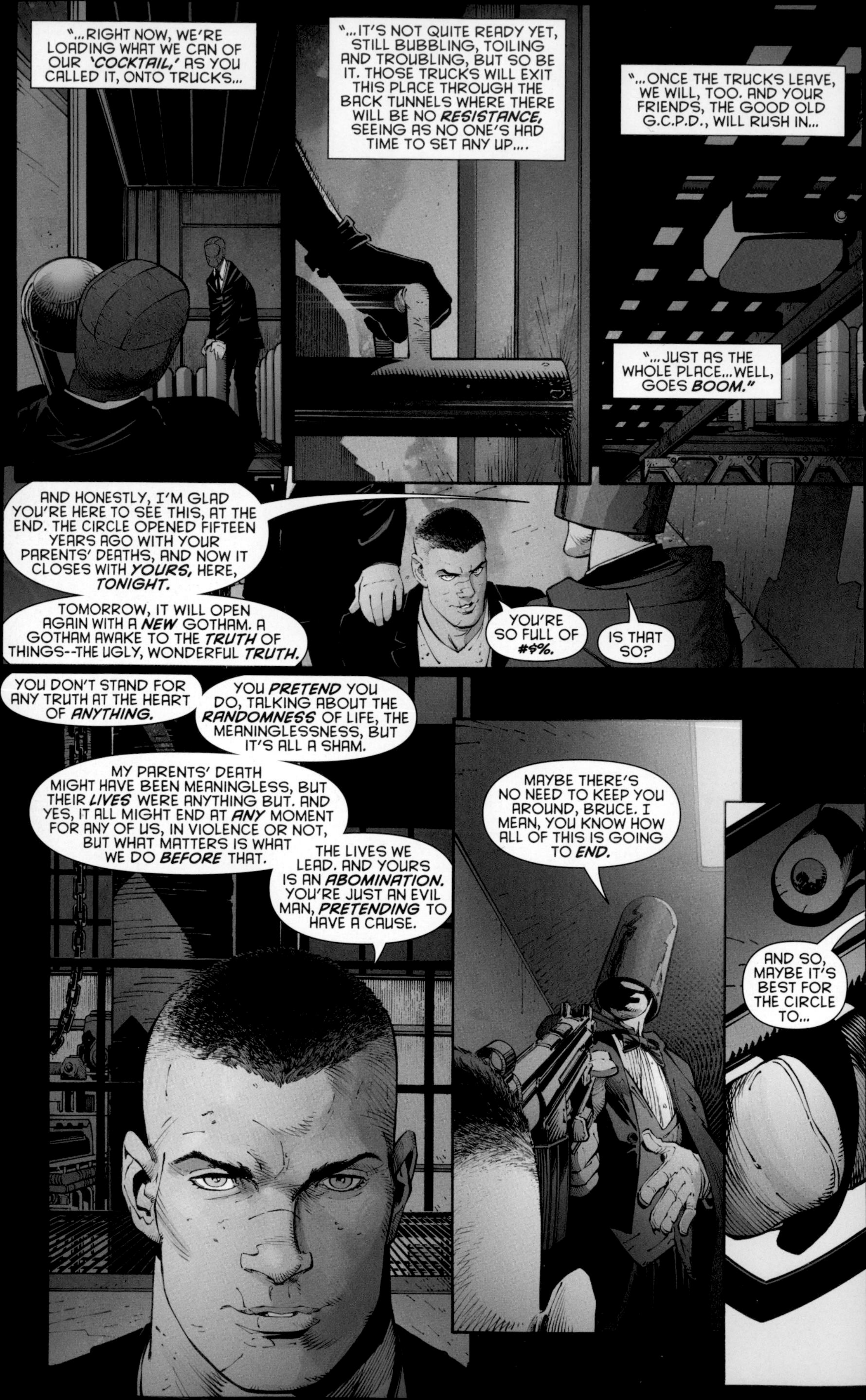
"...RIGHT NOW, WE'RE LOADING WHAT WE CAN OF OUR *'COCKTAIL,'* AS YOU CALLED IT, ONTO TRUCKS...
"...IT'S NOT QUITE READY YET, STILL BUBBLING, TOILING AND TROUBLING, BUT SO BE IT. THOSE TRUCKS WILL EXIT THIS PLACE THROUGH THE BACK TUNNELS WHERE THERE WILL BE NO *RESISTANCE,* SEEING AS NO ONE'S HAD TIME TO SET ANY UP....
"...ONCE THE TRUCKS LEAVE, WE WILL, TOO. AND YOUR FRIENDS, THE GOOD OLD G.C.P.D., WILL RUSH IN...
"...JUST AS THE WHOLE PLACE...WELL, GOES *BOOM."*
AND HONESTLY, I'M GLAD YOU'RE HERE TO SEE THIS, AT THE END. THE CIRCLE OPENED FIFTEEN YEARS AGO WITH YOUR PARENTS' DEATHS, AND NOW IT CLOSES WITH *YOURS,* HERE, *TONIGHT.*
TOMORROW, IT WILL OPEN AGAIN WITH A *NEW* GOTHAM. A GOTHAM AWAKE TO THE *TRUTH* OF THINGS--THE UGLY, WONDERFUL *TRUTH.*
YOU'RE SO FULL OF #$%.
IS THAT SO?
YOU DON'T STAND FOR ANY TRUTH AT THE HEART OF *ANYTHING.*
YOU *PRETEND* YOU DO, TALKING ABOUT THE *RANDOMNESS* OF LIFE, THE MEANINGLESSNESS, BUT IT'S ALL A SHAM.
MY PARENTS' DEATH MIGHT HAVE BEEN MEANINGLESS, BUT THEIR *LIVES* WERE ANYTHING BUT. AND YES, IT ALL MIGHT END AT *ANY* MOMENT FOR ANY OF US, IN VIOLENCE OR NOT, BUT WHAT MATTERS IS WHAT WE DO *BEFORE* THAT.
THE LIVES WE LEAD. AND YOURS IS AN *ABOMINATION.* YOU'RE JUST AN EVIL MAN, *PRETENDING* TO HAVE A CAUSE.
MAYBE THERE'S NO NEED TO KEEP YOU AROUND, BRUCE. I MEAN, YOU KNOW HOW ALL OF THIS IS GOING TO *END.*
AND SO, MAYBE IT'S BEST FOR THE CIRCLE TO...

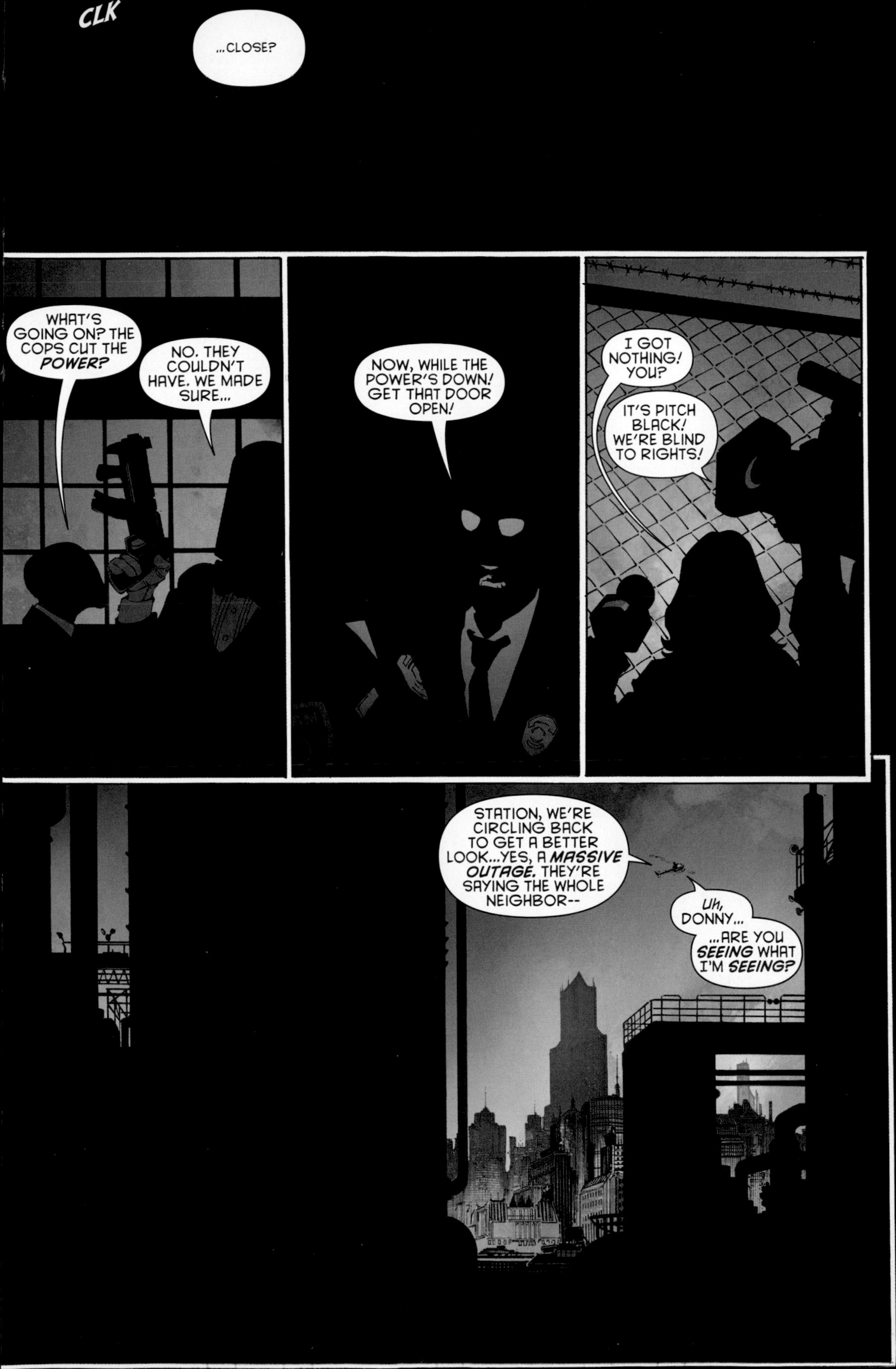
CLK
...CLOSE?
WHAT'S GOING ON? THE COPS CUT THE POWER?
NO. THEY COULDN'T HAVE. WE MADE SURE...
NOW, WHILE THE POWER'S DOWN! GET THAT DOOR OPEN!
I GOT NOTHING! YOU?
IT'S PITCH BLACK! WE'RE BLIND TO RIGHTS!
STATION, WE'RE CIRCLING BACK TO GET A BETTER LOOK...YES, A MASSIVE OUTAGE. THEY'RE SAYING THE WHOLE NEIGHBOR--
Uh, DONNY...
...ARE YOU SEEING WHAT I'M SEEING?

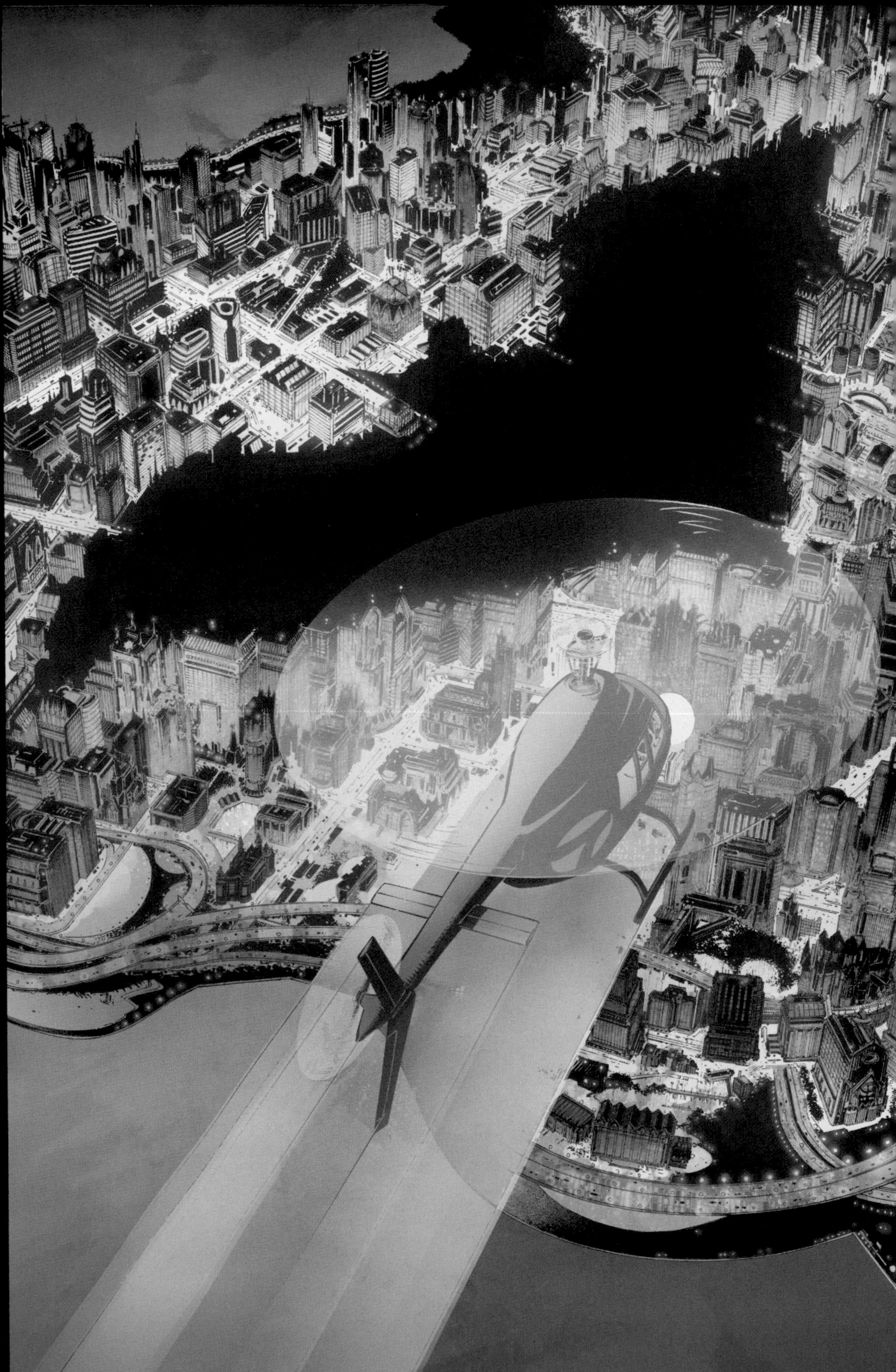

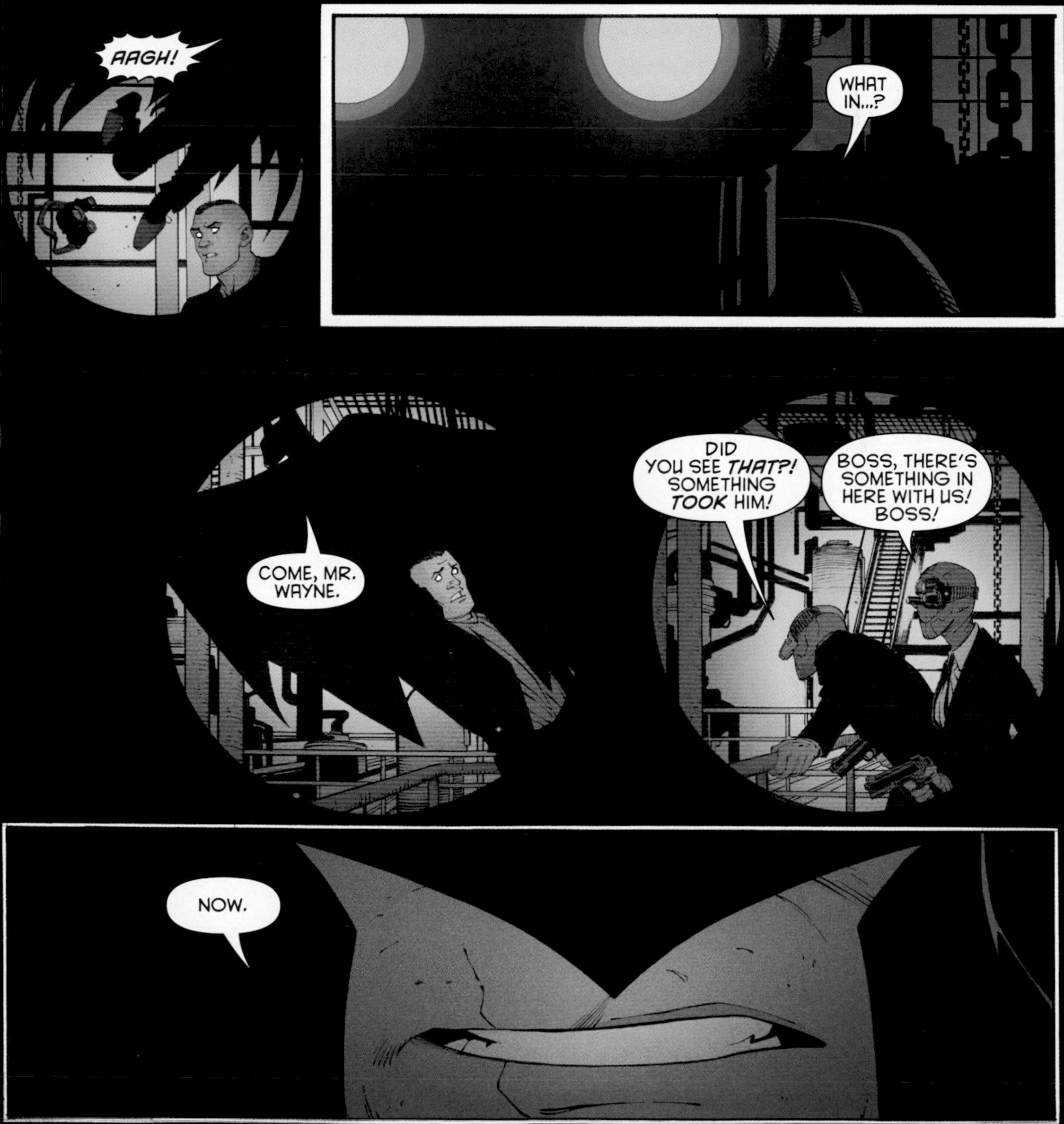
AAGH!
WHAT IN...?
COME, MR. WAYNE.
DID YOU SEE *THAT?!* SOMETHING *TOOK* HIM!
BOSS, THERE'S SOMETHING IN HERE WITH US! BOSS!
NOW.

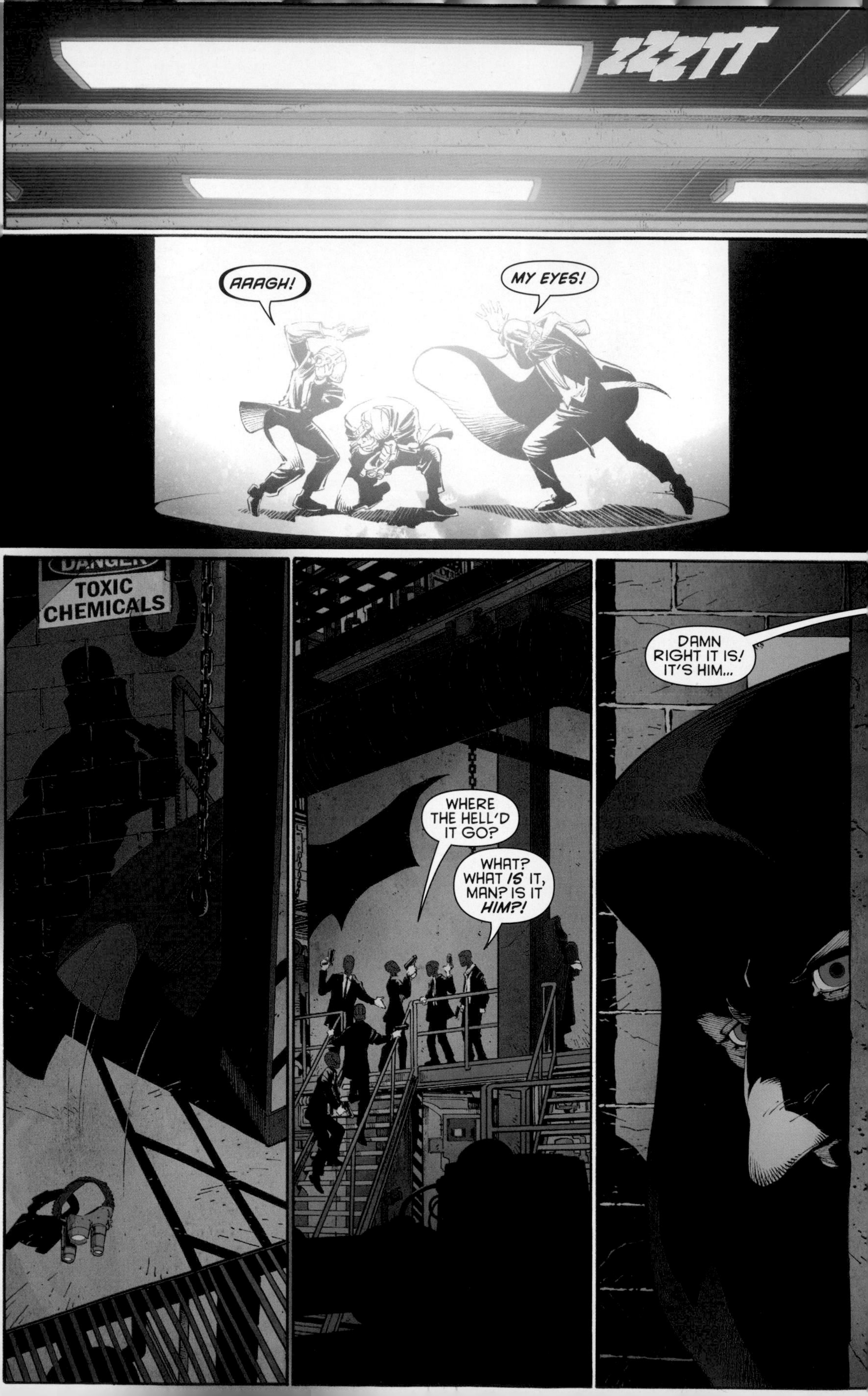
ZZZTT
AAAGH!
MY EYES!
DANGER
TOXIC CHEMICALS
WHERE THE HELL'D IT GO?
WHAT? WHAT IS IT, MAN? IS IT HIM?!
DAMN RIGHT IT IS! IT'S HIM...

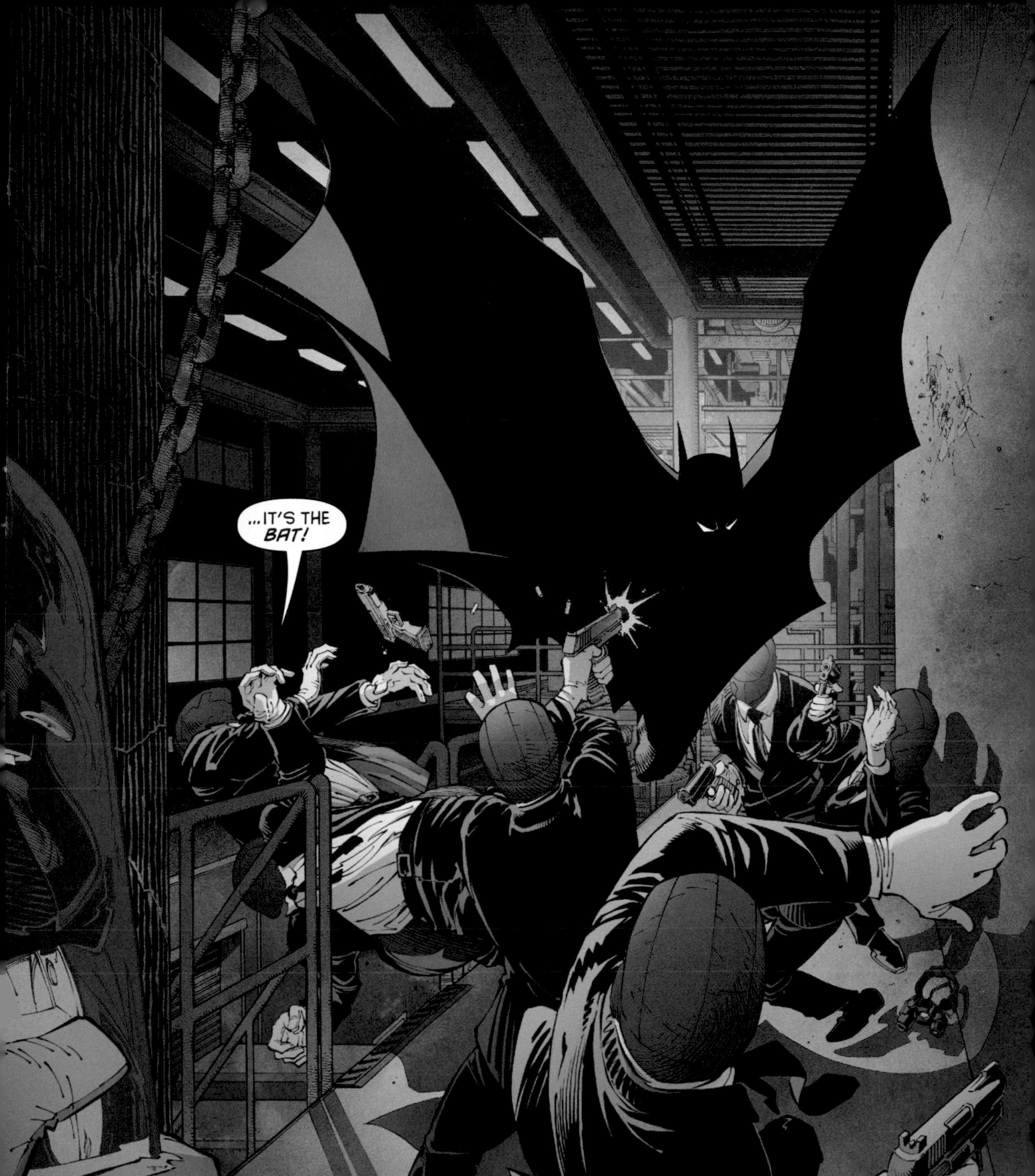
...IT'S THE BAT!
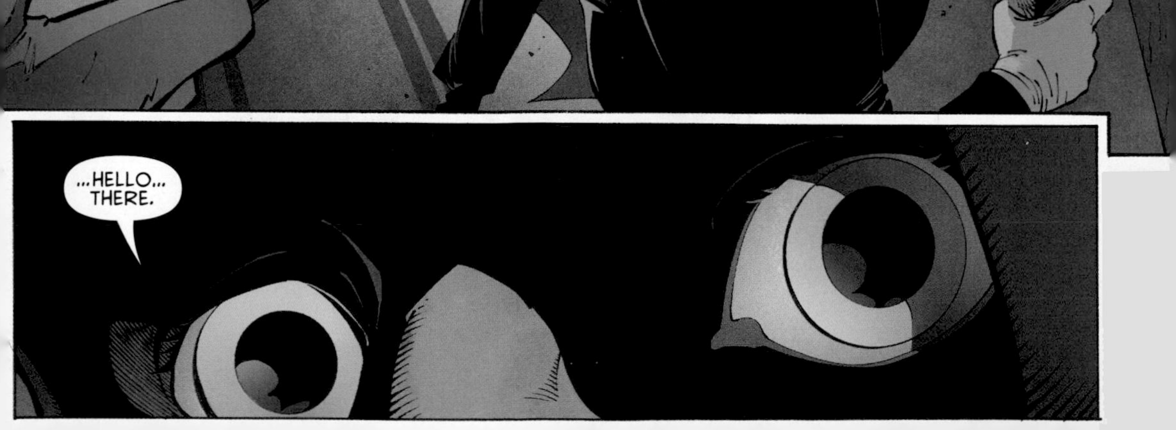
...HELLO... THERE.

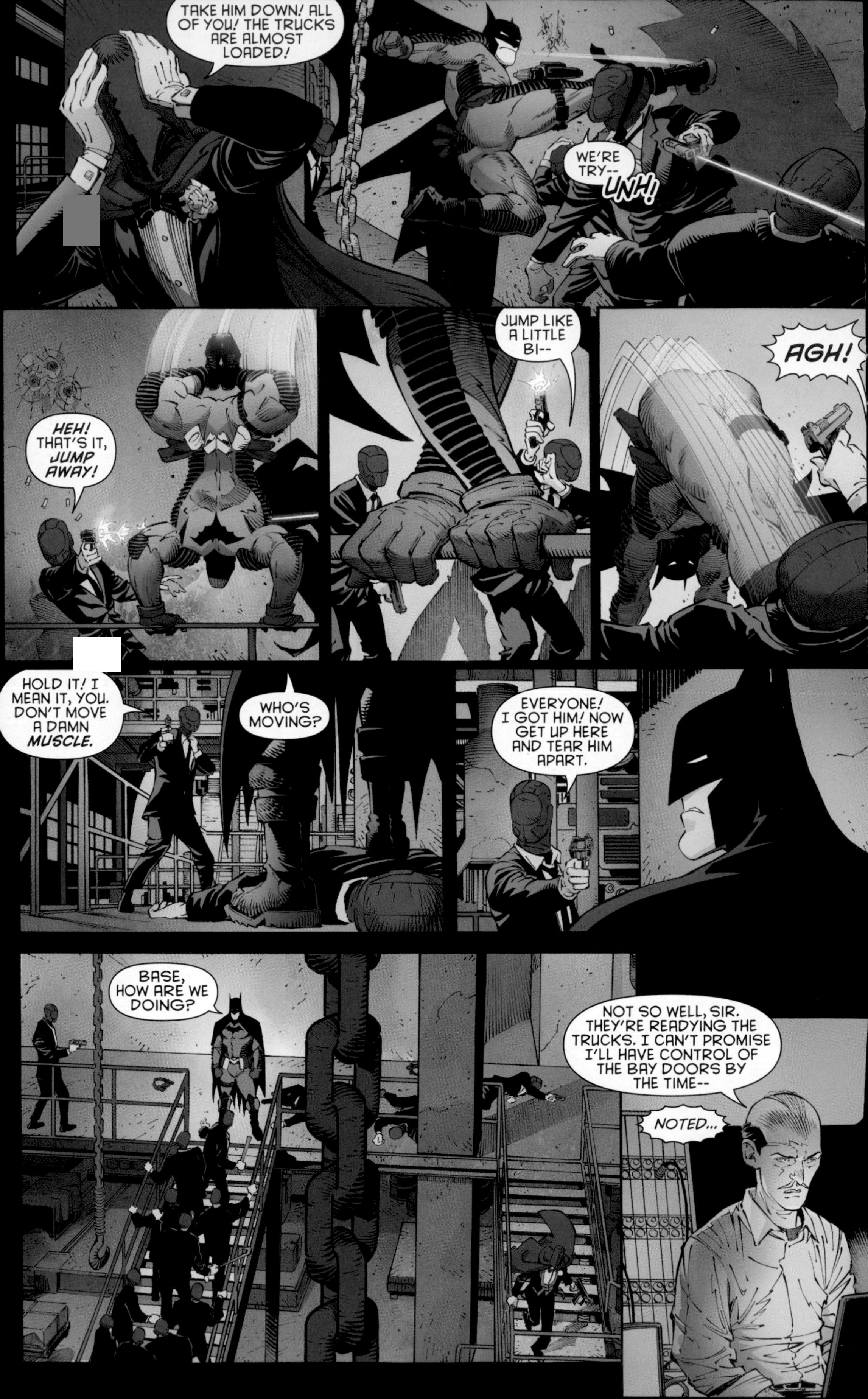
TAKE HIM DOWN! ALL OF YOU! THE TRUCKS ARE ALMOST LOADED!
WE'RE TRY--
UNH!
HEH! THAT'S IT, JUMP AWAY!
JUMP LIKE A LITTLE BI--
AGH!
HOLD IT! I MEAN IT, YOU. DON'T MOVE A DAMN MUSCLE.
WHO'S MOVING?
EVERYONE! I GOT HIM! NOW GET UP HERE AND TEAR HIM APART.
BASE, HOW ARE WE DOING?
NOT SO WELL, SIR. THEY'RE READYING THE TRUCKS. I CAN'T PROMISE I'LL HAVE CONTROL OF THE BAY DOORS BY THE TIME--
NOTED...

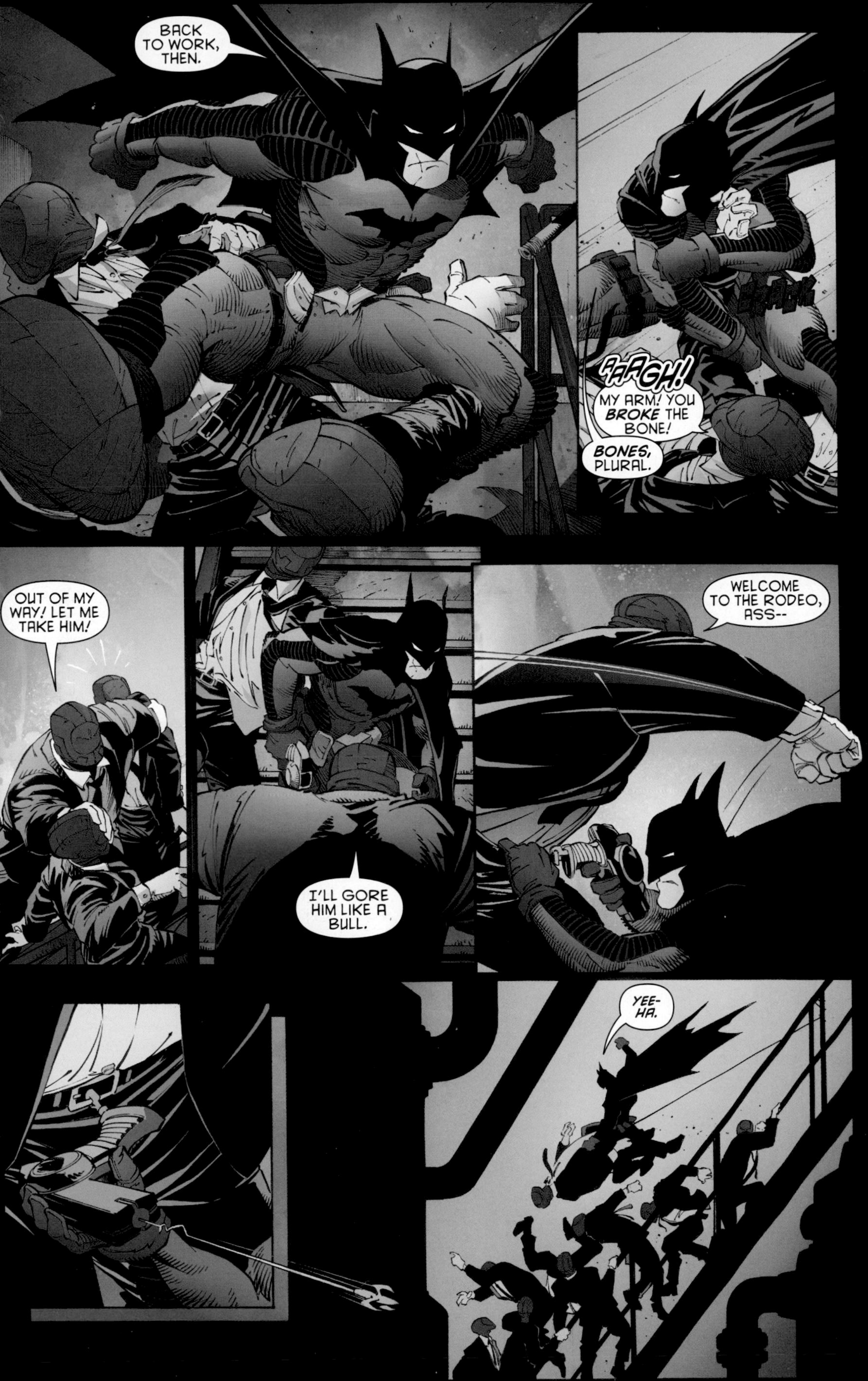

BACK TO WORK, THEN.
AAAGH!
MY ARM! YOU BROKE THE BONE!
BONES, PLURAL.
OUT OF MY WAY! LET ME TAKE HIM!
I'LL GORE HIM LIKE A BULL.
WELCOME TO THE RODEO, ASS--
YEE-HA.

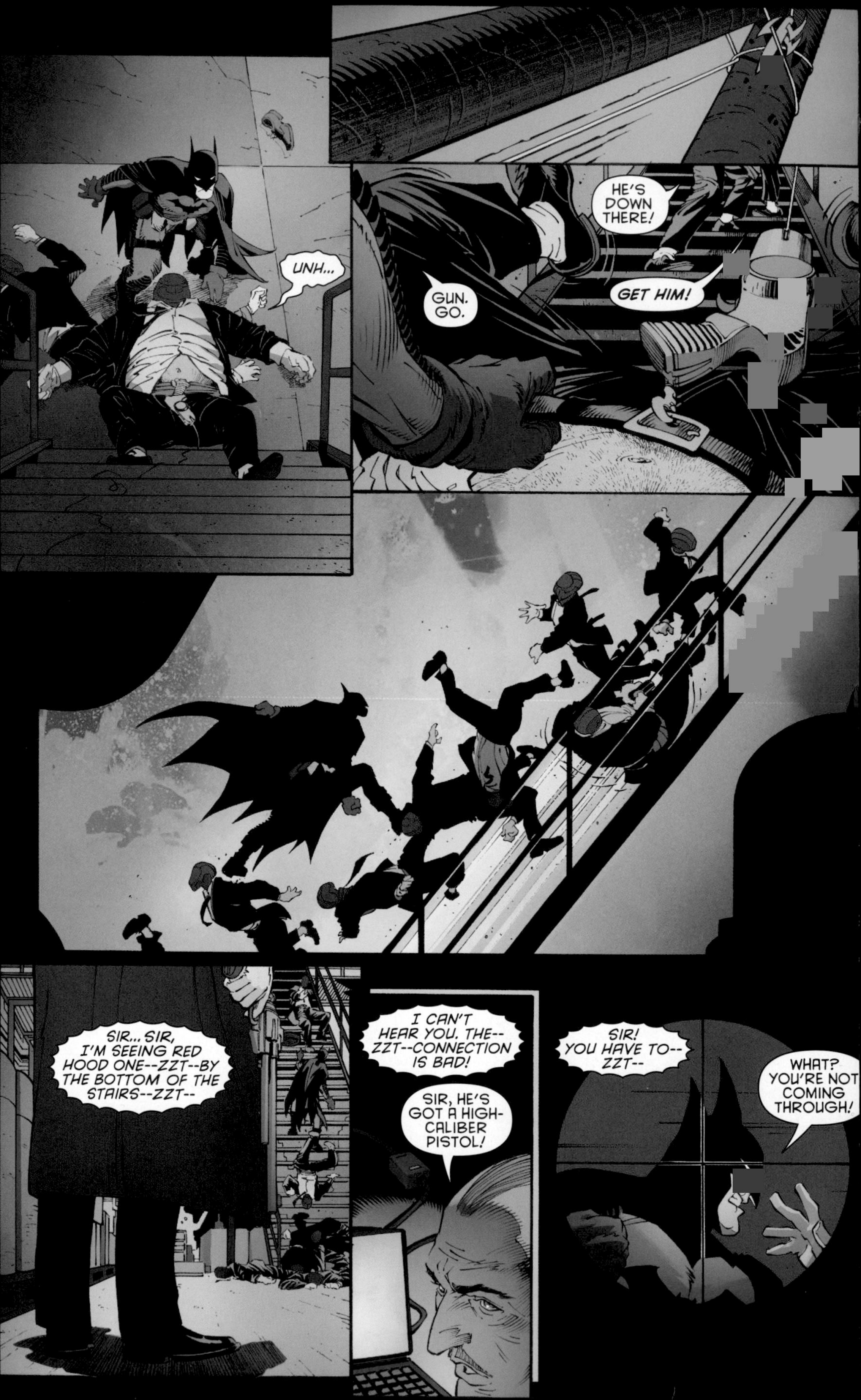
UNH...
HE'S DOWN THERE!
GUN. GO.
GET HIM!
SIR... SIR, I'M SEEING RED HOOD ONE--ZZT--BY THE BOTTOM OF THE STAIRS--ZZT--
I CAN'T HEAR YOU. THE--ZZT--CONNECTION IS BAD!
SIR, HE'S GOT A HIGH-CALIBER PISTOL!
SIR! YOU HAVE TO--ZZT--
WHAT? YOU'RE NOT COMING THROUGH!

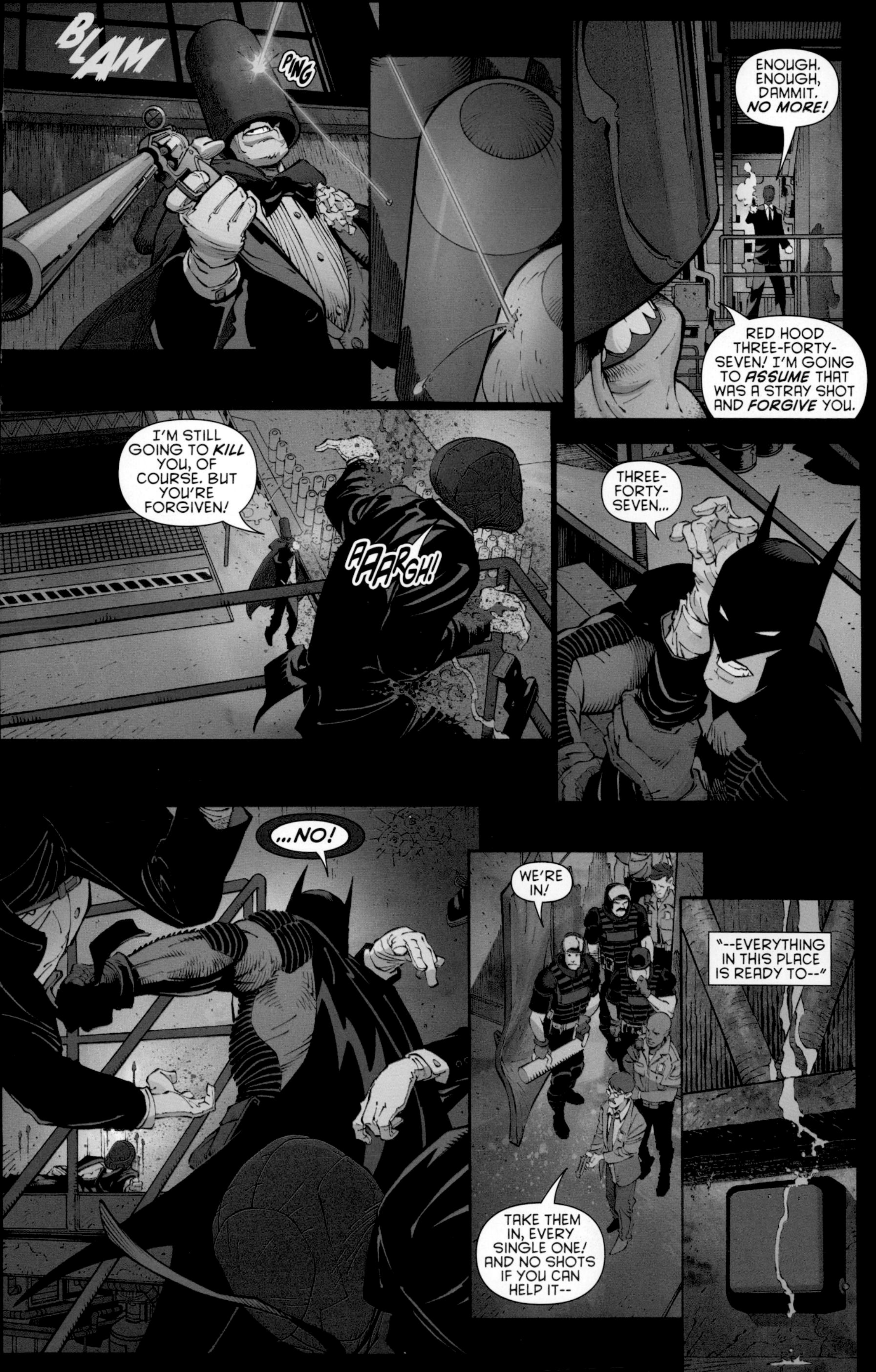
BLAM
PING
ENOUGH. ENOUGH, DAMMIT. NO MORE!
RED HOOD THREE-FORTY-SEVEN! I'M GOING TO ASSUME THAT WAS A STRAY SHOT AND FORGIVE YOU.
I'M STILL GOING TO KILL YOU, OF COURSE. BUT YOU'RE FORGIVEN!
AAARGH!
THREE-FORTY-SEVEN...
...NO!
WE'RE IN!
TAKE THEM IN, EVERY SINGLE ONE! AND NO SHOTS IF YOU CAN HELP IT--
"--EVERYTHING IN THIS PLACE IS READY TO--"

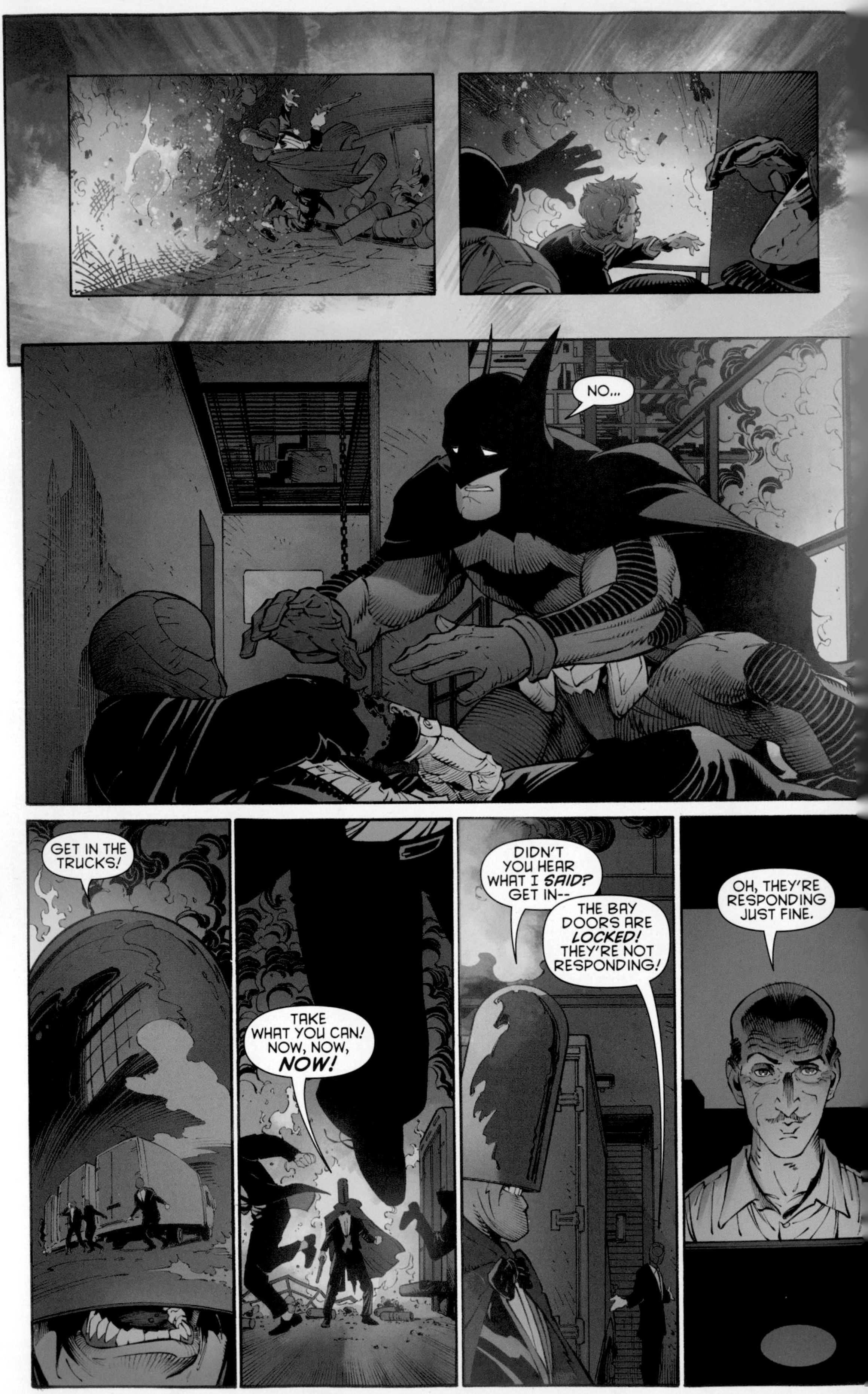
NO...
GET IN THE TRUCKS!
TAKE WHAT YOU CAN! NOW, NOW, NOW!
DIDN'T YOU HEAR WHAT I SAID? GET IN--
THE BAY DOORS ARE LOCKED! THEY'RE NOT RESPONDING!
OH, THEY'RE RESPONDING JUST FINE.

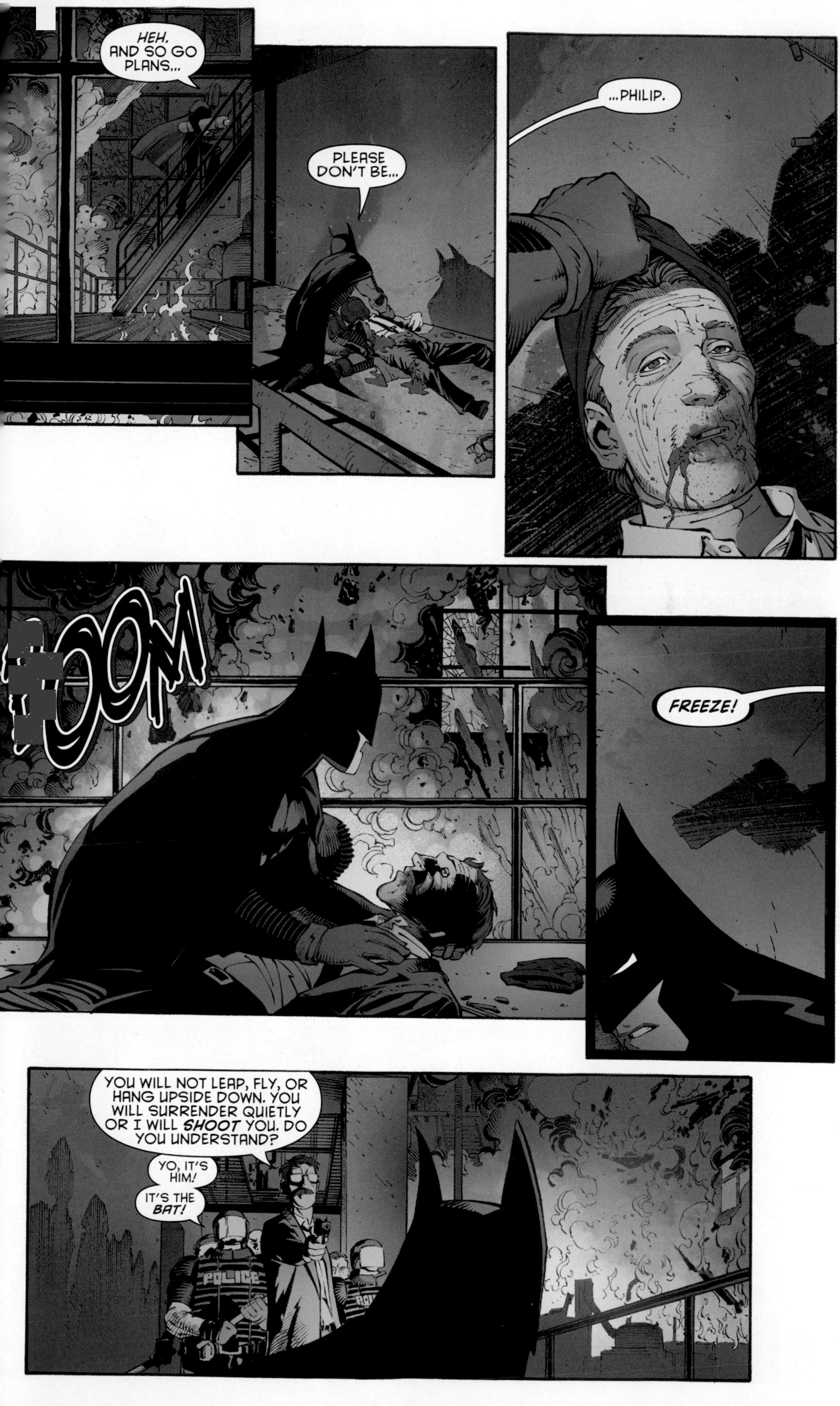
HEH. AND SO GO PLANS...
PLEASE DON'T BE...
...PHILIP.
OOM
FREEZE!
YOU WILL NOT LEAP, FLY, OR HANG UPSIDE DOWN. YOU WILL SURRENDER QUIETLY OR I WILL SHOOT YOU. DO YOU UNDERSTAND?
YO, IT'S HIM!
IT'S THE BAT!
POLICE

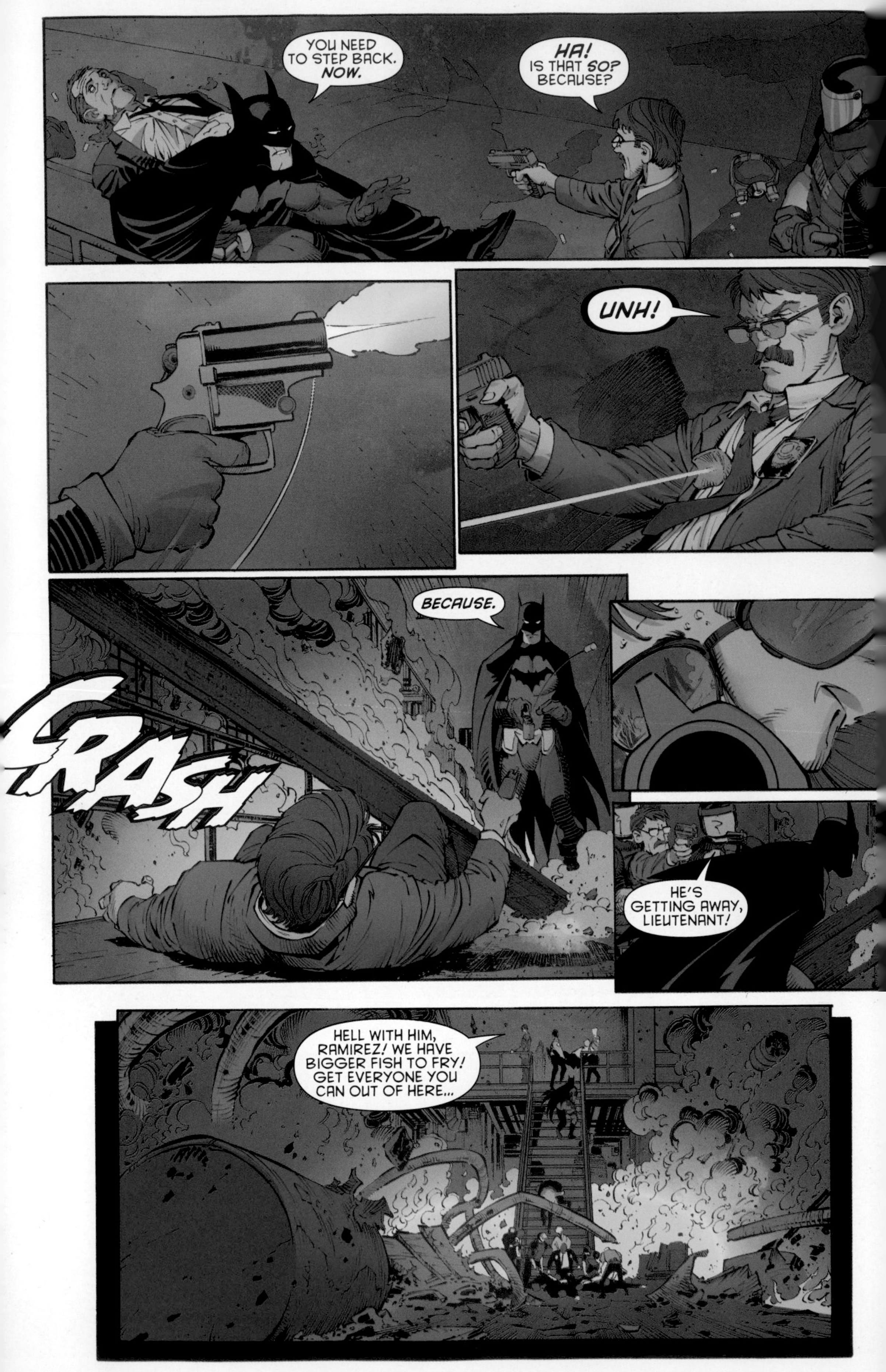
YOU NEED TO STEP BACK. NOW.
HA! IS THAT SO? BECAUSE?
UNH!
BECAUSE.
CRASH
HE'S GETTING AWAY, LIEUTENANT!
HELL WITH HIM, RAMIREZ! WE HAVE BIGGER FISH TO FRY! GET EVERYONE YOU CAN OUT OF HERE...

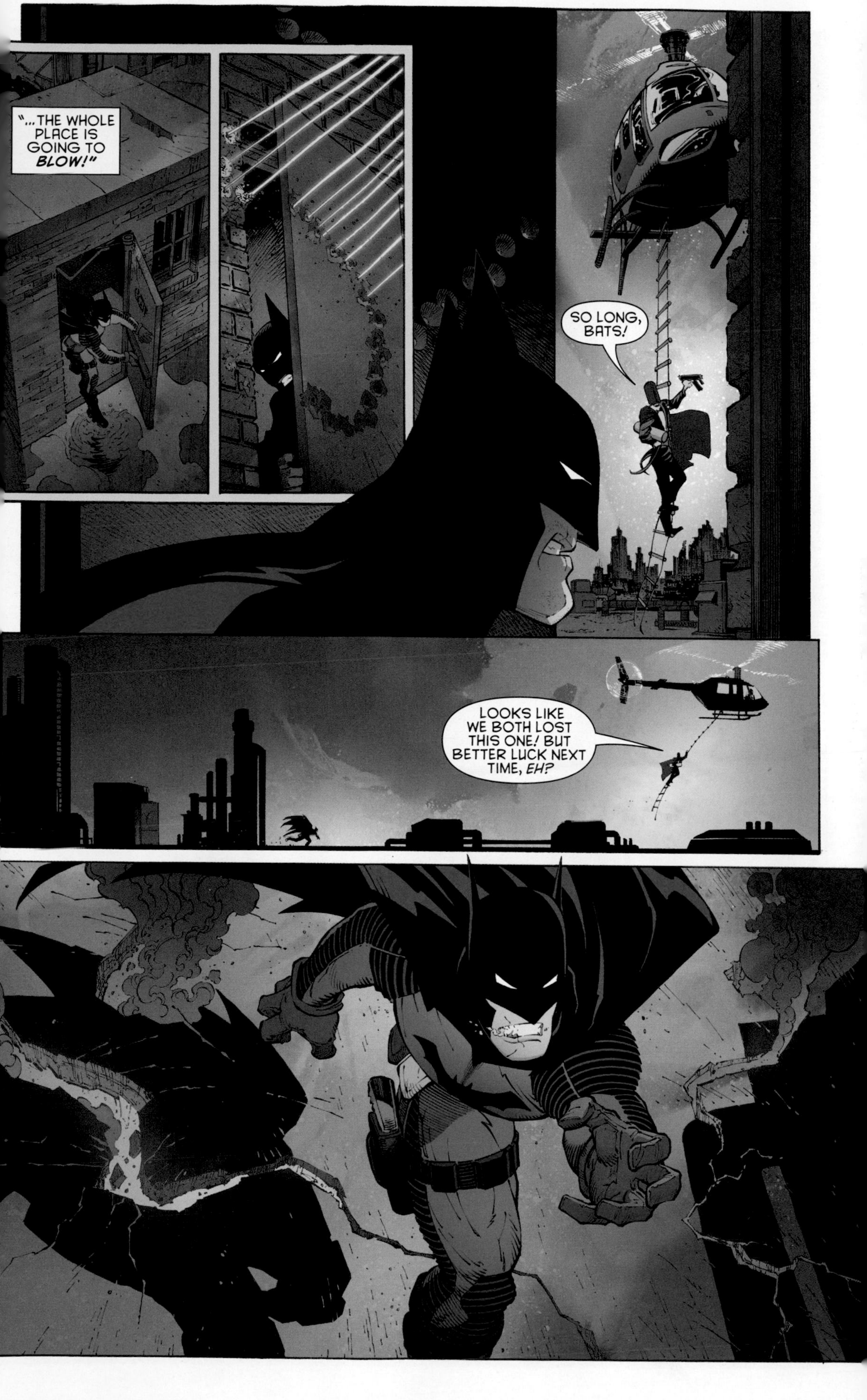
"...THE WHOLE PLACE IS GOING TO *BLOW!*"
SO LONG, BATS!
LOOKS LIKE WE BOTH LOST THIS ONE! BUT BETTER LUCK NEXT TIME, *EH?*

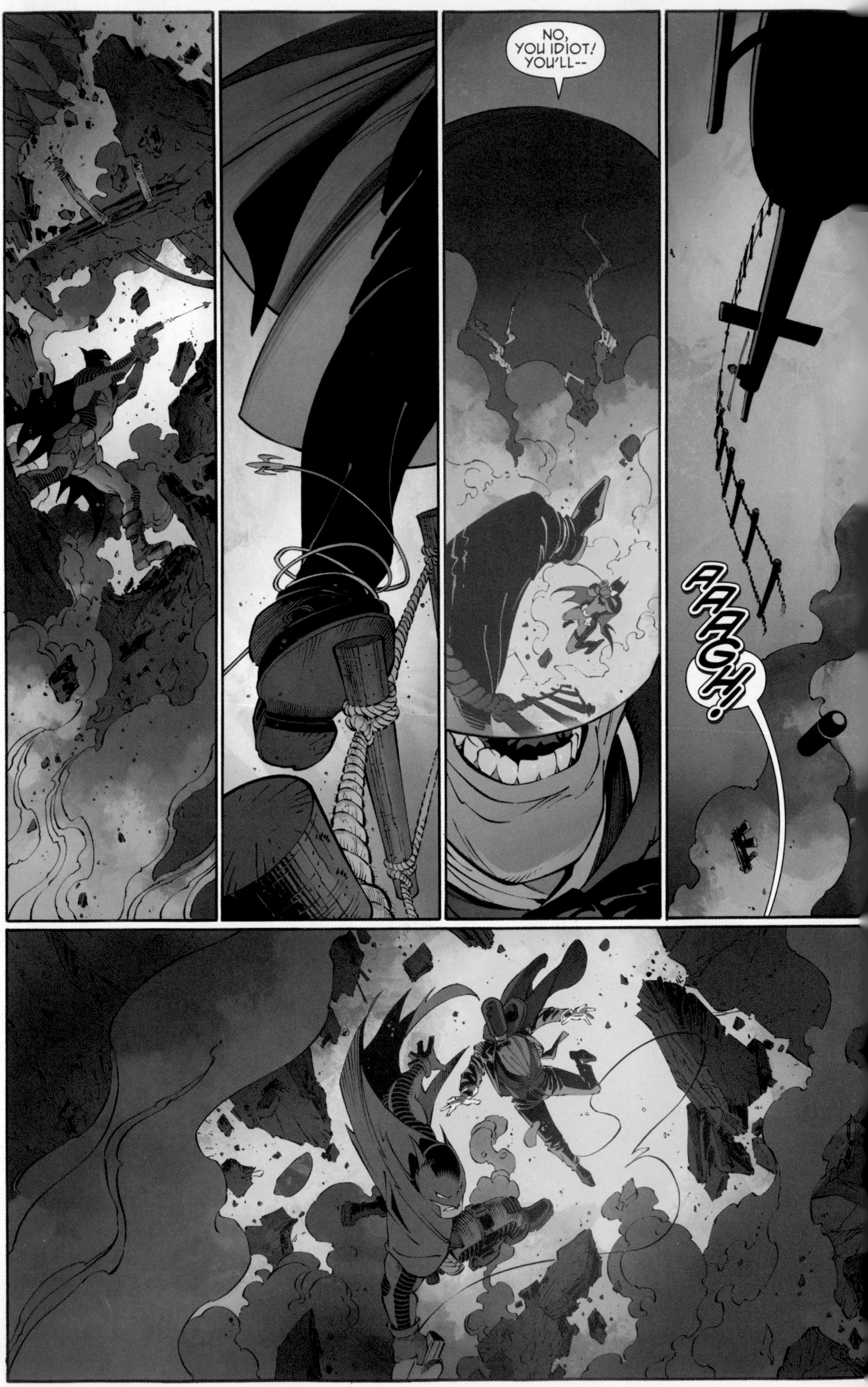
NO, YOU IDIOT! YOU'LL--
AAAGH!

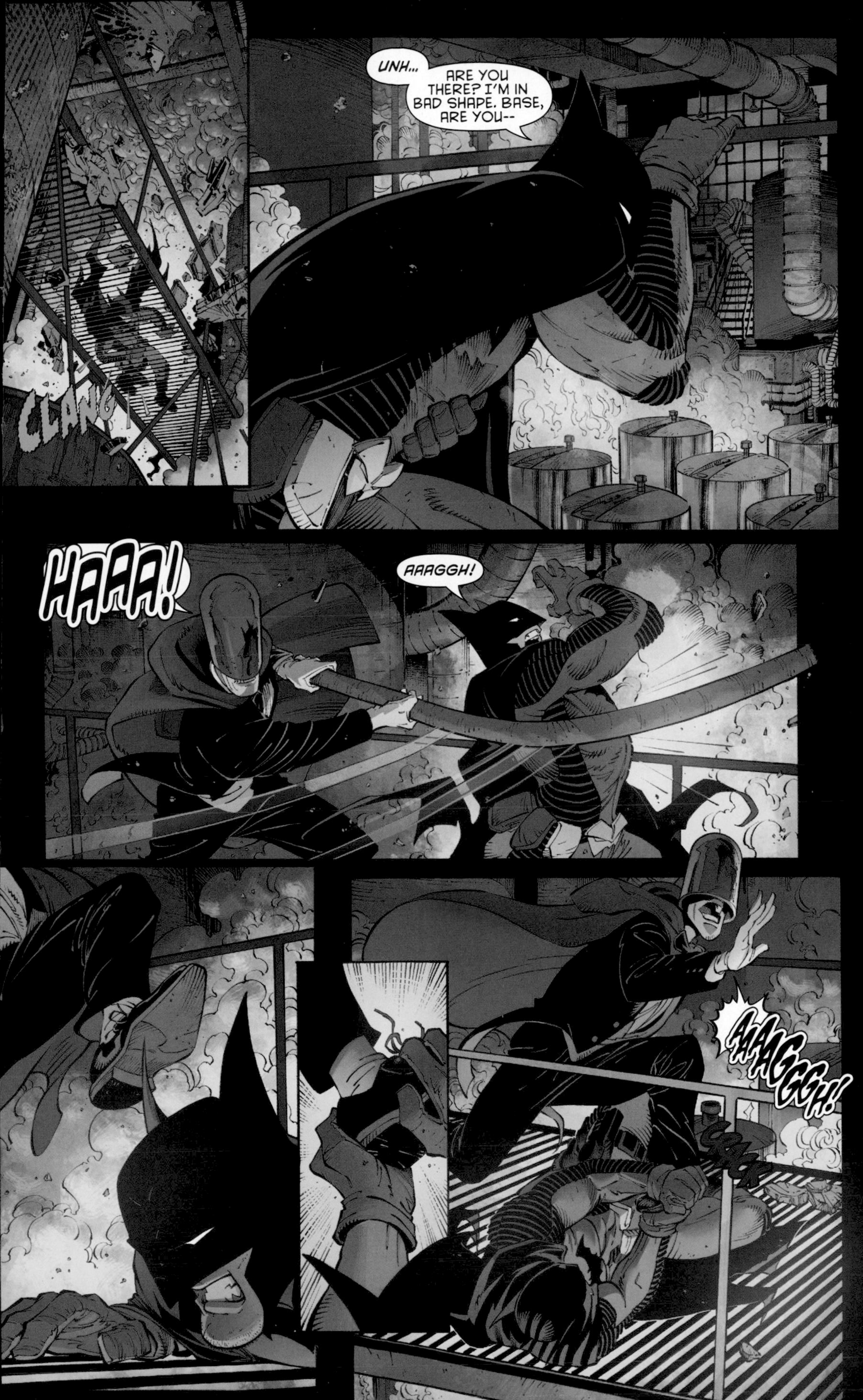
UNH... ARE YOU THERE? I'M IN BAD SHAPE. BASE, ARE YOU--
CLANG!
HAAA!
AAAGGH!
AAAAGGGH!

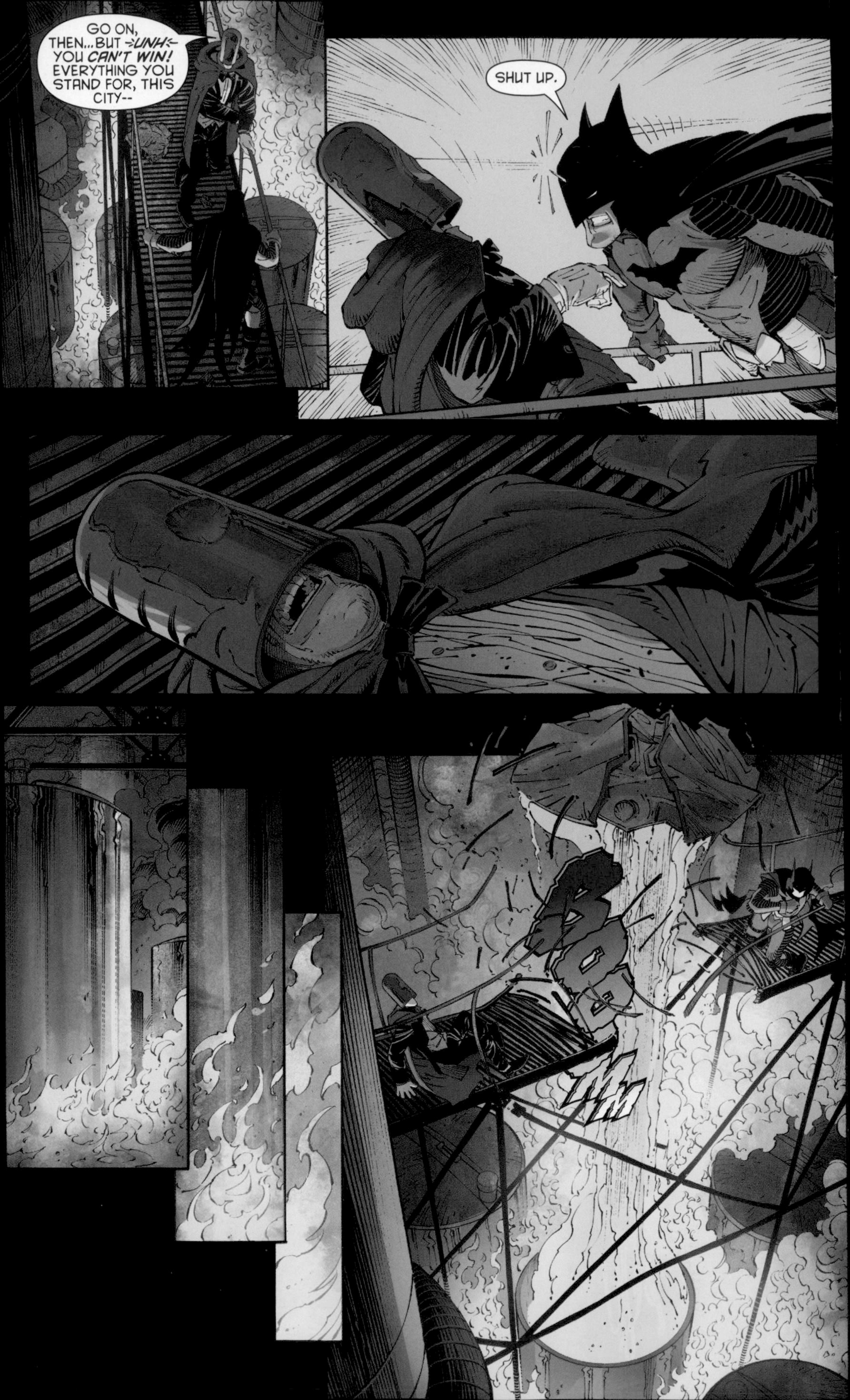
GO ON, THEN...BUT –UNH– YOU CAN'T WIN! EVERYTHING YOU STAND FOR, THIS CITY--
SHUT UP.

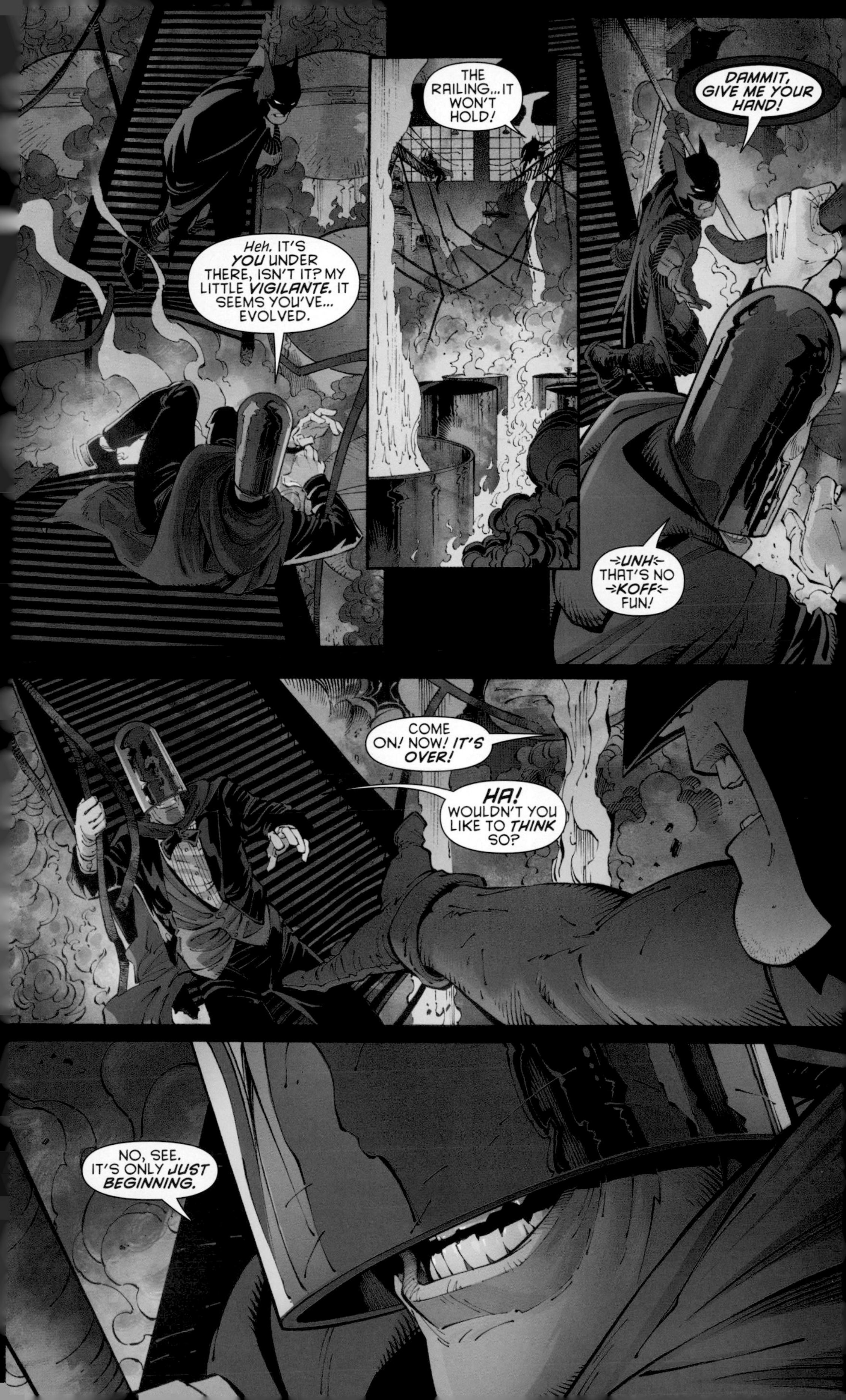

Heh. IT'S YOU UNDER THERE, ISN'T IT? MY LITTLE VIGILANTE. IT SEEMS YOU'VE... EVOLVED.
THE RAILING...IT WON'T HOLD!
DAMMIT, GIVE ME YOUR HAND!
UNH THAT'S NO KOFF FUN!
COME ON! NOW! IT'S OVER!
HA! WOULDN'T YOU LIKE TO THINK SO?
NO, SEE. IT'S ONLY JUST BEGINNING.

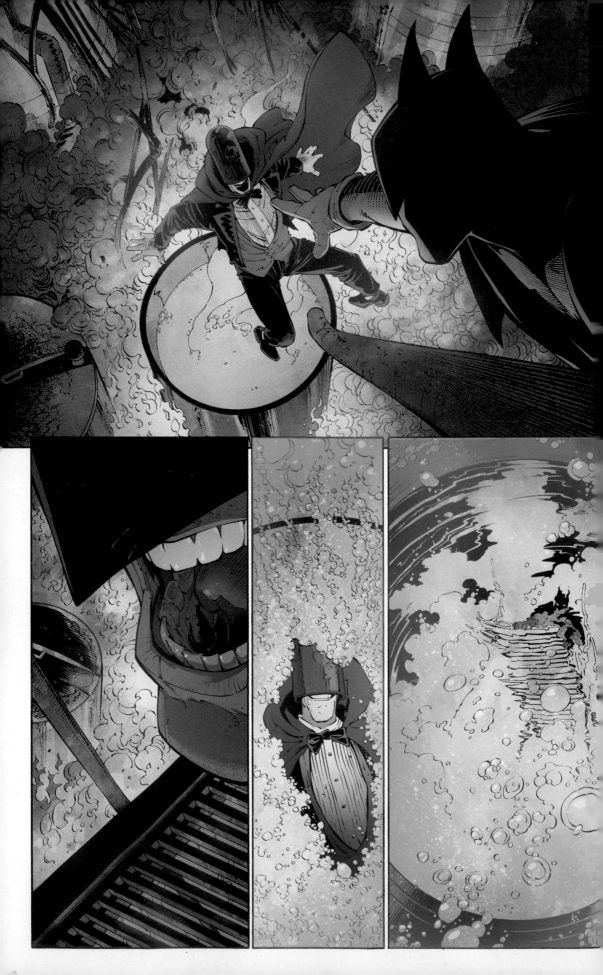

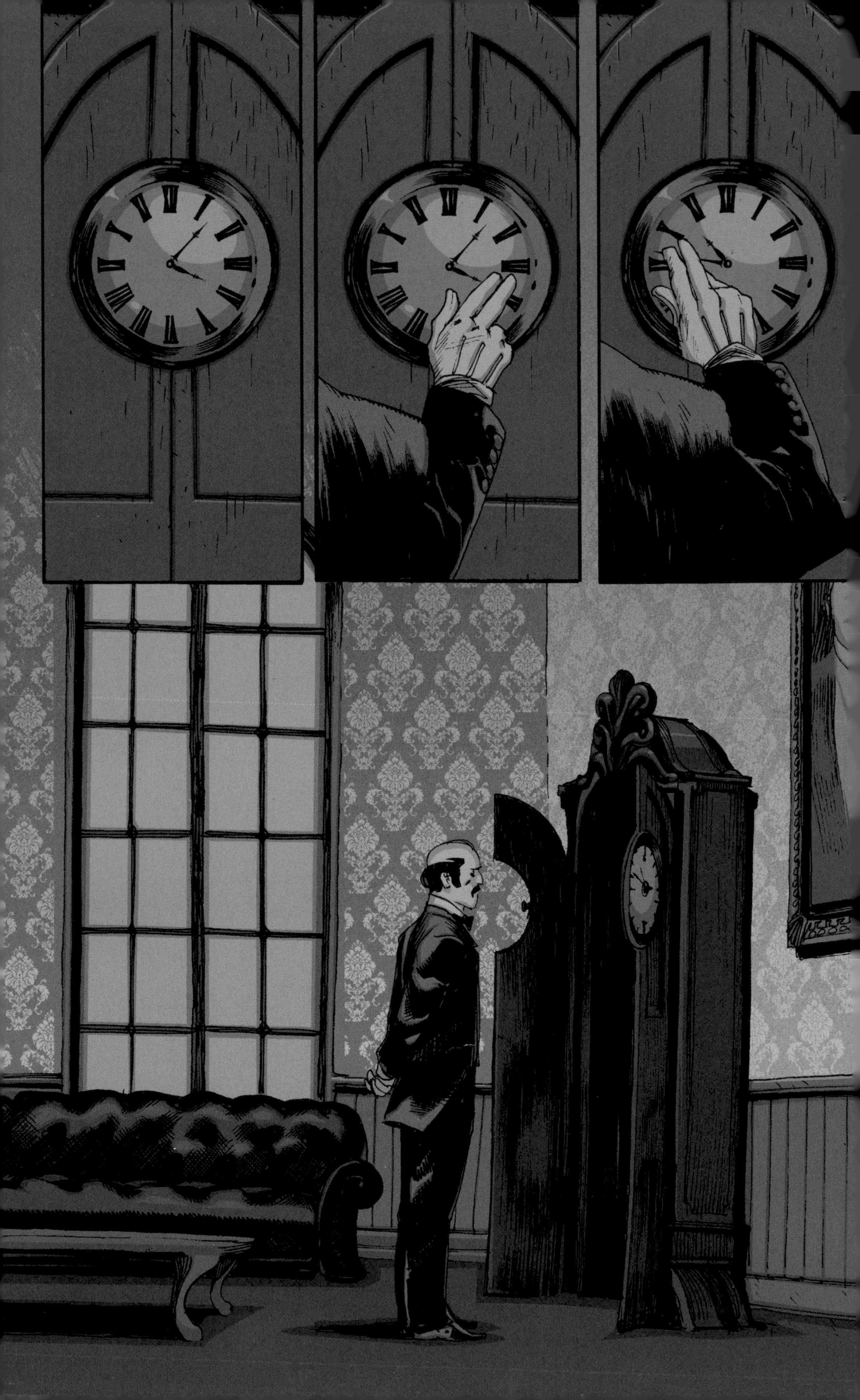

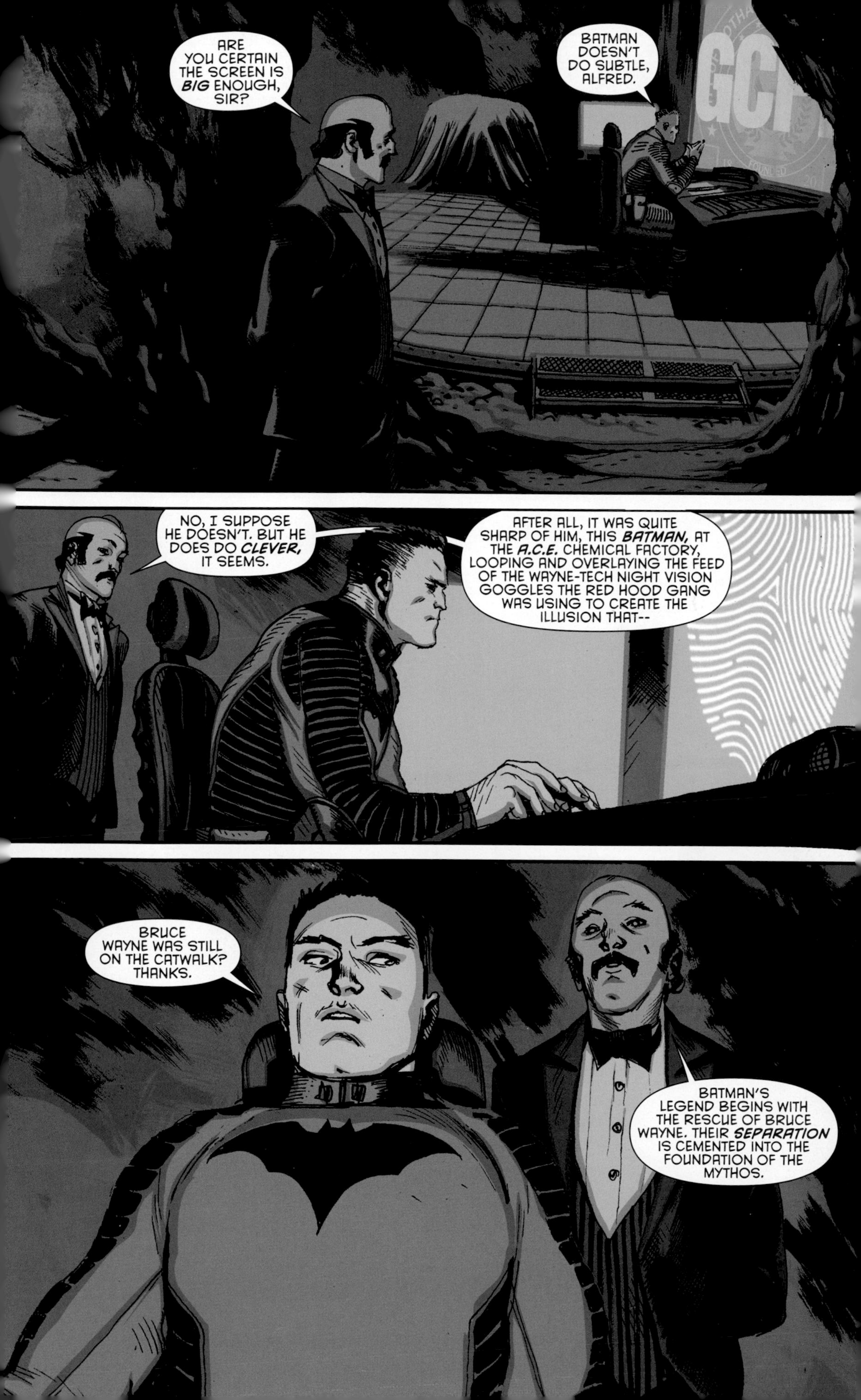
ARE YOU CERTAIN THE SCREEN IS BIG ENOUGH, SIR?
BATMAN DOESN'T DO SUBTLE, ALFRED.
NO, I SUPPOSE HE DOESN'T. BUT HE DOES DO CLEVER, IT SEEMS.
AFTER ALL, IT WAS QUITE SHARP OF HIM, THIS BATMAN, AT THE A.C.E. CHEMICAL FACTORY, LOOPING AND OVERLAYING THE FEED OF THE WAYNE-TECH NIGHT VISION GOGGLES THE RED HOOD GANG WAS USING TO CREATE THE ILLUSION THAT--
BRUCE WAYNE WAS STILL ON THE CATWALK? THANKS.
BATMAN'S LEGEND BEGINS WITH THE RESCUE OF BRUCE WAYNE. THEIR SEPARATION IS CEMENTED INTO THE FOUNDATION OF THE MYTHOS.

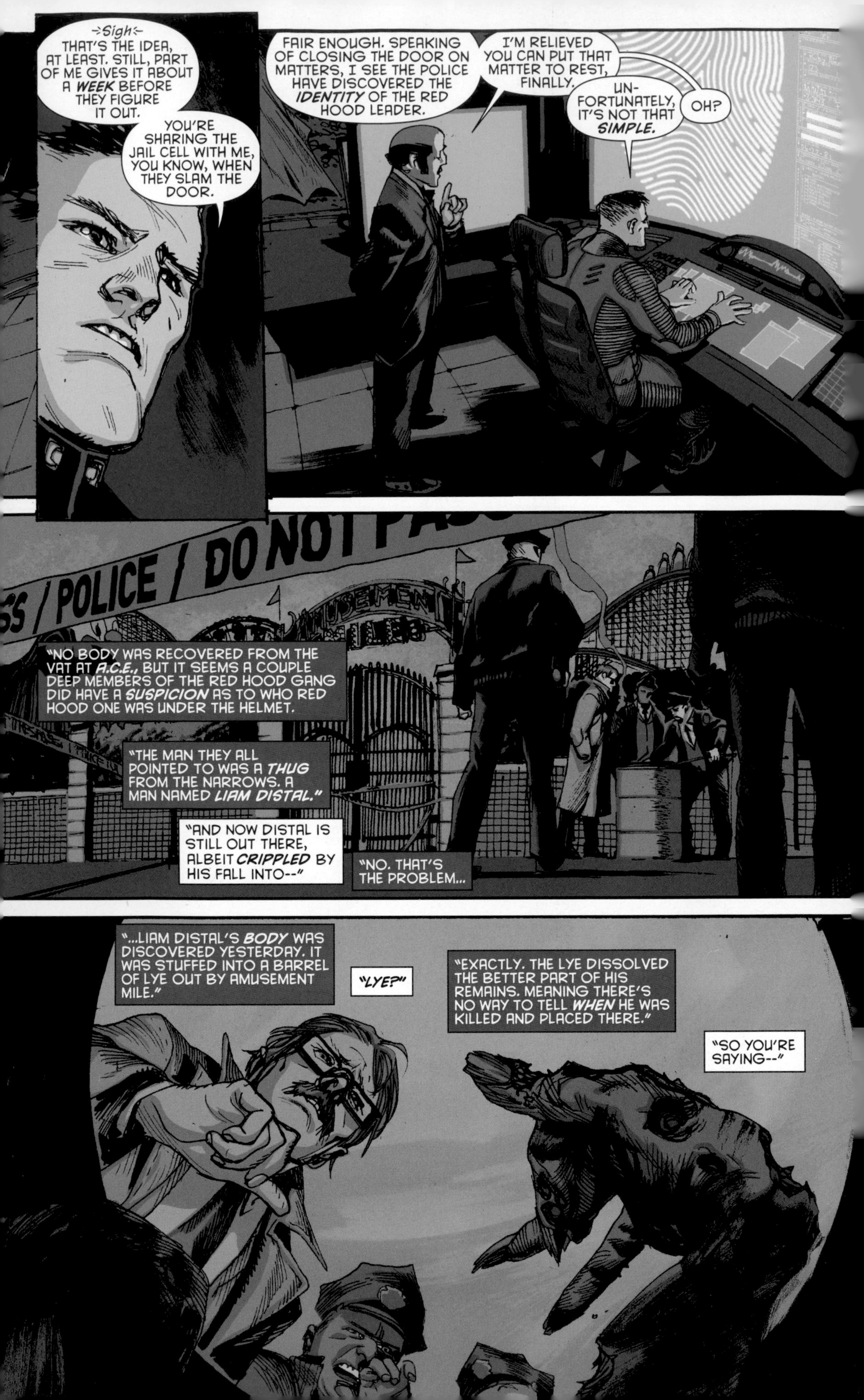

SIGH
THAT'S THE IDEA, AT LEAST. STILL, PART OF ME GIVES IT ABOUT A WEEK BEFORE THEY FIGURE IT OUT.
YOU'RE SHARING THE JAIL CELL WITH ME, YOU KNOW, WHEN THEY SLAM THE DOOR.
FAIR ENOUGH. SPEAKING OF CLOSING THE DOOR ON MATTERS, I SEE THE POLICE HAVE DISCOVERED THE IDENTITY OF THE RED HOOD LEADER.
I'M RELIEVED YOU CAN PUT THAT MATTER TO REST, FINALLY.
UN-FORTUNATELY, IT'S NOT THAT SIMPLE.
OH?
POLICE / DO NOT PASS
"NO BODY WAS RECOVERED FROM THE VAT AT A.C.E., BUT IT SEEMS A COUPLE DEEP MEMBERS OF THE RED HOOD GANG DID HAVE A SUSPICION AS TO WHO RED HOOD ONE WAS UNDER THE HELMET.
"THE MAN THEY ALL POINTED TO WAS A THUG FROM THE NARROWS. A MAN NAMED LIAM DISTAL."
"AND NOW DISTAL IS STILL OUT THERE, ALBEIT CRIPPLED BY HIS FALL INTO--"
"NO. THAT'S THE PROBLEM...
"...LIAM DISTAL'S BODY WAS DISCOVERED YESTERDAY. IT WAS STUFFED INTO A BARREL OF LYE OUT BY AMUSEMENT MILE."
"LYE?"
"EXACTLY. THE LYE DISSOLVED THE BETTER PART OF HIS REMAINS. MEANING THERE'S NO WAY TO TELL WHEN HE WAS KILLED AND PLACED THERE."
"SO YOU'RE SAYING--"

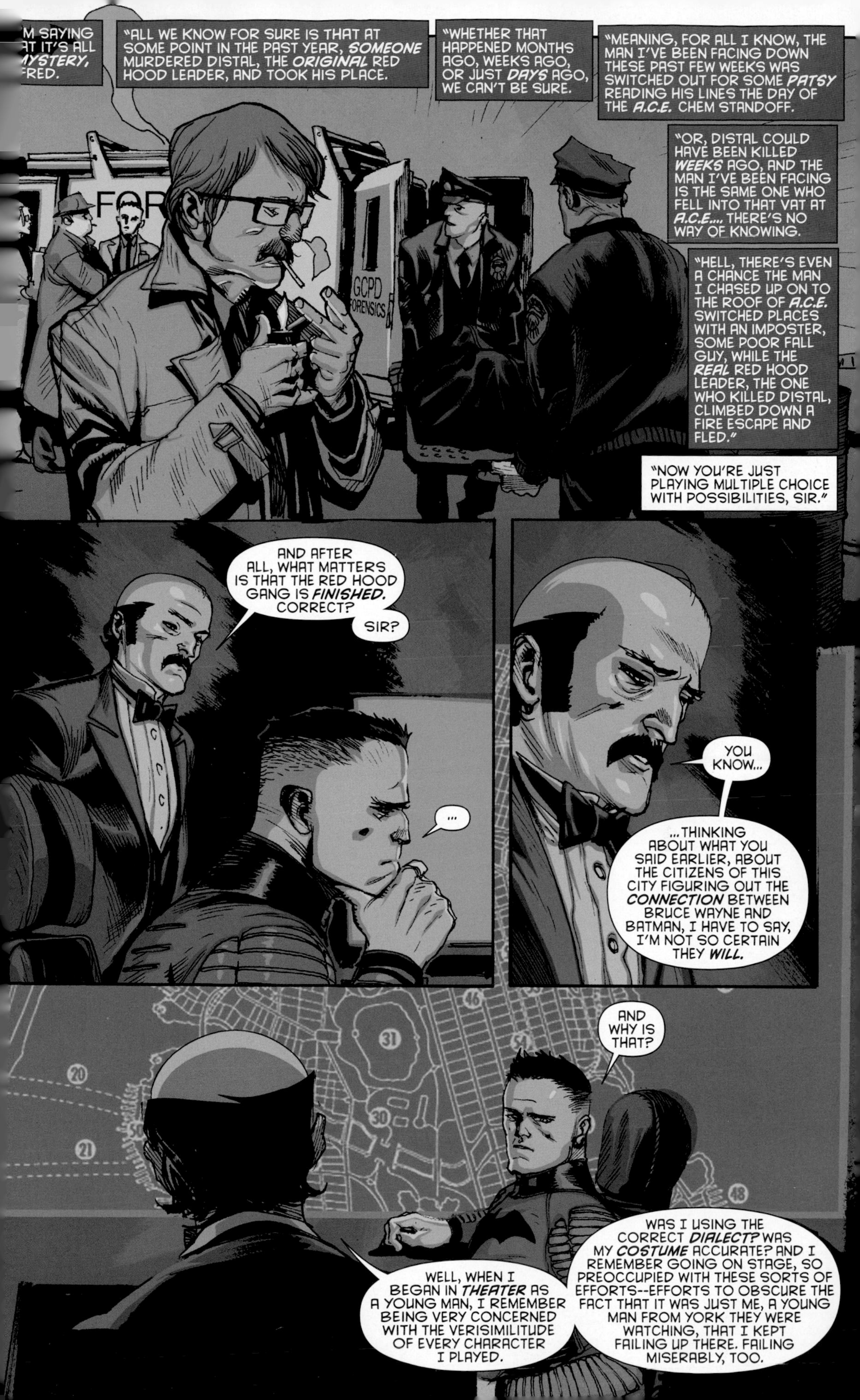
M SAYING AT IT'S ALL MYSTERY, FRED.
"ALL WE KNOW FOR SURE IS THAT AT SOME POINT IN THE PAST YEAR, SOMEONE MURDERED DISTAL, THE ORIGINAL RED HOOD LEADER, AND TOOK HIS PLACE.
"WHETHER THAT HAPPENED MONTHS AGO, WEEKS AGO, OR JUST DAYS AGO, WE CAN'T BE SURE.
"MEANING, FOR ALL I KNOW, THE MAN I'VE BEEN FACING DOWN THESE PAST FEW WEEKS WAS SWITCHED OUT FOR SOME PATSY READING HIS LINES THE DAY OF THE A.C.E. CHEM STANDOFF.
"OR, DISTAL COULD HAVE BEEN KILLED WEEKS AGO, AND THE MAN I'VE BEEN FACING IS THE SAME ONE WHO FELL INTO THAT VAT AT A.C.E.... THERE'S NO WAY OF KNOWING.
"HELL, THERE'S EVEN A CHANCE THE MAN I CHASED UP ON TO THE ROOF OF A.C.E. SWITCHED PLACES WITH AN IMPOSTER, SOME POOR FALL GUY, WHILE THE REAL RED HOOD LEADER, THE ONE WHO KILLED DISTAL, CLIMBED DOWN A FIRE ESCAPE AND FLED."
"NOW YOU'RE JUST PLAYING MULTIPLE CHOICE WITH POSSIBILITIES, SIR."
FOR
GCPD FORENSICS
AND AFTER ALL, WHAT MATTERS IS THAT THE RED HOOD GANG IS FINISHED. CORRECT?
SIR?
...
YOU KNOW...
...THINKING ABOUT WHAT YOU SAID EARLIER, ABOUT THE CITIZENS OF THIS CITY FIGURING OUT THE CONNECTION BETWEEN BRUCE WAYNE AND BATMAN, I HAVE TO SAY, I'M NOT SO CERTAIN THEY WILL.
AND WHY IS THAT?
WELL, WHEN I BEGAN IN THEATER AS A YOUNG MAN, I REMEMBER BEING VERY CONCERNED WITH THE VERISIMILITUDE OF EVERY CHARACTER I PLAYED.
WAS I USING THE CORRECT DIALECT? WAS MY COSTUME ACCURATE? AND I REMEMBER GOING ON STAGE, SO PREOCCUPIED WITH THESE SORTS OF EFFORTS--EFFORTS TO OBSCURE THE FACT THAT IT WAS JUST ME, A YOUNG MAN FROM YORK THEY WERE WATCHING, THAT I KEPT FAILING UP THERE. FAILING MISERABLY, TOO.

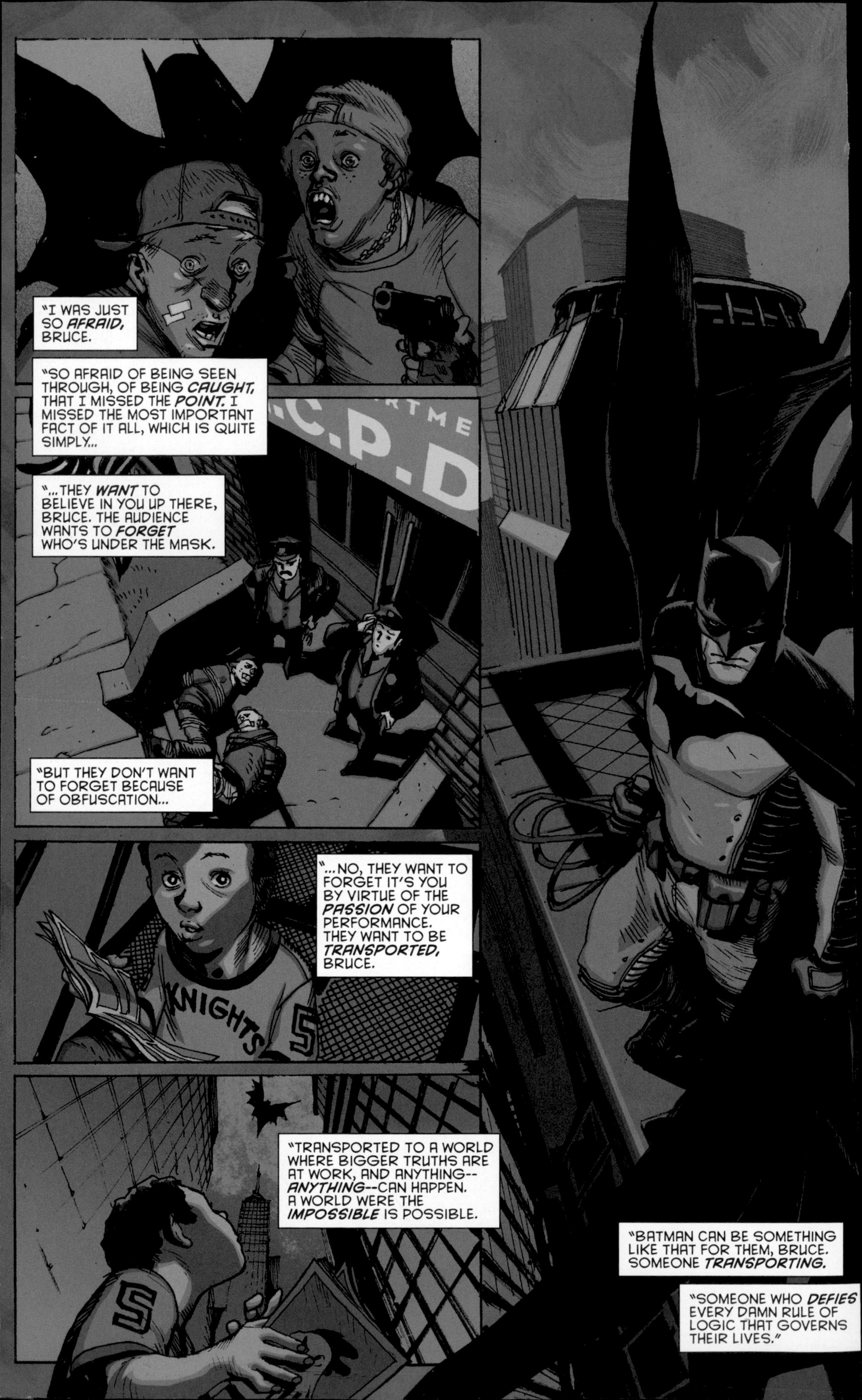

"I WAS JUST SO AFRAID, BRUCE.
"SO AFRAID OF BEING SEEN THROUGH, OF BEING CAUGHT, THAT I MISSED THE POINT. I MISSED THE MOST IMPORTANT FACT OF IT ALL, WHICH IS QUITE SIMPLY...
"...THEY WANT TO BELIEVE IN YOU UP THERE, BRUCE. THE AUDIENCE WANTS TO FORGET WHO'S UNDER THE MASK.
"BUT THEY DON'T WANT TO FORGET BECAUSE OF OBFUSCATION...
"...NO, THEY WANT TO FORGET IT'S YOU BY VIRTUE OF THE PASSION OF YOUR PERFORMANCE. THEY WANT TO BE TRANSPORTED, BRUCE.
"TRANSPORTED TO A WORLD WHERE BIGGER TRUTHS ARE AT WORK, AND ANYTHING--ANYTHING--CAN HAPPEN. A WORLD WERE THE IMPOSSIBLE IS POSSIBLE.
"BATMAN CAN BE SOMETHING LIKE THAT FOR THEM, BRUCE. SOMEONE TRANSPORTING.
"SOMEONE WHO DEFIES EVERY DAMN RULE OF LOGIC THAT GOVERNS THEIR LIVES."

WHAT I'M SAYING IS, IF YOU PLAY BATMAN RIGHT, THEY WON'T *WANT* TO FIGURE OUT WHO'S BENEATH THE COWL.

THAT'S THE KEY. AND YOU'RE DOING IT. YOU'RE PLAYING HIM BEAUTIFULLY, IF I DO SAY SO MYSELF.

ALFRED. I...I NEVER SAID I'M *SORRY.*

NEITHER DID I. BUT LET ME SAY THAT I THINK...

...NO, I *KNOW* YOUR PARENTS WOULD BE PROUD OF YOU, BRUCE.

YOU'RE *STILL* SHARING THE JAIL CELL WITH ME.

AND THAT'S *"MASTER BRUCE"*, ALFRED. SOME ETIQUETTE, PLEASE.

Heh. FORGIVE ME, SIR. I--

AHEM, AHEM! WELL HELLLLO, GOTHAM!

WHAT THE...?

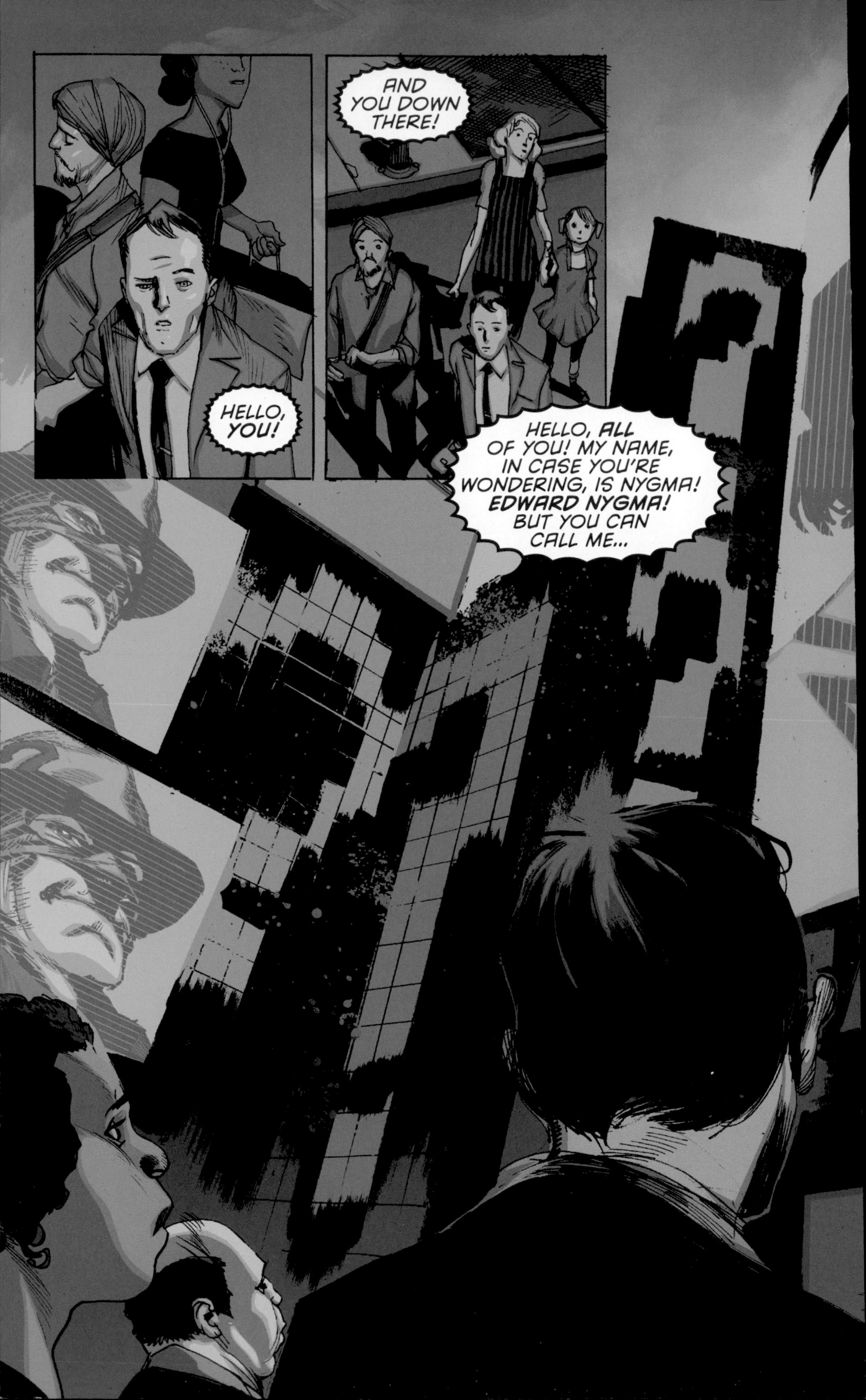
HELLO, YOU!
AND YOU DOWN THERE!
HELLO, ALL OF YOU! MY NAME, IN CASE YOU'RE WONDERING, IS NYGMA! EDWARD NYGMA! BUT YOU CAN CALL ME...

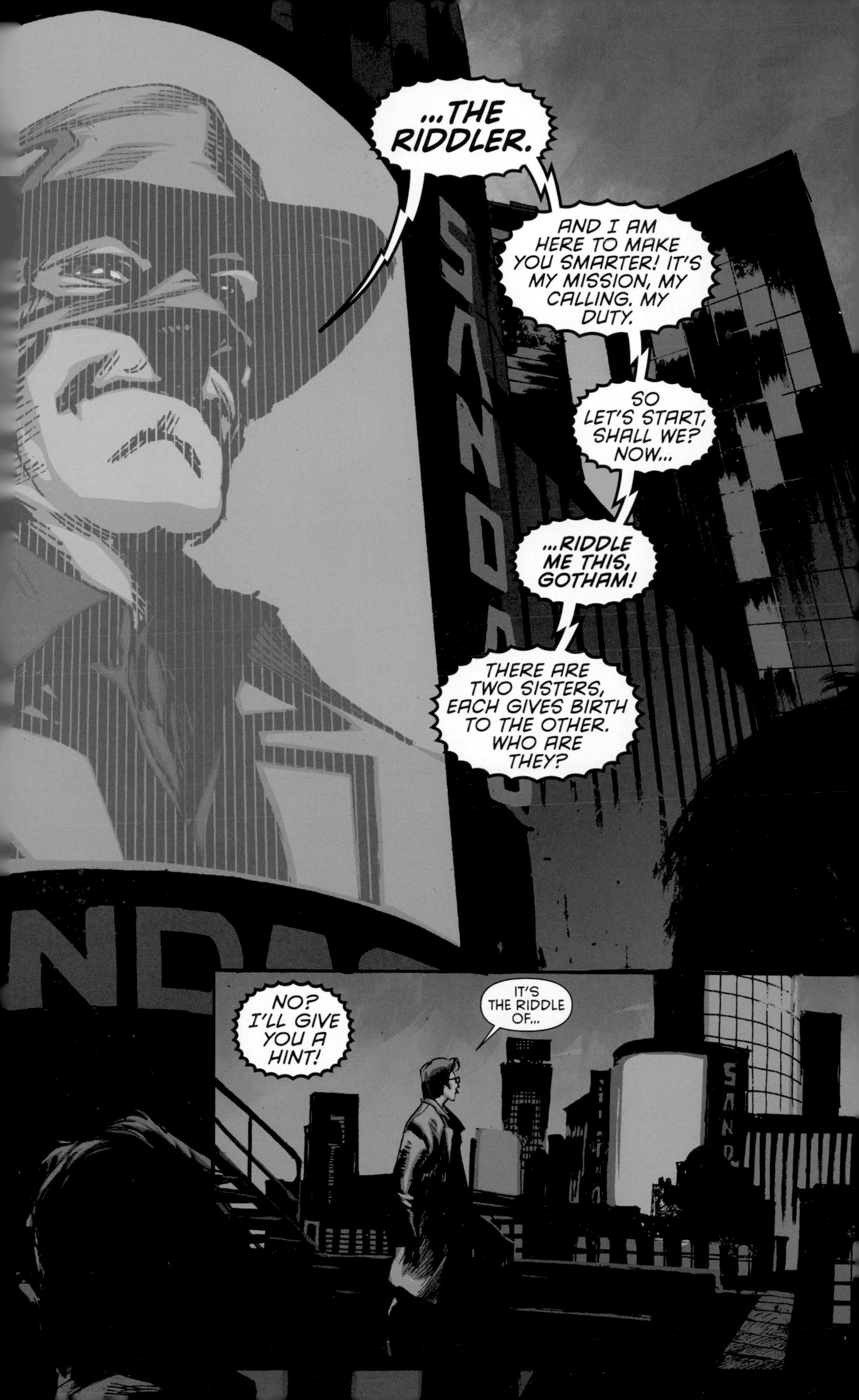
...THE RIDDLER.
AND I AM HERE TO MAKE YOU SMARTER! IT'S MY MISSION, MY CALLING. MY DUTY.
SO LET'S START, SHALL WE? NOW...
...RIDDLE ME THIS, GOTHAM!
THERE ARE TWO SISTERS, EACH GIVES BIRTH TO THE OTHER. WHO ARE THEY?
NO? I'LL GIVE YOU A HINT!
IT'S THE RIDDLE OF...

...THE RIDDLE OF THE SPHINX. THE LESSER-KNOWN SECOND RIDDLE.
HERE'S YOUR HINT. ONE SISTER SAYS...
...I AM THE DAY...
...AND THE OTHER SISTER SAYS...
I AM THE NIGHT.

SO BRING ON THE DARK, DARK NIGHT!
GOTHAM CITY

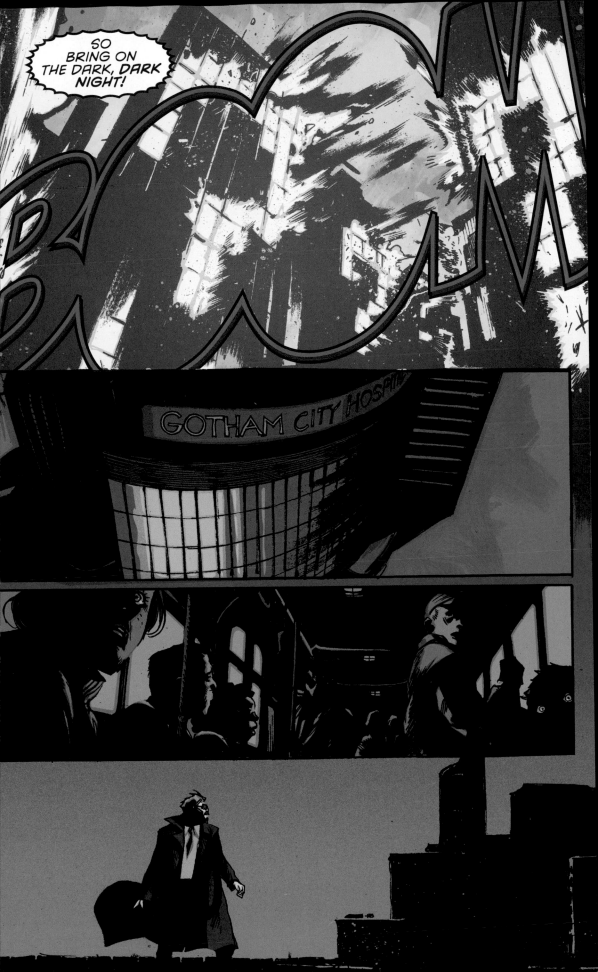

ALL RIGHT, GOTHAM, TIME TO GET SMART!
YOU'RE GOING TO HAVE TO DO BETTER THAN THAT...OR THE CITY **DIES** FOR REAL!
NOW...
...LET THE **GAMES** BEGIN!

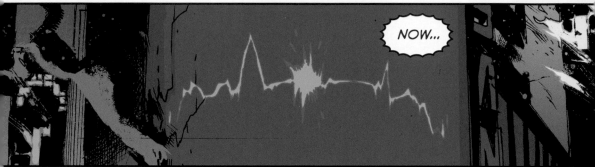

BATMAN #21 variant cover by Jock

RIO DE JANEIRO...
BRUCE. AGE NINETEEN.
BRUCE WAYNE
IN
WHERE THE HELL DID HE LEARN TO DRIVE?!
WRITTEN BY SCOTT SNYDER & JAMES TYNION IV
ART BY RAFAEL ALBUQUERQUE
COLORS BY DAVE McCAIG
LETTERS BY TAYLOR ESPOSITO
THIS IS INSANE, MIGUEL.
YES, MY BOY! THAT IS PRECISELY THE POINT! PRECISELY!
HANG LEFT.

THE CARS WE PRACTICED WITH WERE--
DULL AND PLAIN, I KNOW! GRAY PIGEONS!
I WAS GOING TO SAY INCONSPICUOUS! BUT THIS MONSTER...
...ALL THE TRICKS YOU'VE TAUGHT ME OVER THE LAST SIX WEEKS! COLOR COVER, CROWD DUCKING. HOW DO YOU EXPECT ME TO LOSE THEM IN THIS THING?
SEE, BUT THAT'S TODAY'S LESSON, BRUCE! THE FINAL ONE. I DON'T EXPECT YOU TO LOSE THEM. I EXPECT YOU TO THRILL THEM.
THRILL THEM?! THEY'RE POLICIA, DON MIGUEL! THEY'RE NOT OUT TO BE THRILLED!
I ONCE DROVE MY CAR THROUGH THE NATIONAL GALLERY IN PERU. STOLE $14 MILLION IN INCAN ARTIFACTS WITHOUT EVER DROPPING UNDER 30 MILES PER HOUR.
MY CAR WAS GOLD-PLATED, BRIGHT AS A MIRROR. A SEVEN-HUNDRED-YEAR-OLD STATUE OF INITI, THE SUN GOD, IN THE PASSENGER SEAT. AND YET, THEY DIDN'T CATCH ME. WHY, BRUCE?
BECAUSE WHEN THEY SEE A CAR LIKE THIS, A CAR FROM DREAMS, WITH A TOUCH OF MAGIC TO IT...

...THE TRUTH IS, THEY WON'T CATCH YOU, BRUCE, BECAUSE DEEP DOWN, THEY DON'T WANT TO.
THEY WANT TO CHASE YOU, BUT THEY DON'T WANT TO CATCH YOU! THEY WANT TO BELIEVE IN YOU, SEE? THEY WANT YOU TO GET AWAY!
YEAH, WELL...
...YOU COULD'VE FOOLED ME.
OH, THEY'RE JUST ACTING, BRUCE. THEY WANT US TO BREAK THEIR LITTLE CHAIN.
NOW, LET'S SEE IF THIS BEAUTIFUL DARLING WAS WORTH STEALING IN THE FIRST PLACE.
DAMMIT...

WHAT THE--BOY, WHAT ARE YOU DOING? THAT WEAPON IS WORTH 1.6 LLION DOLLARS! THIS IS NOT WHAT YOU'VE BEEN TAUGHT. YOU ARE BREAKING THE RULES!
I'M MORE OF AN IMPROVISER, MIGUEL.
THEATRO MUNICIPAL
SLOW DOWN! YOU'LL KILL US BOTH!
NO. I WON'T.
AVÉ MARIA, CHEIA DE GRAÇA, O SENHOR É CONVOSCO...

CRASH
NO! I'VE NEVER BEEN TRAPPED IN MY LIFE! YOU IDIOT SCHOOLBOY! I KNEW I SHOULD HAVE REFUSED YOU! BUT I WAS--

WHACK
THANKS FOR THE LESSON, DON MIGUEL.
YOU'VE KILLED TWENTY-THREE POLICE OFFICERS IN THIRTEEN COUNTRIES OVER THE LAST THREE YEARS...
...AND SOME THINGS YOU CAN'T GET AWAY FROM.
IT'S HIM! IT'S REALLY HIM!
DON MIGUEL! WE HAVE HIM!

BATMAN #22 variant cover by Mikel Janin

CATION UNKNOWN.
E TWENTY-ONE...
MY HEAD...
...SERGEI, ARE YOU OUT THERE? I CAN'T SEE A DAMN THING.
WELL, CRAP.
BRUCE WAYNE IN
HAT ONE TIME
WRITTEN BY SCOTT SNYDER & JAMES TYNION IV
ART BY RAFAEL ALBUQUERQUE
COLORS BY DAVE McCAIG
LETTERS BY TAYLOR ESPOSITO

BEFORE...
THESE BLUNT LITTLE TOOLS, YOU'VE BEEN BUILDING THEM FOR MONTHS, BRUCE. TINKER-ING, PERFECTING...AND WHY?
I'M DOING EXACTLY WHAT YOU TAUGHT ME, SERGEI. THIS TECHNOLOGY IS AS SOPHISTICATED AS ANY MILITARY'S IN THE WORLD.
EEK
>Sigh< LITTLE MILITARY TRINKETS I WAS MAKING BACK IN THE COLD WAR. OH, MAXWELL. THE BOY IS HOPELESS.
YOU TOLD ME THE BROAD PARAMETERS OF YOUR FINAL TEST. CLOSED ROOM. LIMITED OXYGEN SUPPLY.
ALL I'LL HAVE WITH ME IS WHA I'VE SPENT TH LAST SIX MONTH WORKING ON T GET OUT, OR I'LL DIE.
I'VE PREPARED FOR EVERY EVENTUALITY. I'VE PERFECTED EACH OF THESE TOOLS. THEY WILL D THE JOB. YOU CAN'T BEAT M HERE. IT'S NOT POSSIBLE.
NOW...
DAMN...HALF THE COMPONENTS ARE MISSING... NONE OF THIS IS OPERA-TIONAL.
QUAKE BOOTS
TASER GAUNTLETS
LASER CUTTER
SONIC RADAR EXTRAVISION GOGGLES

OKAY... NK BRUCE, K...WHAT ARE U GOING TO DO?
YOU'RE GOING TO DIE.
AND THAT CRUSTY OLD RUSSIAN'S GOING TO FEED YOU TO HIS DAMNED MONKEY.
IMPOSSIBLE, EH? THAT IS WHY YOU SOUGHT ME OUT, NO? TO LEARN THE IMPOSSIBLE.
AND YET, YOU ARE SO WRAPPED UP IN THE OUTCOME...IN YOUR PLANNING. YOU ARE INFLEXIBLE.
YOU DO NOT ALLOW YOURSELF TO MAKE NEW CONNECTIONS.
YOU DO NOT ALLOW THE IMPOSSIBLE.
STEADY YOUR BREATHING. YOU CAN MAKE TEN MINUTES OF AIR LAST AN HOUR. YOU KNOW THAT MUCH.
JUST THINK. BE FLEXIBLE. WHAT CAN I DO WITH THIS CRAP?
NO. THERE ISN'T ENOUGH POWER...KEEP THINKING.
MAYBE IF I AMPLIFY THE SONIC BLAST...
...heh. THIS IS CRAZY.

NOT CRAZY *ENOUGH*, BRUCE. THAT IS THE PROBLEM, MAXWELL.

HE IS *SMART*, YES. I WOULD HAVE HIRED HIM AS AN UNDERLING BACK IN THE KREMLIN. GIVEN HIM A LITTLE KERNEL OF THE IDEA. HE WOULD HAVE CRACKED IT. IMPROVED IT.

BUT HE'S NO *DREAMER*. HE WOULD HAVE NEVER PRODUCED SOMETHING *NEW*.

-koff- WANNA *BET*?

I USED THE MOTOR FOR THE QUAKE BOOTS TO OVER-CLOCK THE SONIC RADAR SYSTEM IN THE EYE-SET BY 10,000 DECIBELS. BUILT THEM INTO THE GLOVES.

TOOK A FEW TRIES TO FIND A SHATTER POINT. BUT I BROKE THROUGH. AND *DUG.*

YES! YES! AS IT SHOULD! POWER L... IN THE IMPOSSIBLE. DOING THE IMPOSSIB... IS THE VERY ORIGI... OF THIS ART...

IT WAS *THRILLING*, WASN'T IT?

ACTUALLY, I THINK IT BURST ONE OF MY EARDRUMS...

NOT THE ESCAPE, BOY! THAT *MOMENT*. THAT PERFECT MOMENT YOU LET GO OF YOUR RIGID CONCEPTS OF WHAT WAS POSSIBLE.

WHEN THERE WAS NOTHING LEFT TO DO BUT STEP BEYOND ANYTHING YOU'D LEARNED BEFORE...WHEN YOU STOPPED BEING A POOR MIMIC AND BECAME AN *EXPLORER OF THE MIND*.

HOW DID *THAT* FEEL?

EMPOWERING.

...IMAGINE THE ANCIENTS, WHEN COMPELLED TO DO SOMETHING NEW, FOR THE FIRST TIME...WHEN THEIR MIGHTY KINGS TOLD THEM TO BUILD WONDERS THAT THE WORLD HAD NEVER *SEEN* BEFORE.

THEY COULD NOT *RELY* ON WHAT HAD BEEN DONE *BEFORE*. THEY HA... TO *CREATE*. THEY HAD TO BREAK OUT OF THE RIGID... OF THE CONTEMPORARY MINDSETS...

...THAT IS WHY YOUR TEST WAS *HERE*. THAT IS WHAT I WANTED TO SHOW YOU.
WHEN YOU CAN WIELD THE IMPOSSIBLE...
...YOU CAN CREATE *WONDERS*.

BATMAN #23 variant cover by Gary Frank and Brad Anderso

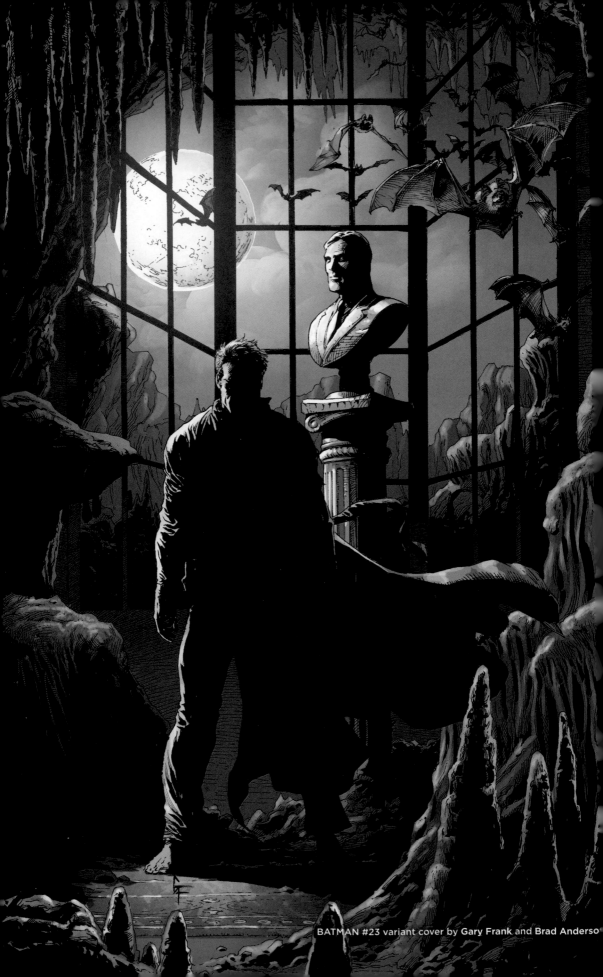

MILES NORTHEAST OF HARSTAD, NORWAY.
A SINGLE DEATH MATCH HAS NEVER LASTED THIS LONG BEFORE.
TWENTY-EIGHT HOURS STRAIGHT...EACH HOUR WE'VE ADDED ANOTHER COMBATANT IN ACCORDANCE WITH THE RULES, BUT WE'VE RUNOUT OF FIGHTERS.
THIS CAN'T CONTINUE MUCH LONGER. YOUR ROUNDS ONLY EVER RAN--
16 MINUTES 34 SECONDS. 12 MINUTES 7 SECONDS. AND THAT'S NOT COUNTING THE TIME I THREW THE LAST PIT MASTER IN AND TOOK THE TOURNAMENT FOR MYSELF.
BUT QUIET NOW, KRISTOFFER. YOU'RE DISTRACTING ME. I DON'T WANT TO MISS IT ALL CRASHING DOWN. I WANT TO SEE IT IN THAT BRAT'S EYES.
WHEN HE REALIZES HE'S GOING TO HAVE TO KILL OR HE'LL DIE.
AGE 24.

≥PANT PANT≥

I CAN PRACTICALLY FEEL THE PAIN *RADIATING* FROM YOUR BODY UP HERE.

YOU KNOW THERE'S ONLY ONE WAY TO MAKE THIS STOP.

IT IS THE LESSO YOU NEEDED T LEARN MOST OF ALL, YOUN MAN.

THIS WAS *NOT* THE LESSON WE DISCUSSED, MY QUEEN.

CRAK

YOU CAME TO *ME*...TO BE TAUGHT HOW TO USE YOUR BODY, THIS SOFT, *WEAK* THING, TO WAGE WAR.

AND I'VE TAUGHT YOU. BUT TO WAGE WAR WITHOUT *DEATH*... THERE'S SIMPLY NO WAY TO *WIN* WITHOUT IT.

YOU MIGHT WIN *BATTLES*, BUT NOT THE WAR. NO, YOUR OPPONENTS WILL KEEP COMING BACK AGAIN, AND AGAIN, AND AGAIN...

...BECAUS THEY KNOW YOU'LL NEV GO ALL TH WAY.

SO KEEP GOING, BANION, OR WHATEVER YOUR *REAL* NAME IS. BY ALL MEANS. IN FACT... HERE. ÷HEH÷

BUT BELIEVE ME WHEN I TELL YOU THAT THIS WAR, HERE IN THIS PIT, IT'S NOT GOING TO STOP BECAUSE YOU *WANT* IT TO.

IT'LL GO ON, AND ON, AND ON, UNTIL YOU LEARN WHAT YOU NEED TO LEARN.

COME ON, THEN.

OR THING.

I SAID, *COME ON!*

KRAK
PTAUGH
PANT PANT PANT

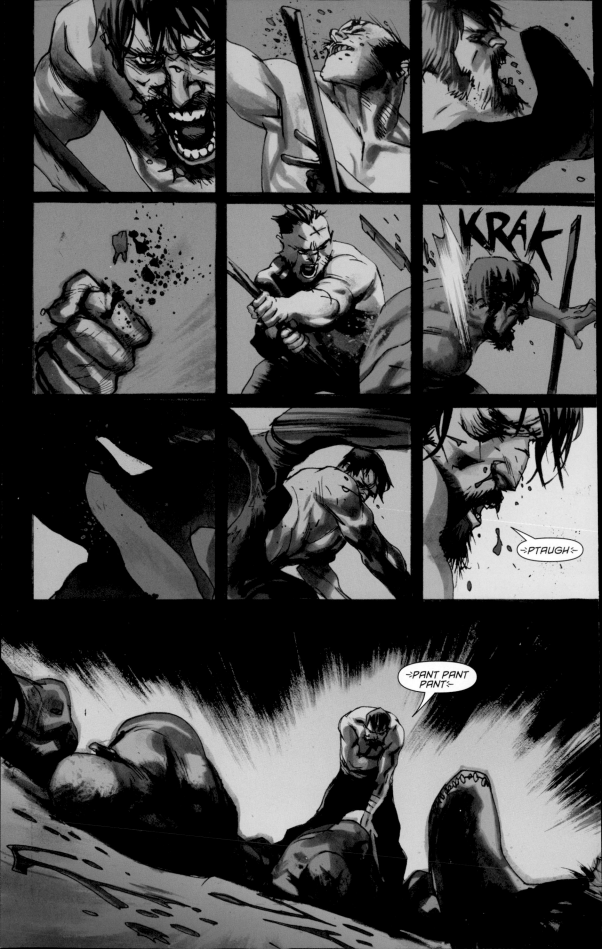

"... ALLOW MORE MEN IN."

"I CAN'T, MA'AM. THEY... THEY WON'T GO."

"...HE'S CRAZY..."

"SOME KIND OF DEMON."

"CAN'T FEEL MY--"

"GET ME OUT OF HERE...GET ME OUT!"

"WHAT DO YOU MEAN? THEY HAVE TO!"

"I'M SORRY. THEY JUST WON'T."

"THEY'RE SCARED OF HIM, MA'AM."

"THEY'RE AFRAID."

BRUCE WAYNE IN THE PIT

SCOTT SNYDER & JAMES TYNION IV
WRITERS

RAFAEL ALBUQUERQUE
ARTIST

DAVE McCAIG
COLORIST

DEZI SIENTY
LETTERER

BATMAN #24 variant cover by Guillem March

BATMAN: ISSUE #21
First Draft

Written by Scott Snyder
2013

Hey guys! One note before we start - the feel of this issue
(and the next three) should be bold, fun, fast, bright!
We want to cut 180 degrees AWAY from the other origin
stories. This is where we'll surprise people and make
something totally our own - our story is organically brighter
and more kinetic and more bombastic, with action,
adventure, even touches of sci-fi! So let's celebrate that!
Innovative cutting, creative paneling, fast storytelling...
I want this to be like an anti-Year One, because it genuinely
is, by nature. That story is intimate, grim, gritty, realistic
and dark, artistically and storywise - it's a masterpiece,
untouchably good, and one of my favorite books ever.
But it's mob, crime, grit, blood, corruption...

Our story is big, huge, city-shaking, action, sci-fi at times,
adventure! This in no way means it's meant to be less deep
or affecting than Year One; on the contrary, I've put more
into this story, between folklore about threads of fate,
riddles, rebirth and redemption tales than anything we've
done. On the surface, though, I want it to feel modern and
bright and fast. Bottom line: we're a very, very different
beast and we should celebrate that fact in the art, the
storytelling, and the tone overall! This is intended as an
innovative, bright, and layered Batman origin for today's
generation.

Okay - to Gotham!

PAGE 1

I'm thinking we do something here reminiscent of our very first page on BATMAN #1! Three vertical panels, with three views of the city that make the place look almost post-apocalyptic. Should be really shocking. Not so crazy it seems totally irreparable, like buildings fallen down. But...definitely windows shattered, streets flooded, tall weeds and grass and vines grown everywhere, up buildings!

1.
The first, like in BATMAN #1, is WAYNE TOWER, but the glass is shattered. The W broken.

Flocks of birds fly by. Many windows are broken.

2.
CRIME ALLEY, tall, waist-high weeds having grown through the sidewalk.

3.
We're inside a SUBWAY STATION (this one is different, I know) – but it's flooded to the roof with water. FISH swim by. Should seem otherworldly.

4.
Small inset - A SPEAR goes through a FISH in the subway.

PAGES 2-3

1.
A young BOY, maybe 10 years old, African American, in ratty clothes, pulls the fish out of the water with his spear, climbing up the flooded subway steps.

> BOY: Gotcha.

2.
As he opens a bag of ice for the fish, from the weeds, behind him, two WHITE-STOCKINGED HEADS slowly rise. These belong to two members of a new gang in Gotham. I imagine us seeing them from behind here, looking past them at the BOY, but if you do front, see the next panel for description of the masks!

3.
The BOY spots the 2 GANG MEMBERS, terrified. We see they wear EYELESS white stocking masks , with GIANT MOUTHS painted on the faces, so it's like their whole faces are these hungry, scary mouths.

> GANG MEMBER: Gotchhhaa...

4.
He starts running! Drops his SPEAR and FISH. They give chase!

5.
CLOSE on a motorcycle wheel cutting through the tall weeds and grasses. (This wheel, of course, belongs to BATMAN'S post-apocalyptic chopper – see next page!)

6.
A BAT-BOLA ties the feet of one of the GANG MEMBERS, tripping him up.

7.
A modernized, cool BILLY CLUB with a BAT SYMBOL on it hits the other GANG MEMBER in the back of the head, knocking him out.

8.
BOY senses a commotion going on behind him.

9.
The BOY turns to see...

PAGE 4

1.
HUGE – BATMAN as we've never seen him before. Militaristic, survivalist, no cape, backpack, straps, gear, a crossbow, rope and grappling hook - badass, like someone living in the wilds.

Greg – of course this design is totally up for grabs! All that matters to me is that it is BADASS and fits the context. We're in a Gotham with no electricity, overgrown and wild. Post-apocalyptic. A dead city. And it has been this way for months. This is the anciently dark, wild, savage, and scary city where BATMAN made his name. A folk-legend... The point is – the description below is just suggestion, brother. If you want a cape, a cloak, whatever, just say and let's talk it out, try it out, brain-storm, and make something cool together!

And he's sitting astride a STEAM-POWERED MOTORCYCLE.

The image should be imposing, intimidating, awe-inspiring. BATMAN – even in ruins, he's saying, this is MY city.

As for the bike, anything you think, Greg, so long as it looks sort of post-apocalyptic.

Or something more train/tank-like:

The key though, is NOT to have the bike overpower BATMAN himself. I really feel like BATMAN in his gear should be the focus. The bike is like an accessory, you know? BATMAN is the star survivalist.

2.
BATMAN hands the boy his fish on the spear, which he dropped.

     BATMAN: You dropped your fish.

3.
The BOY, scared, in awe.

     BOY: Thank...Thank you.

     BOY: He's telling everyone you're dead.

PAGE 4 CONTINUED

4.
BATMAN.

   BATMAN: Good. Then he won't see me coming.

PAGE 5

Guys, I'm thinking of a BACK CARD page, that reads "BATMAN: THE ZERO YEAR" with three, thin, HORIZONTAL SLASH/STRIP BANNER PANELS that are close-ups that don't make sense yet, but will later.

The SUPER-CLOSE, mystery images being:

1.
DETAIL of a RED THREAD going down into the darkness. Greg, we can talk about this - it's the thread the DEVICE BRUCE uses to map the caves is dangling from.

2.
A BONE finger against black brick. [REDACTED] This is just a bone finger, super close.

3.
DETAIL of a LION EYE peering through leaves. This is from the scene when [REDACTED]

PAGE 6

1.
RH LEADER! His shiny red helmet gleaming. Bright, modern, badass! He's pointing a SEMI-AUTOMATIC GUN (UZI maybe?) at US/the camera (and BRUCE) - confrontational- his gang behind him if you can fit them.

[REDACTED]

As for the larger situation itself, we're on the roof of a parking garage in a nice business area of Gotham, right by the water. BRUCE, in escaping the RED HOOD GANG, has driven a TRUCK he stole from them (the truck secretly contains HOSTAGES they were going to murder), up onto the garage roof. It's a fifteen-story building or so.

Facing off with him, the RED HOOD GANG. The LEADER in front, carrying a semi-automatic. Looking badass. There are about 20 of them up here, standing outside cars - nice black cars, like Mercedes, a couple of nice motorcycles. The gang is high-class, is the idea. all in suits like in #0. Those awesome leather masks you designed! And as a reminder, the RED HOOD GANG as an entity is all about terrifyingly random and senseless violence. The leader, RH ONE, he believes that there is no meaning to it all, the plans and designs and lives we make, and he wants people to accept this by joining the gang. The gang is the bloody red truth of things, in his mind, and he is passionate and ruthless. As he represents meaninglessness, so BRUCE will have to combat him by becoming something meaningful, a mad symbol of achievement and the obsessive belief that one person can make a difference.

PAGE 6 CONTINUED

Also, there is a HEAVY-DUTY CRANE on the building just beyond this building – BRUCE is facing it; it's behind the RH GANG, on the next building, closer to the water.

> RH LEADER: Oh we're **going** there.

> RH LEADER: Feel free to take it personally.

2.
BRUCE in the TRUCK, peering out of a fake face. Squinting. The face is tattered and should look weird - a synthetic face like he wore in our #0 issue, but tattered, ripped at the bottom, revealing his own mouth and chin beneath the shredded synthetic skin.

> RH LEADER (OP): We're coming for the men in the back of that truck, amigo, and we're going to kill them in all manner of creativity. And then we're going to deal with you.

> ALFRED (VIA INT.): Master Bruce, please, if you make a break for the—

> BRUCE: Not now.

3.
The SCENE.

> RH LEADER: Now I admit, you've put up a good chase. Frankly, I don't know where the hell you learned to drive like that.

> RH LEADER: But you're at the end of the alley now, nowhere left to run. After all the weeks of trouble, we've got the cans tied on your tail, little guy. The city belongs to the Red Hood.

4.
BRUCE, furious.

> BRUCE: ...

> ALFRED (VIA INT.): Master Bruce, don't!

5.
BRUCE'S foot slams the gas.

6. [if you can fit it comfortably, Greg – if not, kill this panel!]
RH LEADER, truck reflected in his helmet...

> RH LEADER: Well, well.

PAGE 7

1.
The TRUCK barrels forward toward the RH GANG...

> ALFRED (VIA INT.): What...what are you doing?!

> BRUCE: All part of the plan.

2.
BRUCE takes a GRAPPLING HOOK CANNON from a BAG OF COOL GEAR on the passenger seat. I picture this as a kind of mini-bazooka-looking grappling gun – it's heavy duty!

> ALFRED (VIA INT.): What plan? You can't be serious!

3.
BRUCE puts the base against the wall behind him.

> ALFRED (VIA INT.): But you said yourself, the tensile strength of the grappling cable is—

> BRUCE: It'll hold.

4.
POOM! The GUN ANCHORS itself by firing heavy anchoring hooks/bolts into the wall behind BRUCE – Greg, for this panel I was thinking we could be with the MEN in the back of the truck, seeing the BOLTS come through. They're BUSINESSMEN – 6 of them – who are tied up, in their work clothes, sitting handcuffed, blindfolded (but with their feet free – they'll need to be able to swim).

5.
BRUCE FIRES the GRAPPLING CANNON HOOK forward, through the windshield at the CRANE on the next building.

> ALFRED (VIA INT.): Forgive me, sir, but you're not counting the weight of six men in the back of the truck! Average weight for a grown man is--

> BRUCE: They're underfed!

The RH GANG dives out of the way of the TRUCK! LEADER diving right by us. As the TRUCK roars off the roof.

> ALFRED (VIA INT.): Your math is wrong! I'm telling you--

> BRUCE: It'll hold!

> ALFRED (VIA INT.): Master Bruce, you're going to--

> BRUCE: Alfred...

6.
The TRUCK roars off the roof!

> BRUCE: ...Would you kindly shut up!

PAGE 8

Greg, however you want to show this awesome moment, SPLASH, couple panels, go for it - the TRUCK, swinging up B'way towards the water. BRUCE is hanging on the door of the truck, dangling, as the truck swings up the street – a truck playing Spider-Man (BRUCE has a remote in his hand by the way – something really small, so not important to show in any big way)... PEOPLE inside office buildings look and see this phenomenon. Maybe you can show this from their POV in a panel?

1.
When the TRUCK is dangling over the water, at the farthest point of its swing, before it swings back the other way, back toward the garage, dangling BRUCE pushes a button on a remote in his hand...

2.
...Blowing the back open, causing the HOSTAGES to tumble out.

3.
The rope SNAPS, the TRUCK tumbling, with BRUCE.

4.
Everything hits the water!

5.
BRUCE surfaces, the hostages around him, treading water... A POLICE boat is nearby.

6., 7.
The RH LEADER looking at him, saluting.

8.
BRUCE gives him the FINGER – let's bleep this out with a censored panel. Again, guys, we're going for a stylish, wild, cool book! Let's do this!

PAGE 10

Greg, this page is a MONTAGE of YOUNG BRUCE – age 10, days before his PARENTS are killed.

It's just him exploring the city – loving Gotham! Part of this story is about why Bruce loves the city – after all, he grew up across the river. What is it he loves about it? Let's show the childhood joy he found in exploring it. This should be exuberant young BRUCE, thin, inquisitive, eager, a boy with floppy black hair, bright blue eyes...he loves being anonymous in the city, getting to explore without anyone knowing he's BRUCE WAYNE, "prince of Gotham."

As for how he looks, dress-wise, I imagine he's wearing his school uniform, navy blue pants, a white button-down, a jacket with a crest. His tie is way loose, shirt unbuttoned at the collar. And he could be wearing a GOTHAM RAIDERS cap.

Near the top of the page, running across it, I'd love a BANNER, like white lettering that reads: "What do you love about the city, Bruce?" That's the only text on this page! Again, let's be bold, fun!

The images:
1.
BRUCE happily riding the BUS with everyday PEOPLE who don't know who he is.

2.
BRUCE examining a busy fish market in Chinatown, where all sorts of fish are packed in ice.

3.
BRUCE looking up at a beautiful rain of SPARKS falling as a TRAIN passes overhead on the EL.

4.
BRUCE walking across a GOTHAM BRIDGE, taking pictures with an old camera. **And, Greg, if you want to do some kind of cool composition, go for it, maybe a GOTHAM TOKEN at the center of the 4 images?**

PAGE 11

Now we're in the SECRET BASE inside the brownstone in Crime Alley (as seen in #0). BRUCE is at the COMPUTER and on the desk in front of him, it'd be cool if there were a bunch of FAKE FACES (MASKS) on mannequin head stands. Like all the disguises he uses.

BRUCE is hanging upside down, wearing magnetic shoes, attached to a metal scaffolding or bar. He's testing how well they hold him, as he increases the weight. But the idea should be that he's also sort of a resting bat, hanging upside down, becoming...

As for how he looks, I imagine that BRUCE in casual clothes wears mostly black, but he's young, so clothes are rugged – he needs to be active. No suits, no pants and jackets. More like black jeans, cool black sneakers, black T-shirt, and over it, a gray motorcycle jacket with yellow or black detailing (not garish though – he doesn't want to be noticed!) with a black hood he puts up when he leaves. And (also when he leaves) a black GOTHAM RAIDERS baseball cap. This is young, angry, dark BRUCE! No suits, no ties, this is a driven, angry 24-year-old BRUCE. Not wanting to draw attention to himself.

1.
On the computer screen is footage of the RED HOOD LEADER, zoom in so we're close on his helmet.

> BRUCE (OP): He could be anyone, Alfred. Whoever the Red Hood Gang Leader is, he never takes off the helmet in front of them. None of them know his identity. That much I'm sure of.

2.
Big. The scene, BRUCE hanging upside down. Looking bat-like. He's in his jeans, bare-chested.

> BRUCE: Not only is he faceless to the gang, but they're generally faceless to each other.

> ALFRED: Weights, sir?

> BRUCE: Fifty, please.

3.
ALFRED hands him a fifty-pound weight.

> BRUCE: Anonymity. It's the foundation of the gang's success. The six newest members of the gang, inducted last week, all of them were strong-armed in by him.

> BRUCE: Men and women he blackmailed. He must have a core of dedicated followers, but overall, the gang is a phalanx, a collection of agents who can be activated by him at any time.

PAGE 11 CONTINUED

4.
A DETAIL of the MAGNETIC SHOES BRUCE is wearing. The small wires along the sides...they should look like awesome sneakers, with lighted veins of wires.

> BRUCE (OP): A wife, a husband...he gets something on them, gives them a mask, and they're now part of the Red Hood. Two more fifties, please?

5.
ALFRED hands BRUCE another 50 lbs.

> BRUCE: It's impossible to get a read on how many of them there are. Anyone could be a member.

PAGE 12

1.
BRUCE is now holding 200 lbs. upside down. Straining.

> ALFRED: Speaking of anonymity, Master Bruce, forgive me, but isn't it about time you consider letting the city know Bruce Wayne has returned?

> BRUCE: (straining) Unh. To Gotham? I get that you don't approve, Alfred, but Bruce Wayne is legally dead, and that's how he's going to stay.

> ALFRED: Master Bruce--

2.
CLANG. BRUCE drops the weights.

> BRUCE: Alfred, just call me Bruce, will you? Please?

3.
BRUCE flips down.

> ALFRED: I'm afraid I can't do that, sir. When you first asked me to join you in this madness of yours, the truth is, I did so to have your ear. To talk some sense into you.

4.
BRUCE puts some MASKS in a hard black carrying case, like a briefcase, but really hard material.

> BRUCE: I'm more effective in this war against crime like this.

5.
ALFRED.

> ALFRED: It's strange, for years I waited every day for some word of you Master Bruce. Every day, I waited, believing you were still alive. And when you showed up, out of the blue, six weeks ago, I was filled with such...joy.

PAGE 12 CONTINUED

6.
BRUCE, a moment with ALFRED.

> BRUCE: And I want you to know, Alfred, there wasn't a week that
> went by while I was traveling that I didn't think about writing
> you. But the truth is, for all I knew, I wouldn't live a month past
> any letter I sent. And I didn't want to hurt you any worse.

> BRUCE: I can't tell you what it means to have you by my side
> here. But I'm not bringing Bruce Wayne back to life.

PAGE 13

1.
BRUCE, coming through the entrance from the PRIVATE BASE into the
PUBLIC BASE, carrying the case, and also dressed now.

Here's the description from our #0 issue: I imagine it as classy, pre-war,
antique but bachelor-ish – a little more antique-ish, library, study, etc.,
than you'd expect a young man to have, but this is for the contrast with
the glassy modern base, cool?

> BRUCE: Now the men the Red Hood Gang were going to execute.
> All of them were lower-level executives, businessmen who
> refused to join.

2.
BRUCE moving through the BASE to the door to PUBLIC part of the
BROWNSTONE.

> BRUCE: I might not know his name, but I know the man on that
> screen well enough to say he won't be deterred by what I did
> earlier.

> BRUCE: I need to watch them, they'll lead me back to him.

3.
We're nearing the door of the PUBLIC BROWNSTONE that leads to the
street.

> ALFRED: Just answer me this, please. To what end, Master
> Bruce?

> BRUCE: How can you ask that?

> ALFRED: Easily. You do all this for what?

4.
BRUCE, turns, angry, but not furious. Not yelling, just frustrated.

> BRUCE: Dammit, Alfred, so no one has to go through what I did
> that night, right there, in that alley! That's why. That's the
> mission. How can you even ask that?

5.

ALFRED: I'm sorry, sir, that's not what I meant. I was referring to--

BRUCE: Look. I have to go.

ALFRED: Very well, I'll get the car.

6.

BRUCE puts on a GOTHAM RAIDERS baseball cap at the door.

BRUCE: Actually, I'll drive myself.

PHILIP (OP): Let me give you a lift, BRUCE.

PAGE 14

1.

Large - outside the door is UNCLE PHILIP KANE. Greg, I see him in his late 50s, large in the shoulders, fit. Close-cropped gray hair. I imagine him wearing a nice suit – he's CEO of WAYNE ENT. after all! Let's talk design – love to give him a bit of flair.

Greg, as always, I'm going to leave the composition here up to you – you make conversations exciting somehow, so I'll stay out of your way!

BRUCE: Uncle Philip.

BRUCE: How did you...

2.

PHILIP: Find you? I've had a search on you since the moment you left. In all that time, I only got two sightings of you. Seven years ago, I got a report about someone who looked like you arrested for base jumping at Meru Peak. One more about three years ago. A man resembling you again, for killing a man in Lagos, Nigeria, during a marathon death fight of some kind.

3.

BRUCE: I didn't kill anyone.

PHILIP: Yes, well. All that searching, and deep down I always knew that the way to find you was to follow Mr. Pennyworth. If you were back, he'd come to you.

4.

ALFRED: Forgive me, but you have no business being here, Mr. Kane.

BRUCE: It's all right, Alfred.

PAGE 14 CONTINUED...

5.
A shot as though we're under the lamp where BRUCE'S parents were killed, the BROWNSTONE where PHILIP and BRUCE are standing in the distance.

> PHILIP: God, I haven't been here since the year after it happened. It was right there, too, wasn't it?

> BRUCE: How can I help you, Uncle Philip?

6.
Back with PHILIP and BRUCE.

> PHILIP: Give me a few minutes of your time. Take a quick drive with me.

> BRUCE: Uncle Philip, I--

> PHILIP: Just a few minutes...

PAGE 15

Greg, again, I'm going to largely leave the composition of these pages up to you! For the most part, they're really just talking in front of the PENNY. The one thing is, when PHILIP describes what's happening in the building, the projects being worked on, I'd love insets or small slash panels that show details from the projects he's describing. For example, when he talks about [REDACTED] research, a splash panel of a cyclotron would be great. Like a close-up glimpse.

The CAR is parked outside WAYNE ENT. And in front of WAYNE ENT. is the GIANT PENNY from the cave. It's like a statue erected in front of the building. And the building itself is crowded around by other big skyscrapers, too. So it's like a statue commemorating the financial strength and vibrancy of Gotham.

1.
The CAR in front of the PENNY.

> PHILIP CONT.: "...I want to show you something."

2.
Inside the car. PHILIP is surprised BRUCE doesn't know the building.

> BRUCE: I'm sorry, but I don't understand, Uncle Philip. You brought me here to see a statue?

> PHILIP: ...

> PHILIP: No, the building behind it, Bruce.

3.
The BUILDING. WAYNE ENT. Shiny and new.

> PHILIP (OP): It's the new Wayne Enterprises. I thought you knew.

4.
In the car.

>BRUCE: I've seen pictures. I haven't actually seen the place since coming back.

>PHILIP: We've been doing some incredible work these last few years. We finally merged the families, you know. Kane Chemical is now part of Wayne Industries.

>PHILIP: With our resources pooled, we've become a real giant, Bruce. Not just here in Gotham, but nationally. The research we're doing, from tissue growth to sonic deterrents...we've become a leader in protective technology.

Greg – some INSETS or SPLASH PANELS wherever on the page you think is most striking and is still clear this is in WAYNE ENT.

A.
A CYCLOTRON (we can see it's huge if you put a MAN next to it, what do you think?).

B.
TISSUE DIFFERENTIATION and GROWTH (bone being grown).

5., 6., 7.

>PHILIP: So will you come inside, let me show you around?

>BRUCE: I'm sorry, Uncle Philip.

>PHILIP: You don't approve of what I've done with the company?

>BRUCE: I don't have an opinion.

>PHILIP: You have no opinion. How can you have no--

>BRUCE: I think what you're doing is dangerous, housing R&D in and around the city. I agree with the sentiment there. But you said it yourself, it's your company.

PAGE 16

1.

>PHILIP: But I don't want it to be, Bruce. That's why I brought you here. It's YOUR company. Your mother knew me well enough to understand I'd make a terrible father. But I like to think that this is how I've cared for her, and for you, in my own way. Building up the company.

>PHILIP: It's why I had you declared dead, Bruce. I needed to, in order to take care of what was left. To make it into something that would live on.

2.

PHILIP: Now this city has always had a hard time trusting the Kanes. We've had more than our share of scandal and controversy. This new round of attacks isn't surprising.

PHILIP: Your namesakes, The Waynes, they were the chosen sons and daughters of this city. It's why we were all so excited when your father married my sister. The Waynes and the Kanes, together at last. But for whatever reason, your parents had different, less ambitious callings.

PHILIP: You can't underestimate how powerful a symbol it would be to see a Wayne back at the top of this company. You can't.

3.

BRUCE: That's not why I came back.

PHILIP: You're really not going to come inside, are you?

BRUCE: ...

PHILIP: I guess I did come to show you a penny then.

4., 5.

PHILIP: One hundred percent copper, you know. I oversaw its construction directly.

PHILIP: I don't know if you know this about me, but I studied to be a geologist. I was on an expedition in Cueva de los Cristales in northern Mexico when my father, Roderick, learned he was dying. He flew there, to (heh) to the bald scrub of Mexico to find me and tell me it was time to come home.

PHILIP: You see, some of us have a responsibility, Bruce, a chance to take this city by the horns and shape it. I understood. I took over Kane Chem four months later, and I'm proud of the work we've done there.

PHILIP: Your mother and father, they followed their callings. And certainly, I admired their charitable work, and what your father did every day in the hospital. But they could have done so much more.

6.

PHILIP: And so can you.

BRUCE: I'm sorry, Uncle Philip. That's just not what I'm here to do. It's not who I am.

PHILIP: Then who are you?

PAGE 17

This scene is a FLASHBACK to the day BRUCE fell into the caves. The same day we saw him running around the city on PAGE 10. So he's dressed the same as we saw.

We're in the garage – ROWS of AWESOME VINTAGE CARS – have fun, Greg. Most of the cars are 1920s, 30s, 40s and 50s. Motorcycles, too. This should be any vintage car buff's DREAM garage...amazing, pristine Fords, Rolls-Royces, just beauties, all in a row.

The one THOMAS WAYNE is standing by, which can be pulled out from the line of them if you want, in the center of the room, is a 1939 roadster. The idea, Greg (and Mike and Katie!) is that [REDACTED]

1.
BRUCE approaching his father, standing by the LINCOLN.

> BRUCE: You fixed the Lincoln, Dad?

> THOMAS: Just about. I'm not the car man my father was, but this one, it's hard to stay away from.

> BRUCE: It is. You wanted to see me?

2.
> THOMAS: I did. What do you love about Gotham, Bruce?

3.
> BRUCE: What do you mean?

4.
> THOMAS: I'm just...I'm just curious. I know you're sneaking off to the city after school.

5.
> BRUCE ...

> BRUCE: You had me followed?

PAGE 18

1.
> THOMAS: Bruce, when you're from a family like ours, it isn't safe to--

> BRUCE: That's why, though.

> THOMAS: That's why what?

PAGE 18 CONTINUED...

2.

BRUCE: That's why I love Gotham, Dad. Because it's a place where you can be anyone. You can become who you want. Where I can be...not Bruce Wayne. I mean nobody knows who I am there, Dad. Not like school.

THOMAS: And who did Gotham tell you to be?

BRUCE: I don't know...no one, really.

THOMAS: (heh) Well, just know that whoever you are, wandering around the city, you'll still be Bruce Wayne.

3.

THOMAS: And we're a part of the city, too, Bruce. Our family. And the river that feeds the city, it runs right through the caves beneath the house. We're not apart from it, or above it. We're all Gothamites is all.

BRUCE: I guess. Yeah.

THOMAS: Look, go easy on yourself, will you, Bruce? Give your self some room. My great-grandfather, Alan, he used to say that fate forms in the dark. And speaking of the dark....take a look at this.

4.

THOMAS produces a small sphere. It should look like something Mac would make, sleek, black glass, with a laser-camera inside to map things. The idea with this device is that it is lowered into treacherous areas, villages where there've been mudslides, earthquakes, etc., to see if there are people in need of medical help. It holographically maps the area, producing a 3-D replica in perfect hologram when replayed. A long red thread released from its back that you hold onto, as it lowers itself or spins into the collapsed area. Cool? Symbolically, it has a touch of the witch's eye from Oedipus (and the Clash of the Titans). The eye that sees the future, that sees fate...

We're looking at the DEVICE here.

BRUCE: What is it?

THOMAS: A crazy idea Lucius helped me build. It's called the Witch's Eye. It sees the future!

BRUCE: Shut up.

THOMAS: Ha! Okay, it can see the present. It's actually a visual mapper, see? There's a three hundred and sixty degree camera inside.

PAGE 18 CONTINUED...

5.
A laser mapper?

THOMAS: That's right. It's designed for first responders at a disaster site. Firefighters, EMTs, doctors, like me. If a building has collapsed, or a whole village even, if a town has been swallowed up by a mudslide, and it's not safe to approach, you roll this device in, and it maps the unseen spaces. It can tell responders if anyone is alive inside. It actually creates a three-dimensional map of the affected area that can be played back. Cool, eh?

6.

BRUCE: Meh. I could build a better one.

THOMAS: I thought we could use it to--

THOMAS: Ugh.

THOMAS: That's the hospital, I have to make a call, Bruce. Hang on.

7.
BRUCE left alone.

PAGE 19

1.
We're back in the present, with BRUCE, sitting in a car of his own, outside the MANOR.

2.
BRUCE, looking at the old abandoned house, the overgrown grounds.

3.
BRUCE looks at the FAKE FACES in his case, the disguises – the idea is a sort of "who are you?" feel.

4.
He closes the case.

5.
And drives off.

PHILIP CONT.: "He's not coming around..."

PAGE 20

We're now at WAYNE ENT. We're in a top office – this is actually the office of EDWARD NYGMA, the RIDDLER before he's RIDDLER, Greg – though the reader won't realize that it's him until the next page. This page is mostly about showing his office, how odd it is, how smart he is, and what his relationship is to PHILIP. Technically EDWARD is a corporate consultant. A genius strategist, responsible for the rise of multiple companies in the last decade. He's in his late 20s. He looks like classic RIDDLER in terms of hair, face, physique. He's NOT in costume yet. Right now, he wears a green short-sleeve button-down, but all else is relatively normal. He's like a slightly younger version of the EDWARD we know. Before the pomp. He has the same ego, same chip on his shoulder, but not the massive ambition yet. He has a touch of something off, socially. For example, he admits to wearing green because it's known in nature to attract the female eye. He's boastful and annoyingly egotistical, but socially he's an egghead.

As for his office - this is the fun part - at the center is a chair a tiny bit evocative of a question mark, but not too much.

And leading off from the chair's desk (where there are multiple computer screens, too) are dozens, even hundreds of strings of different colors, fanning out across the room, zigzagging, whirling into circular patterns and then straightening out again, a maze of different color strings with each string representing a factor only EDWARD understands – the idea is that this is one big spatial equation – a kind of visual 3-D algorithm for the health and happiness of WAYNE ENT. There should be Post-Its hanging from the strings in various places, sheets of paper marked up, off objects, even, to weigh certain strings down – a snow globe with a Post-It on it labeled "tomorrow's weather." A balloon tied to one string, giving it a bump, with the words "attractiveness of secretaries." Overall, it should look at once brilliant and crazy, all fanning out from the one chair.

On the walls, multiple degrees. EDWARD gets degrees in things for fun, when he feels like it. He has about fifteen is the idea.

1.
WAYNE ENT.

    EDWARD: I figured as much.

    PHILIP: You figured as much. Well, thanks for letting me know.

    EDWARD: I don't understand why you're being so biting, Philip.

2.
PHILIP talking to someone in this crazy office. We can't see who he's speaking with yet.

    PHILIP: It's called sarcasm.

    EDWARD: Precisely, from the Greek, "sarkasmos," meaning, to rip, tear the flesh. Bite. Biting.

3.
We see a stack of framed diplomas gathering dust on the floor. Above them on the wall, A SWORD (not unlike the sword he was holding in Death of the Family - BATMAN #15)

> PHILIP: Well then perhaps I'm being biting because I hired you as my top strategist. And yes, you've helped me take this company to new heights.

> EDWARD: And then some, yes.

4.
PHILIP reaches out to touch a string.

> PHILIP: Fine. But we've stalled is the issue.

> EDWARD: Please don't touch, Philip. That string represents [need something out there] The algorithm is spatial. You breathing on a string like that...disturbs things.

5.
PHILIP, looking angry. A cold anger though. Not explosive.

> PHILIP: You know what disturbs things? A public image problem for one, which we have. The Red Hood Gang exploiting that, stealing from us on both ends, which it's doing. So tell me, with your strings and your strategy, what the hell are we doing next? What's the answer to the mystery?

6.
PHILIP takes the SWORD off the wall.

> PHILIP: I'm getting the feeling you're not listening to me. So allow me to speak loudly by cutting your little cat's cradle to--

PAGE 21

1.
HUGE - Now EDWARD NYGMA – the big reveal. Everything spinning out of him.

> EDWARD: It's not a mystery, Philip. It's a riddle. After all, riddles always seem complicated but have very simple, hidden answers.

2.
EDWARD looking at him over the sword. PHILIP is no longer trying to cut anything down.

> EDWARD: ...and this one has a simple answer, too...

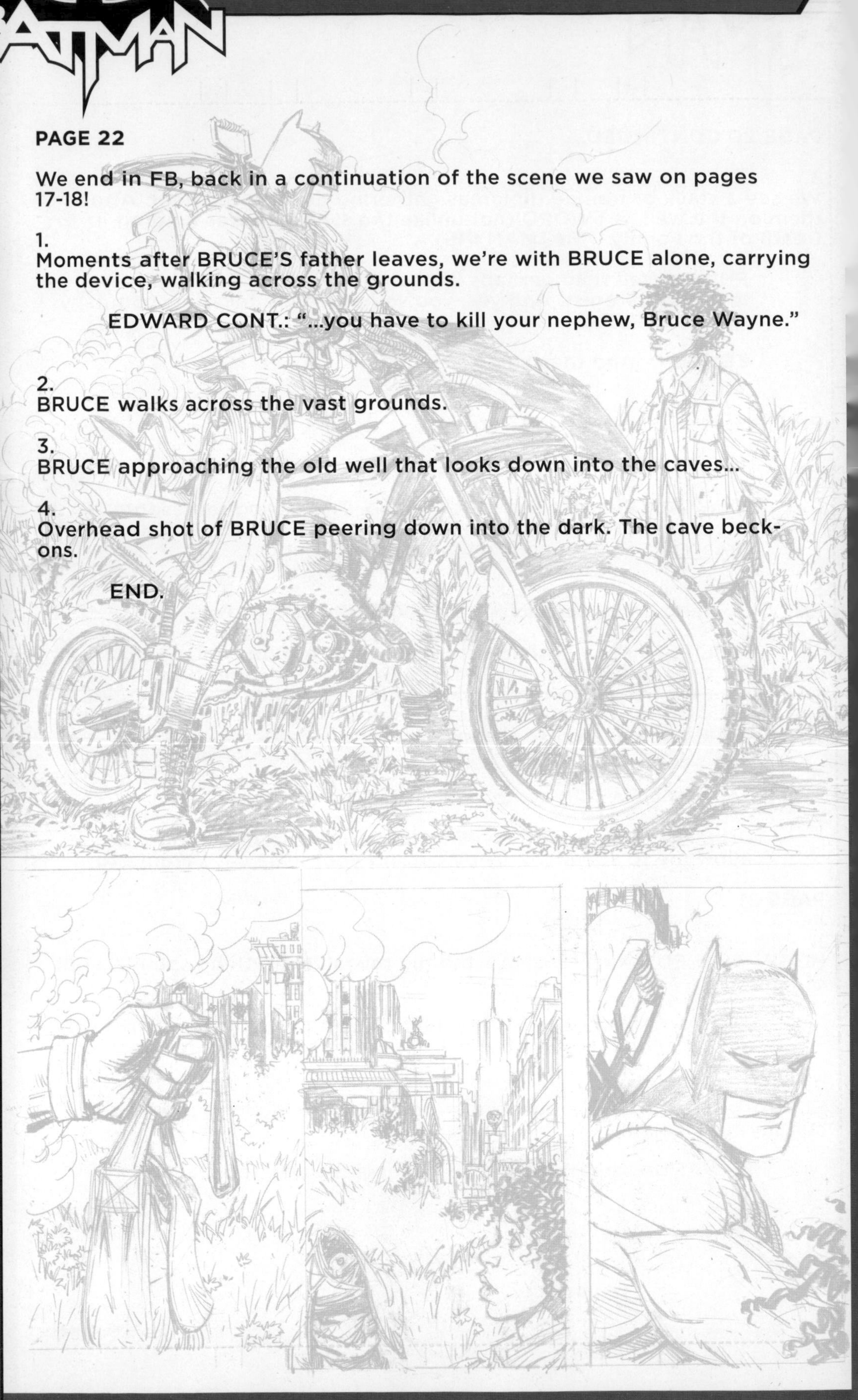

PAGE 22

We end in FB, back in a continuation of the scene we saw on pages 17-18!

1.
Moments after BRUCE'S father leaves, we're with BRUCE alone, carrying the device, walking across the grounds.

EDWARD CONT.: "...you have to kill your nephew, Bruce Wayne."

2.
BRUCE walks across the vast grounds.

3.
BRUCE approaching the old well that looks down into the caves...

4.
Overhead shot of BRUCE peering down into the dark. The cave beckons.

END.